DELAY AND DISRUPTION IN CONSTRUCTION CONTRACTS

FIFTH EDITION: FIRST SUPPLEMENT

CONSTRUCTION PRACTICE SERIES

Remedies in Construction Law
2nd Edition
Roger ter Haar
(2017)

International Contractual and
Statutory Adjudication
Andrew Burr
(2017)

Construction Law
Second Edition
Julian Bailey
(2016)

Construction Insurance and UK
Construction Contracts
Third Edition
Roger ter Haar QC, Marshall Levine
and Anna Laney
(2016)

The Law of Construction Disputes
Second Edition
Cyril Chern
(2016)

Delay and Disruption in
Construction Contracts
Fifth Edition
Andrew Burr
(2016)

Adjudication in Construction Law
Darryl Royce
(2016)

Chern on Dispute Boards:
Practice and Procedure
Third Edition
Cyril Chern
(2015)

Construction Contract Variations
Michael Sergeant and
Max Wieliczko
Holman Fenwick Willan LLP
(2014)

FIDIC Contracts: Law and Practice
Ellis Baker, Ben Mellors, Scott Chalmers
and Anthony Lavers
(2010)

DELAY AND DISRUPTION IN CONSTRUCTION CONTRACTS

ANDREW BURR
(MA) (Cantab), ACIArb, FFAVE, Barrister,
Adjudicator and Arbitrator

with editorial assistance from Annabella Matute Castro and Clelia Zotti

FIFTH EDITION
FIRST SUPPLEMENT

informa law
from Routledge

First published 2018
by Informa Law from Routledge
2 Park Square, Milton Park, Abingdon, Oxon OX14 4RN

And by Informa Law from Routledge
711 Third Avenue, New York, NY 10017

Informa Law from Routledge is an imprint of the Taylor & Francis Group, an Informa business

British Library Cataloguing-in-Publication Data
A catalogue record for this book is available from the British Library

Library of Congress Cataloging-in-Publication Data
Delay and disruption in construction contracts. — Fifth Edition.
    pages cm. — (Construction practice series)
    ISBN 978-1-138-94066-6 (hbk) — ISBN 978-1-315-67395-0 (ebk)
 1. Construction contracts.   2. Construction contracts—England.
I. Burr, Andrew editor.
    K891.B8D449 2016
    343.07'862—dc23
    2015033967

ISBN: 978-1-138-23989-0 pbk
eISBN: 978-1-315-10373-0 ebk

Typeset in Plantin
by Apex CoVantage, LLC

MIX
Paper from
responsible sources
FSC™ C013985

Printed in the United Kingdom
by Henry Ling Limited

CONTENTS

**Ancora per
Alexander Matteo, Thomas Jacopo e Alice**

PREFACE TO THE FIRST SUPPLEMENT
TO THE FIFTH EDITION

Just as the saying goes: "You know you're getting old when policemen start looking young", so the same goes for the London Technology and Construction Court judiciary. The two judicial luminaries cited so admiringly on pages xx and xxi of the fifth edition having retired to the international arbitration conference circuit (September 2016 saw Sir Robert Akenhead addressing the Society of Construction Law in Leeds, whilst Sir Vivian Ramsey spoke at the Society's "samba" party in São Paulo!), the "changing of the guard" at the Rolls Building has seen the injection of several pints of young blood, namely Fraser, O'Farrell and Jefford JJ; it is particularly good (at long last) to welcome two female members to the TCC judiciary.

It should also be noted that 2015 saw four hugely significant decisions by the United Kingdom Supreme Court on the interpretation of commercial contracts, the over-arching theme being that courts will not generally rewrite agreements between parties and will only (in exceptional circumstances) permit commerciality at the time of interpretation to override the natural meaning of the words used in the original bargain. Courts will not usually intrude in order to imply terms and the rule on contractual penalties has been rewritten; the fundamental autonomy of contracting parties is reinforced by respecting the natural meaning of the words originally deployed: see the landmark decisions in *Arnold v Britton*[1]; *Marks and Spencer plc v BNP Paribas Services Trust Co (Jersey) Limited*[2], *Cavendish Square Holdings BV v Makdessi*[3] and *ParkingEye Limited v Beavis*.[4]

Now (even more so), it is therefore crucial for parties drafting and entering into commercial agreements (and their legal advisers) to:

- Adopt clear and unambiguous drafting techniques;
- Clearly define the parties' principal obligations under the contract;
- Understand (with clarity) the natural and ordinary meaning of the phraseology adopted and the overall purpose of each separate clause and the agreement as a whole;
- Give due consideration to any available remedies in the event of future contractual breach;
- Take careful advice on the prospects of successfully challenging the terms of a clearly-drafted contract.

---

1 [2015] UKSC 36: please see 2-090(1) below. *Arnold v Britten* was recently considered in *Wood v Capita Insurance Services Limited* [2017] 2 WLR 1095, at [8]–[15], in which the Supreme Court reaffirmed the principle that the court's task is to ascertain the objective meaning of the language which the parties have actually chosen to express their agreement, the starting point being the words themselves.

2 [2015] UKSC 72: please see 2-090(2) below.

3 [2015] UKSC67: please see 21-224(3) below.

4 [2015] UKSC67: please see 21-232(1) below.

As with the fifth edition, this *First Supplement* is Illustration led: Annabella Matute-Castro has produced a raft of these with her usual aplomb and Katie Lee (of 3 Paper Buildings, Inner Temple) has kindly now taken up the case reporting baton; other recent signings have also played their part on the re-seeded pitch (with Dave Owen, for example, introducing a number of Canadian cases), whilst many of the original specialist editorial team have again made magnificent contributions to the final product.

In a publication whose stock-in-trade is the pathological project, it is particularly heartening to record a significant success story for a change: on a Turkish Airlines flight to Johannesburg, South Africa (to address MDA Associates' annual "Collective Wisdom" lecture[5] on the subject-matter of this book), the author (following a tearful viewing of Disney's latest version of *The Jungle Book*[6]) was cheered to read a report in the Turkish newspaper *Daily Sabah* (under the heading "Third bridge to open, completed in record-breaking time"):

> "The Yavuz Sultan Selim Bridge was completed within a recent-breaking 27 month time frame, nine months ahead of schedule, according to Transportation, Maritime and Communications Minister Ahmet Arslan. The project, which is worth TL 8.5 billion, is the first of its kind completed in such a time frame and could break a world record, according to Arslan."[7]

This is glowing testament to the fast-developing globalisation of international construction law as reflected by the inclusion in this *First Supplement* of a new introductory chapter to Nordic construction law (chapter 27, contributed by Assistant Professor Sylvie Cavaleri of the University of Copenaghen). Closer to home, the specialist editorial team has significantly developed the coverage of construction delay insurance (in chapter 26, contributed by Francis Barber) and has completely replaced the chapter on disruption (chapter 17, contributed by Derek Nelson), whilst focussing (in new appendix 5) up on the measured mile approach to the assessment thereof (contributed by Robert Gemmell).

Finally, just as the page proofs were being checked, Fraser J gave judgment in *North Midland Building Limited v Cyden Homes Limited*,[8] in which he delivered a masterfully incisive summary of the prevention principle in the context of concurrent delay.

Much thanks are due to all those who have made such extremely valuable contributions to this *First Supplement* (as more fully particularised in the editorial team biographies below).

Much as Paolo Hewitt commented in an interview (at www.oasis-recordinginfo. co.uk/?page_id-1719), the present author also aspires continuously to "up his writing" and very much hopes to have done so herein.

ArbDB Chambers, 150 Fleet Street, London, EC4A 2DQ
4 July 2017
Andrew Burr
andrew.burr@arbdb.com

---

5 With heartfelt thanks to Vaughan and Jacky Hattingh for their immensely generous hospitality and to all of Vaughan's colleagues at MDA Associates (particularly Tiffany Widlake) for the kind warmth and generosity of their welcome.

6 The cartoon colourist for Baloo (the bear) and Shere Khan (the tiger) was Katreena Erin Bowell, the immensely talented artist and folk musician, who kindly performed (along with her great friend, Aoife McMahon) at the book launch of the fifth edition held in the City of London (precisely one year ago) on 29 February 2016. The author commends to his readers two particular tracks from the movie (voiced respectively by Bill Murray and Christopher Walken (channelling his "Kill Bill" character)) (both available on YouTube), namely "The Bare Necessities" and "I'm the King of the Jungle").

7 "Istanbul's third bridge to open this week, completed in record-breaking time" Daily Sabah (Istanbul, 22 August 2016).

8 [2017] EWHC 2414 (TCC).

PREFACE TO THE FIFTH EDITION

The fourth edition of *Delay and Disruption in Construction Contracts* by Keith Pickavance LLB (Hons), Dip Arch, Dip IC Arb, RIBA, PPCIOB was published by Sweet and Maxwell/ Thomson Reuters (Legal) Limited in 2010, with editorial assistance from Andrew Burr MA (Cantab), ACI Arb, Barrister, Nick Lane (then at Olswang, London) and David Tyerman MBA, LLM, Planning Director.

Since that time, a considerable amount of water has flowed under the construction law bridge. A number of important judgments have been handed down in the Technology and Construction Court (TCC) (both in London and throughout England and Wales), the Scottish judiciary (thankfully, still within a part of the United Kingdom!) have remained active in the field and civil courts worldwide appear ever more acutely aware of the necessity to develop a coherent body of case law, which can be accessed by an increasingly "interweb savvy" global construction bar, ever eager to draw cross-legal – cultural comparisons, where appropriate and relevant (hence the conscious decision to appoint several civil lawyers and international correspondents to the team of specialist advisory editors). We have endeavoured to reflect case law developments by the use of illustrations throughout the text.

Probably the most significant construction law decision in England and Wales in the last five years has been Akenhead J's 660-paragraph *tour de force* in *Walter Lilly and Co Limited v Mackay*,[1] which merits detailed consideration for its masterful dissection of the JCT standard form of building contract 1998 edition private without quantities (incorporating various specific amendments), as modified by the contractor's designed portion supplement without quantities 1998 edition (revised November 2003) as amended ([102]–[126]), the JCT extension of time provisions ([362]–[392]), including a discussion of "criticality" [379], "prospective" *versus* "retrospective" analysis [380] and the carrying out by experts of "cross checks" [381], the quantification of loss and expense under the JCT contract ([461]–[473]), "global" (or "total") cost claims ([474]–[508]), head office overheads and profit ([540]–[554]), reasonable settlement ([562]–[569]) and contractual and statutory interest ([650]–[657]).

As observed by the learned judge at first instance,[2] the project in question was almost certainly a "disaster waiting to happen" and the Court of Appeal paid notably short shrift to the subsequent attempt to overturn Akenhead J's sterling judgment.[3]

---

1 [2012] EWHC 1773 (TCC).
2 [2012] EWHC 1773 (TCC), at [1].
3 By way of postscript, the London *Evening Standard* reported on 9 April 2015 that the site upon which Mr Mackay's property was built was purchased in 2001 by three developers (including Mr Mackay) for £13m. They accepted Walter Lilly & Co's tender to build three houses on the site for £15.3m. In December 2014, one of the three houses was sold to a Bermuda-registered company for £51.17m (with stamp duty of £7.6m and an Annual Tax on Enveloped Dwellings of £218,000).

Of similar (but perhaps marginally less well-publicised) intensity and scholarship is Ramsey J's decision in *Vivergo Fuels Limited v Redhall Engineering Solutions Limited*.[4] Again, the following paragraphs of his judgment should probably be required reading for any serious practitioner, or student, of construction law: [343]–[375] (material breach: programming), [376]–[407] (failure to proceed regularly and diligently), [408]–[420] (notices: the law), [421]–[498] (notices: failure to proceed regularly and diligently), [504]–[513] (repudiatory breach) and [514]–[519] (acceptance thereof).

As regards recent amendments and revisions to the standard forms of construction contract so comprehensively reviewed and analysed by Mr Pickavance in the fourth edition, there has been insufficient time in which to update his masterful cross-referencing service. This will be attempted for the supplement to the fifth edition, but, meantime, Mr Pickavance (together with Mr Lane) has himself kindly provided a comparison of the CIOB Complex Projects Contract (the CPC) (drafted by himself, Mr Lane and others) with the JCT Major Projects Form (the MPF). This follows their *Construction Law Journal* article,[5] comparing and contrasting the CPC with the MPF, which article also comes highly recommended. As regards other contracts, the following table may assist readers:

Contract	Website	Publisher
ECC3 – April 2013 update	www.netcontract.com/products/bookshop_main.asp?page=Bookshop_main.asp&ISBN=9780727758675&NEC=True&UK4TJTV63YD2CH5XUFYH=.aspx?page=1	Institute of Civil Engineers
ICE7 – now equals ACE/CECA Infrastructure Conditions of Contract (2011)	www.acenet.co.uk/infrastructureconditionsofcontract/65f	CECA
IChemE – now 5th edition, 2013 (the International Red Book, 1st edition was 2007, but that is not mentioned in the table)	www.icheme.org/shop/books/contracts/printable%20forms-of-contract-electronic-redbook-uk5th-edition.aspx	Institute of Chemical Engineers
IGBW09	http://constructionprocurement.gov.ie/contracts/	Construction Procurement NPPU, Department of Public Expenditure and Reform
JCT 2011 revisions	www.jctltd.co.uk/cdm-amendment-sheets.aspx	JCT
MF/1 – Revision 5,2010	www.theiet.org/resources/books/model/mf1-explanation.cfm?type=pdf	Institute of Engineering and Technology
NZ03- NZS 3910 2013	http://shop.standards.co.nz/catalog/3910:2013(NZS)/view	New Zealand Standard Council
SGC95–6th edition, December 2008	www.bca.gov.sg/PSSCOC/others/1_psscoc_ConstnWks.pdf	Building and Construction Authority, Singapore
SIA80–9th edition, September 2010	www.sia.org.sg/building-contracts/109-main-contract-lump-sg	Singapore Architects Association

4 [2013] EWHC 4030 (TCC).
5 (2015) 31 Const LJ 295.

This fifth edition also includes a significantly expanded section on "Building Information Modelling", contributed by David-John Gibbs, an up-and-coming expert in the field (and which has also appeared recently as an article in *Construction Law Journal*[6]).

February 2013 saw the publication by the Task Force of Building Information Modelling of a range of contractual and related documents relevant to the UK government's intention to require the use of collaborative 3D BIM on all its projects by 2016. These documents include the CIC Building Information Model (BIM) Protocol (CIC/BIM Pro, first edition February 2013), a supplemental document to be incorporated into professional services appointments and construction contracts: see the website[7] for the Task Force's guidance on the use of the protocol.[8] The BIM protocol creates an information management rôle and a Scope of Services for Information Management was also published (again, see the website[9]). Careful consideration needs to be given when incorporating the protocol into standard form contracts in order to ensure consistency with existing terms. The Task Force has also published the BIM Employer's Information Requirements (EIR), which are intended to form part of the appointment and tender documents on BIM projects: see the website for the EIR to cover the employer's technical, management and commercial requirements for a project.[10]

BS1192:2007 (entitled *Collaborative Production of Architectural, Engineering and Construction Information* in its 2012 update) is a code of practice providing guidance on the technical aspects of the structuring and exchange of CAD data, as well as how to implement collaborative work. The Task Force has published the PAS1192–2 Specification for information exchanges specific to a BIM environment to supplement the BS1192:2007: see the website for further guidance.[11]

Due to uncertainties as to how existing professional insurance arrangements may respond to projects using collaborative 3D BIM to maturity level 2, the Task Force also published a Best Practice Guide for Professional Indemnity Insurance when using Building Information Models (CIC/BIM Ins, first edition February 2013): again, see online.[12] It is recommended that policyholders should check their cover with their broker prior to entering into contracts where BIM processes are being used.

Furthermore, there is an expanded commentary on adjudication in the United Kingdom (again in a new chapter), a new chapter on dispute boards (by Chris Miers) and a new chapter on the civil law dynamic (by Wolfgang Breyer). Finally, there are two new appendices, comprising Julian Bailey's seminal analysis of the SCL Protocol and Nuhu Braimah's excellent discussion of his model for the selection of an appropriate method of delay analysis.

As Keith Pickavance put it so eloquently in his Introduction to the third edition of this book: "The result has been a team effort but, in the event that nonetheless it could be improved upon, then that is my fault." Put another way, as Simon and Garfunkel might have sung (back in the day): "All my words come back to me, in shades of mediocrity."

Atkin Chambers, 1 Atkin Building, Gray's Inn, London, WC1R 5AT
31 December 2014
Andrew Burr
aburr@atkinchambers.com

---

6 (2015) 31 Const LJ 167.
7 BIM Task Group: *www.bimtaskgroup.org/*.
8 Protocol: *www.bimtaskgroup.org/bim-protocol*.
9 Scope of Services for Information Management: *www.bimtaskgroup.org/bim-protocol*.
10 EIR cover: *www.bimtaskgroup.org/bim-eirs*.
11 PAS: *www.bimtaskgroup.org/pas11922-overview/*.
12 Best Practice Guide: *www.bimtaskgroup.org/professional-service-indemnity-insurance-guidance/*.

ACKNOWLEDGMENTS TO THE FIFTH EDITION

In his effusive review[1] of the fourth edition of this publication, John Dorter (the renowned Australian construction lawyer and editor of *Building and Construction Law Journal* (BCLJ)) wrote as follows:

> "What a wonderful, well-rounded and in-depth work this very authoritative text has matured into.
>
> The very learned author has given the profession a splendid encyclopaedia on not just his vast expertise in respect of delay and disruption but also in respect of the several relevant risk categories. . .
>
> The treatment of time and cost is far from just theoretical; quite to the contrary, there is very helpful advice on the necessity for appropriate and proper drafting, well illustrated by quotation from Pascal, viz: 'words differently arranged have a different meaning, and meanings differently arranged have different effects. . .'
>
> The treatment of authorities is both well up to date and extensive. . .
>
> Construction lawyers and others will be greatly helped in the fundamental issues of cause and effect. . .
>
> Similar significance in more recent times of proportionality is recognised and well covered.
>
> The author's great expertise in respect of float is not only well known but exemplified in almost every aspect. . .
>
> The ripple effect is dealt with, including the healthy reminder that the 'ripple effect works both ways'. The fine analysis of the many aspects of delay includes the reminder of the distinction between concurrency and parallelism.
>
> Global claims and their related ones are also well analysed. . .
>
> Technically, the publication is very considerably enhanced. For example, despite the unfortunate modern trend to a brief and mechanical index, this one is detailed and very helpful."

Keith Pickavance is an extremely "hard act" to follow, but the new editorial team wish him all the very best in his well-deserved retirement with Roz on Providenciales, Turks and Caicos, and will do their level best to emulate the breadth and depth of his coverage of the above topics, which are central to every commercial construction lawyer, both in the United Kingdom and abroad (as so eloquently described by Mr Dorter).

The "new kids on the block" are led by Andrew Burr (barrister, arbitrator and adjudicator, at Atkin Chambers, Gray's Inn, and general and articles editor of *Construction Law Journal*), assisted by Annabella Matute-Castro (a qualified foreign lawyer, with the right to advocate at the Supreme Court in Peru).

The expert team of specialist advisory editors now comprises Francis Barber (insurance) (of Cunningham Lindsey, London), Wolfgang Breyer (civil law) (of Breyer Rechtsanwälte, Stuttgart), Steve Briggs (time) (of Hill International, London), Joe Castellano

---

1 (2013) 29 Const LJ 186, first published in BCLJ and reprinted with kind permission.

(North America) (of FTI Consulting, New York), David-John Gibbs (BIM), Wendy MacLaughlin (Pacific Rim) (of Hill International, Perth), Chris Miers (dispute boards) (of Probyn-Miers, London), Robert Palles-Clark (quantum) (of Blackrock PM, London) and Keith Pickavance (of Providenciales, Turks and Caicos). Stuart Wilks (of Hill International, London) has provided invaluable administrative support, as has Andrew Burrows, Mr Burr's Practice Manager at Atkin Chambers. Joshua Wells at the new publishers has given first-rate encouragement. Last (but by no means least), Freda Broderick and Doreen Bruce (of Atkin Chambers, Gray's Inn) have managed (as always) to decipher Mr Burr's hieroglyphics in order to produce the manuscript, any and all remaining errors being those of him alone.

EDITORIAL TEAM BIOGRAPHIES
FOR THE FIRST SUPPLEMENT
TO THE FIFTH EDITION

Francis Barber is a chartered civil engineer and chartered insurance loss adjuster, who has worked in the field of engineering insurance for over 30 years and has written and lectured extensively on the topic of delay insurance.

Andrew Burr, adjudicator, arbitrator, barrister and mediator, was a member of Atkin Chambers from 1983 until May 2016. He now practises as a third party neutral at ArbDB Chambers, Fleet Street, in the City of London and is Legal Counsel at Synthesis Chambers Solicitors, at Stratford City. He specialises primarily in construction and technology matters and is also an affiliated foreign lawyer with Pr1mus (Vilnius, Lithuania). Andrew is past chair of the European Branch of the Chartered Institute of Arbitrators and has worked throughout Europe and internationally on a wide range of construction and infrastructure matters. He is general and articles editor of *Construction Law Journal* and recently sat on the advisory committee for the revision of the ICC's *Dispute Board Rules*. Andrew is a listed arbitrator at the Beijing Arbitration Commission and the Vilnius Court of International Arbitration and is a member of the Independent Standards Board of the International Mediation Institute. Andrew was assistant editor of the third and fourth editions of this publication.

Sylvie Cavaleri is a Swiss and Danish qualified attorney, specialising in international commercial dispute resolution and international contract law, with a particular focus upon construction law. She holds a PhD from the University of Copenhagen and is currently employed there as an assistant professor at the Faculty of Law.

Robert Gemmell is a chartered quantity surveyor, chartered arbitrator and adjudicator with over 20 years' experience in the construction industry in Australia, Hong Kong, Malaysia, Singapore and the United Kingdom. He is also a visiting lecturer on the Master of Construction Law programmes of the University of Melbourne, an approved tutor for the Chartered Institute of Arbitrators, Oceania and a member of the Society of Construction Law Australia. Robert has recently published *Quantification of Delay and Disruption in Construction and Engineering Projects* (Thomson Reuters (Professional) Australia Limited/Lawbook Co 2017).

David-John Gibbs holds a master's degree in civil engineering and is undertaking an engineering doctorate at Loughborough University with industrial support from DAQS Limited and Hill International. His research investigates how BIM can assist with the proactive management and retrospective analysis of delays on construction projects.

Katie Lee has broad experience in commercial law, with particular expertise in construction, technology, engineering and property damage. Prior to commencing practice as a self-employed barrister, Katie worked offshore as a commercial litigator in the Channel Islands.

Chris Miers is principal of Probyn-Miers, one of the UK's leading firm of forensic architect. Chris has many years' experience in expert witness work, sits on the DRBF Council and practises extensively on dispute boards, particularly in South America.

Derek Nelson is a Chartered Quantity Surveyor and Chartered Engineering Surveyor, with over 35 years of construction and engineering experience. He has acted as expert in international disputes, addressing delay, disruption and quantum, having held senior contract and commercial management positions for international contractors and developers across Europe and Asia. His expertise covers quantity surveying practice, valuation, damages, contract administration, contract management, commercial management and cost management, which he combines with his tested planning and delay analysis capabilities. Derek also provides contractual advice and claims preparation and contract administration services worldwide, specialising in the preparation, negotiation and settlement of claims (whether for disruption, acceleration and prolongation), or the investigation, assessment and settlement of claims. Derek seeks rapidly to resolve, or avoid, disputes in a cost-effective and timely manner, having acted in arbitration, conciliation, litigation and mediation and as an expert determiner. He has been cross-examined and given concurrent evidence in disputes from Belize to Brunei and Scotland to Singapore and, alongside working on ongoing projects, Derek undertakes the rôle of "project neutral", independently reviewing international projects in preventative, on-the-job dispute resolution. Derek delivers training and seminars on contractual problems, claims preparation, negotiation and dispute resolution and was described as "a gifted quantum expert" and highly commended in *Who's Who Legal: Construction 2016*.

Dave Owen is a delay analyst, specialising in construction delay. He has 19 years of hands-on site experience in the UK construction industry, working at project management level upon a number of high profile building projects across London. He holds an MSc in Construction Law and a BEng (Hons), being currently employed as a delay analyst with DCTO Consulting.

Rob Palles-Clark is a director of Blackrock Project Management in London and has a broad practice as an independent expert on time and money issues, having particular expertise in the analysis and proof of quantum claims.

TABLE OF ACRONYMS

A201/07	AIA Standard Form of Building Contract, 2007.
A201/97	AIA Standard Form of Building Contract, 1997.
A201SC/07.07	AIA Federal Supplementary Conditions of Contract, 2007.
AACE	Association for the Advancement of Cost Engineers International.
ACA	Association of Consultant Architects.
ACA82	ACA Building Contract 1982 Edition, 1992 Revision.
ACA98	ACA Building Contract, 1998 Edition, 1999 Revision.
ACE	Association for Consulting and Engineering
ADM	Arrow Diagramming Method.
ADR	Alternative Dispute Resolution.
AIA	American Institute of Architects.
AS2124	Australian Standard Conditions of Contract 4th Edition. 1992 Edition, 2000 Revision.
AS4000	Australian Standard Conditions of Contract 1997 Edition, 2000 Revision.
ASCE	American Society of Civil Engineers.
BOO	Build, Own and Operate, a form of arrangement for securing private finance for public projects.
BOOT	Build, Own, Operate and Transfer, a form of arrangement for securing private finance for public projects.
BOT	Build, Operate and Transfer, a form of arrangement for securing private finance for public projects.
C	Contractor (and, where the context requires it, the claimant).
C21/03	Government of New South Wales, General Condition of Contract.
C21/09	New South Wales Government GC21 (Edition 1) General Conditions of Contract July 2003 including revisions to October 6, 2009.
CA	Contract Administrator.
CDM	Construction, Design and Management Regulations, 2007.
CE06	JCT Constructing Excellence Contract, 2006 Edition, 2009 Revision.
CIOB	Chartered Institute of Building.
CM08	JCT Construction Manager Appointment, 2008.
CMS	PFE Change Management Supplements, for use with the 1998 Edition of JCT contracts, 2003, Pickavance Consulting and Fenwick-Elliott.
CPC	Complex Projects Contract (see now: TCM15).
CPM	Critical Path Method.
CPR	Civil Procedure Rules.
CTS	"Count the Squares", The Central Unit on Purchasing Guidance No 7, Project Sponsorship: Planning and Progress (1986, Central Unit on Purchasing, HM Treasury).
DAB	Dispute Adjudication Board.
DB05	JCT Standard Form of Design and Build Contract, 2005 Edition, 2009 Revision.

DB16	JCT Standard Form of Design and Build Contract, 2016 edition.
DBFO	Design, Build, Finance and Operate, a form of arrangement for securing private finance for public projects.
DCMF	Design, Construct, Manage and Finance, a form of arrangement for securing private finance for public projects.
DOM/1	JCT Standard Form of Sub-Contract for Domestic Subcontractors for use with JCT98
DRB	Dispute Review Board.
ECC2	NEC Engineering and Construction Contract, 2nd Edition 1995, 1998 Revision.
ECC3	NEC Engineering and Construction Contract, 3rd Edition. 2005.
Eng	Engineer
EVA	Earned Value Analysis.
EVM	Earned Value Management.
FIDIC	Fédération Internationale des Ingénieurs-Conseils.
FIDIC/Build98	FIDIC Conditions of Contract for Building and Engineering Works Designed by the Employer, Test Edition 1998 (the "Red Book").
FIDIC/Build99	FIDIC Conditions of Contract for Building and Engineering Works Designed by the Employer, 1st Edition 1999 (the "Red Book").
FIDIC/DB95	FIDIC Conditions of Contract for Design-Build and Turnkey, First Edition, 1995 (the "Orange Book").
FIDIC/DB99	FIDIC Conditions of Contract for Design Build and Turnkey, First Edition, 1999 (the "Silver Book").
FIDIC/M&E87	FIDIC Conditions of Contract for Electrical and Mechanical Works, 3rd Edition, 1987, 1988 Revision (the "Yellow Book").
FIDIC/PD + B99	FIDIC Conditions of Contract for Plant and Design-Build for electrical and mechanical plant and for building and engineering works (the "Yellow Book").
FIDIC/SF98	FIDIC Short Form of Contract for projects of relatively small value (the "Green Book").
FIDIC4	FIDIC Conditions of Contract for Works of Civil Engineering Construction, 4th Edition 1987, 1992 Revision, (the "Red Book").
GC/Works/1	General Conditions of Contract for Building & Civil Engineering – Lump Sum with Quantities, 3rd Edition. 1989, 1990 Revision, Department of the Environment.
GC/Works/1/98	General Conditions of Contract for Building & Civil Engineering – Major Works with Quantities, 1998. Property Advisers to the Civil Estate, Central Advice Unit.
GC/Works/1DB	General Conditions of Contract for Building & Civil Engineering – Design & Build Version, 1993. Department of the Environment.
GC/Works/1DB98	Contract for Building & Civil Engineering – Design & Build Version, 1998. Property Advisers to the Civil Estate, Central Advice Unit.
GC/Works/2	General Conditions of Contract for Building & Civil Engineering – Minor Works, Second Edition, 1980 (revised 1989). Department of the Environment.
GC/Works/2/98	General Conditions of Contract for Building and Civil Engineering – Minor Works, 1998. Property Advisers to the Civil Estate, Central Advice Unit.
GMP	Guaranteed Maximum Price.
HGCRA	Housing Grants, Construction and Regeneration Act 1996.
HK05	Hong Kong Special Administrative Region of the People's Republic of China, General Conditions of Contract for Building Works, 2005.
HK86	Standard Form of Building Contract with Quantities, 1986, 1999 Revision, RICS Hong Kong,
HKGC99	Hong Kong Special Administrative Region of the People's Republic of China, General Conditions of Contract for Civil Engineering Works, 1999.

HMSO	Her Majesty's Stationery Office.
ICC	International Chamber of Commerce.
ICC14	Infrastructure Conditions of Contract 2014.
ICE	Institute of Civil Engineers.
ICE/DC	ICE Design and Construct Conditions of Contract, 6th Edition, 1993, 1998 Revision.
ICE/DC01	ICE Design and Construct Conditions of Contract, Measurement 2nd Edition, 2001.
ICE/MW95	ICE Conditions of Contract – Minor Works, 2nd Edition, 1995, 1998 Revision.
ICE6	ICE Conditions of Contract, 6th Edition, 1991, 1998 Revision.
ICE7	ICE Conditions of Contract, Measurement Version, 7th Edition, 1999.
IChemE	Institute of Chemical Engineers lump sum contract, 4th Edition, 2001 (the "Red Book").
ID	Identity Data.
IFC05	JCT Intermediate Building Contract, 2005 Edition, 2009 Revision.
IFC84	JCT Intermediate Form of Building Contract, 1984 Edition, 1995 Revision.
IFC98	JCT Intermediate Form of Building Contract, 1998.
IFWCD/05	JCT Intermediate Building Contract, With Contractor's Design, 2005 Edition, 2009 Revision.
IGBW/09	Irish Government Public Works Contract for Building Works Designed by the Employer, 2009.
IGCE/09	Irish Government Public Works Contract for Civil Engineering Works Designed by the Employer, 2009.
IGCEDB/09	Irish Government Public Works Contract for Civil Engineering Works Designed by the Contractor, 2009.
IGDB/09	Irish Government Public Works Contract for Building Works Designed by the Contractor, 2009.
IGMW/09	Irish Government Public Works Contract for Minor Works, 2009.
IRS	Information Release Schedule (issued by D), or Information Required Schedule (issued by C), as the sense requires it.
JCT	Joint Contracts Tribunal.
JCT05	JCT Standard Form of Building Contract – Private with Quantities, 2005 Edition, 2009 Revision.
JCT63	JCT Standard Form of Building Contract, Private Edition with Quantities, 1963, 1976 Revision.
JCT80	JCT Standard Form of Building Contract, Private Edition with Quantities, 1980, 1995 Revision.
JCT98	JCT Standard Form of Building Contract, Private Edition with Quantities, 1998, 2003 Revision.
JCT16	JCT Standard Form of Building Contract, Private Edition with Quantities, 2016.
JCTSub/05	JCT Standard form of sub-contract, 2005 Edition, 2009 Revision.
LNG	Liquefied Natural Gas.
M&E	Mechanical and Electrical.
MC	Management Contractor.
MC08	JCT Management Building Contract, 2008.
MC87	JCT Standard Form of Management Contract, 1987.
MC98	JCT Standard Form of Management Contract, 1998.
MF/1	Institution of Engineering and Technology, Model Form 1, lump sum contract, 4th Edition, 2000.
MP05	JCT Major Projects Construction Contract 2005 Edition, 2009 Revision.
MTC08	JCT Standard Form of Measured Term Contract, 2008.
MTC89	JCT Standard Form of Measured Term Contract, 1989 Edition 1994 Revision.
MWA05	JCT Agreement for Minor Building Works, 2005 Edition, 2009 Revision.

MWA80	JCT Agreement for Minor Building Works, 1980 Edition, 1994 Revision.
MWA98	JCT Agreement for Minor Building Works, 1998.
NEC	An ICE form of contract written in the present tense, in which the parties agree to work in a spirit of mutual trust and good faith.
NEC/SF99	NEC Short Form 1999.
NEDO	National Economic Development Office.
NPO	Non-Productive Overtime.
NRM	RICS, New Rules of Measurement: Order of Cost Estimating and Elemental Cost Planning, 2009.
NRM 13	New Rules of Measurement 2013.
NS	Nominated Subcontractor
NZ03	New Zealand Standard Form of Contract for Building and Civil Engineering Work, NZS 3910:2003.
OGC	Office of Government Commerce.
PCC06	JCT Prime Cost Building Contract, 2006, Revision 2, 2009.
PCC92	JCT Standard Form of Prime Cost Contract, 1992 Edition, 1995 Revision.
PCC98	JCT Standard Form of Prime Cost Contract, 1998.
PDM	Precedence Diagramming Method.
PERT	Programme Evaluation and Review Technique.
PFI	Private Finance Initiative.
PM	Project manager.
PMI	Project Management Institute.
PMICoS	Project Management Institute, College of Scheduling.
PPC2000	ACA Standard Form of Contract for Project Partnering, 2000, 2008 Edition.
PQS	Private Quantity Surveyor (the QS employed by D used to distinguish from the QS employed by C).
QS	Quantity Surveyor.
RFI	Request For Information.
RIBA	Royal Institute of British Architects.
RICS	Royal Institution of Chartered Surveyors.
RP/FSA	AACE, Forensic Schedule Analysis, International Recommended Practice No. 29R-03 (2009).
SC	Subcontractor.
SCL	Society of Construction Law.
SGC95	Singapore Public Sector Standard Conditions of Contract for Construction Works, 1995, March 2005 Edition.
SIA80	Singapore Institute of Architects Lump Sum Contract (1980) 1999 Revision.
SMM7	RICS, Standard Method of Measurement, 7th Edition, 1998.
SPV	Special Purpose Vehicle.
TC08	JCT Construction Management Trade Contract, 2008 Edition.
TCM15	CIOB Time and Cost Management Contract 2015.
TQ	Technical Query.
VAT	Value Added Tax.
VO	Variation Order.
WBS	Work Breakdown Structure.
WC	Works Contractor.
WC/08	JCT Management Works Contract, 2008.
WC/87	JCT Works Contract Conditions (Works Contract/2), 1987.
WC/98	JCT Works Contract Conditions (Works Contract/2), 1998.
WCD81	JCT Standard Form of Building Contract With Contractor's Design, 1981 Edition, 1995 Revision.
WCD98	JCT Standard Form of Building Contract With Contractor's Design, 1998.

TABLE OF CASES

TABLE OF LEGISLATION

TABLE OF CONTRACT CLAUSES

ONLINE RESOURCES

The fifth edition of *Delay and Disruption in Construction Contracts* (together with *Supplement* thereto) is supported by over 100 bespoke figures that further illuminate some of the concepts in the book. They have all been made available as downloads, which you can access at your convenience from the book's homepage. Whenever you see a reference to a figure in the text please go to *www.routledge.com/9781138940666* and select the file you would like see from the Resources tab.

If you would like permission to use any of the illustrations in *Delay and Disruption in Construction Contracts*, please contact our Permissions department at –: mpkbooks permissions@tandf.co.uk.

LIST OF FIGURES

Figure 11.2 (referred to on p 489 of the main text) is fundamentally incorrect, since the prolongation damages ought properly to be for the period occupied by the disruption damages and the disruption damages are not necessarily limited solely to the delay period, paragraph 21–023 stating the correct position with regard to prolongation costs.

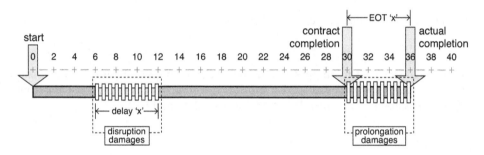

Revised figure 11.2 Reimbursable disruption and prolongation

Similarly, figure 11.3 (again referred to on p 489 of the main text) limits the disruption damages, which may extend further. Paragraph 11–125 incorrectly states that the delay/prolongation damages are **within** the acceleration damages; however, there are no prolongation damages and the acceleration damages are the costs in excess of the production and time-related costs, which would otherwise have been expended.

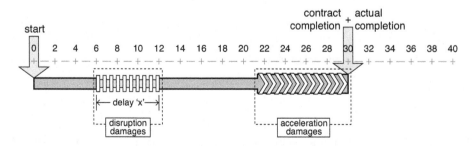

Revised figure 11.3 Reimbursable disruption and acceleration

xlix

Figure 11.4 (also referred to on p 489 of the main text) again limits the disruption damages and overlooks the prolongation damages, which arise in the delay "x" period for the amount of time shown between contract completion and actual completion (namely two months).

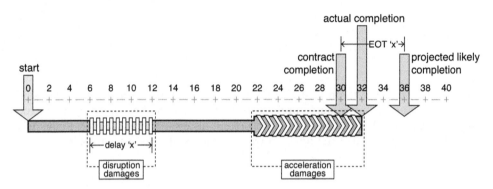

Revised figure 11.4 Reimbursable disruption and ineffective acceleration

Figure 21.10 (referred to on pp 882 and 884 of the main text) ought properly to show the site overheads and the head office overheads spanning from months 1 to 4, the labour and materials graph being intended to be a representation of fact.

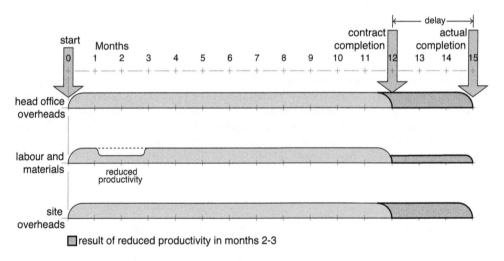

Figure 21.10

Figure 21.11 (again referred to on pp 882 and 884 of the main text) should similarly be redrawn, but the text should not alter.

1

Figure 21.12 (also referred to on pp 882 and 884 of the main text) should likewise be redrawn so that the darker extensions of site and head office overheads coincide with the time frame of the additional work, as is noted under paragraphs 21–109 and 21–110. It should be noted (with regard to the above) that some costs may need to be ascertained as arising in the overrun period, in the event that staff receive salary increases, or site accommodation prices increase, or the like, in like manner to the observations made in paragraphs 21–043 and 21–052.

CHAPTER 1

Introduction and terminology

Introduction

> *"Construction changes, delays and claims are a major problem for public work agencies, developers and facility managers – and for contractors and designers building their projects. Delays and claims siphon off a significant portion of the available funds for construction, often cost contractors and designers a significant portion of their anticipated profit, and sometimes create a loss, or even destroy a contractor and the owner's lifetime savings."[1]*

1–012 Add a new footnote 8A at the end of the phrase in round brackets:
See *Valedictory speeches on the retirement of His Honour Judge Toulmin CMG QC*, (2011) 27 Const LJ 399.

1–014 Add at the end of footnote 10:
See J Winter, *John Doyle v Laing Management: Is it good English law? Is it good English practice?* (2007) 23 Const LJ 89.

This is the Supplement One to the Fifth Edition of Delay and Disruption in Construction Contracts, and follows the structure of the main work. Each chapter of this supplement begins with the mini table of contents from its corresponding chapter in the main work. If the content under a heading has been amended in any way, that heading is marked in the mini table of contents with a symbol.

1 S S Pinnell, "Survey of scheduling practices and results". Risk assessment and best practices in scheduling, an occasional paper given to the PMI College of Scheduling (May 2005), p. 2.

1–023 Add at the end of footnote 37:

The Association for Consultancy and Engineering (ACE) has recently published an amendment sheet for its suite of professional appointments for engineers, namely the *ACE Agreements, 2009 edition (ACE Agreements 2009)*, in order to incorporate CDM 2015; that amendment sheet is freely available to download online.

1–030 Add at the end of footnote 51:

See also I Wishart, "Delay and disruption – a separable duo" (2012) 28 Const LJ 570.

1–032 Add the following Illustration:

Facts: The City of Hamilton (D) sought bids for the installation of a leachate drainage system at a live landfill site owned by D. The project involved trenching through land filled refuse up to 16m in depth with maximum trench depths reaching 30m in order to install the drainage pipework. The tender package issued to prospective bidders included a requirement for a description of the proposed site investigation and construction methodologies for approval by the Employer. No work could commence without the requisite approval. Also included in the tender specification were a number of further requirements, which included a clear statement that "time was of the essence" and that work was to proceed immediately following the award of the contract. The tender also called for an irrevocability period of 60 days from lodging the tender.

Bre-ex Limited (C), a groundwork contractor, responded to the tender on 6 November 2001; this therefore resulted in the irrevocability period expiring on 6 January 2002. C was one of seven bidders and, on 11 December 2001, D accepted C's tender and authorised the award of the resulting construction contract to C. C's successful tender was based upon an ingenious construction method and the tender detailed the methodology as required.

By early 2002, after no further contact from D, C contacted D regarding the contract. C was subsequently called in for what turned out be a pre-construction meeting on 24 January 2002, at which a letter communicating the contractual award was issued. This was some 18 days after the expiry of the irrevocability period. What followed were a number of discussions between C and D, together with D's advisers. A number of technical issues were discussed both at the meeting and in subsequent discussions. One issue concerned odour control, in response to which, C stated it would conduct the majority of the work during cold winter months.

A second issue arose surrounding the wording of the contract and C's insistence upon the inclusion of the approved construction methodology. Discussions between the parties continued. On 19 March 2002, a letter of understanding [**LoU**] was agreed by the parties and was to be inserted into the contract to be executed. D did not issue the agreed contract and, after a period, C himself drafted a contract incorporating the LoU. This was executed by C on 12 April 2002, with D executing on 12 June 2002. The work was originally planned to be carried out in the winter months and it was, therefore, agreed to split the contract period, with site investigation commencing on 21 May 2002 and the balance of work being completed over the 2002 / 2003 winter period. The work was successfully completed with no further issues.

C subsequently sought damages from D by reason of delay in approving the commencement of work following the award of the contract. Prior to trial, both parties agreed that a binding contract came into being on 11 December 2001, which was the date of tender acceptance.

Held: That there were two delay periods, namely that of the delay in communicating the award of the contract to C and, secondly, the issues surrounding the wording of the contract. Due to the express provision for time to be of the essence, the court held that the resulting delay period ran from 6 January 2002 (crucially, prior to the execution of the contract); this was the date at which the irrevocability period expired and C was to have started work.

On the second issue, the court stated that C was correct to insist that the contract included its methodology, with the contract not being executed until 12 April 2002. Therefore, it was held that the damages were to be calculated on the period of delay from 6 January 2002, until 12 April 2002. The court went on to make a further award of damages in favour of C: *Bre-ex Limited v The Corporation of the City of Hamilton* (2012).[2]

---

2 [2012] ONSC 147.

The risk of development

Introduction

> *"No construction project is free of risk. Risk can be managed, minimised, shared, transferred or accepted. It cannot be ignored."*[1]

2–040 Add at the end of footnote 49:
    See also P Mead, "Current trends in risk allocation in construction projects and their implications for industry participants" (2007) 23 Const LJ 23 and F P Phillips, "Drafting dispute management clauses: principles of risk management for commercial contracts" (2009) 25 Const LJ 199.

---

1 Sir M Latham, *Constructing the Team* (London: HMSO, 1994), Final Report of the Government/Industry Review of Procurement and Contractual Arrangements in the Construction Industry, at para. 3.7.

Add the following Illustrations

(1) *Facts*: C commenced adjudication proceedings against D, in relation to its application for payment. No pay less notice had been served by D. D raised various challenges to the adjudicator's jurisdiction, but the latter rejected them, eventually ordering D to pay C the sum claimed. During the adjudication, D had put before the adjudicator some of the email exchanges between the parties during settlement negotiations. C contended that it should not have done so, as these documents were all "without prejudice", being evidence of negotiations to resolve a dispute. Since the dispute was not resolved, C submitted none of the documents should have been put before the adjudicator. D argued that the adjudicator had exceeded his jurisdiction by awarding a sum in excess of the "cap" referred to in paragraph 2(4) of Part II of the *Scheme*, which seeks to provide a cap on the amount of any stage payments. *Held*: that (1) the exchanges between the parties had not been referred to in either the notice of adjudication, or the referral notice; some of them were set out for the first time in the response. C had therefore not waived the "without prejudice" protection. Further, some of the emails upon which D relied were not referred to even in its response. (2) The cap was described as the difference between the contract price and the aggregate of the instalment stage payments. The challenge failed on the "very simple" ground that D had not shown what the contract price was. H had submitted that it was the original contract sum, notwithstanding the fact that it had certified a far greater amount as being the value of the work undertaken so far: *RMC Building & Civil Engineering Limited v UK Construction Limited (Rev 1)* (2016).[2]

(2) *Facts*: Rob Purton (C) carried out some works on site for Kilker (D) at the Dorchester Hotel between 22 September and the last week of October 2014. Preparatory steps were taken before and during the week of 9 June 2014, there being a specified list of itemised work, with reference to a price of £350,000. A dispute arose and C, in the name of his company, brought the case to adjudication. D disputed that any contract had been made with C and the adjudicator, accepting that submission, resigned. C issued a second adjudication in his sole name, on the basis that, on 9 June 2014, an oral contract had been agreed. The adjudication decision dated 12 May 2015 ordered D to pay C £147,223 within seven days and ordered D to pay his fees and expenses of £4,184. C brought proceedings for summary judgment. C resisted enforcement on the same previous basis that there was no contract concluded between the parties and therefore the adjudicator did not have jurisdiction to give his decision. *Held*, by Stuart-Smith J: that beyond argument, there was a contract between the parties, since: (1) there was substantial "performance" on both sides, with C doing the works and D making payments to the tune of £654,000; and (2) an original scope of works was agreed (regardless of the price being agreed) in the knowledge that further works may be added later through a formal process or variation orders and concluded that C was entitled

---

2 [2016] EWHC 241 (TCC).

to summary judgment in the sum of £151,407, plus interest at the rate of 8% from 19 May 2015 to date and continuing at the judgment rate until payment, or further order, and to its costs of the action to be assessed on the standard basis if not agreed: *Purton v Kilker Projects Limited* (2015).[3]

(3) *Facts*: This case concerned the terms of a sub-contract, under which RBL was to provide vibro compaction at the site on which D was contracted to build a warehouse for C. The contentious clause was one of RBL's standard terms, which required the notification of any claim for defective works to be made in writing within 28 days of the appearance of the defect, and in any event to be notified within one calendar year of completion. The failure of the ground piles did not manifest until over ten years after completion, and so the issue was whether RBL's limitation would be effective to prevent CML's recovery against them. Edwards-Stuart J had to determine whether such a limitation would be reasonable for ground works of the sort provided by RBL. *Held*: that such a limitation was not reasonable: there would often be a substantial lapse of time between the carrying out of the work and the occurrence of any visible cracking to the fabric of a building. Whilst it was possible for ground treatment works to fail whilst the sub-contractor was still on site, the potential for a claim was reduced because the sub-contractor would probably put the work right straightaway. Where the failure of ground, or piles, occurred under load, experience suggested that it seldom occurs instantaneously: *Commercial Management (Investments) Limited v Mitchell Design and Construct Limited* (2016).[4]

2–042 Add the following Illustration:

Facts: Bloomberg (C) entered into a lease agreement with regard to 15 Finsbury Square (the property), receiving collateral warranties from various contractors (Sandberg (D), Buro Happold and Malling Pre-cast Limited (Malling)), with regard to the works being carried out in the property. In 2001, two cladding tiles fell from the building and Malling carried out remedial works after investigative works and a condition survey were done. In 2013, a soffit cladding tile fell from the property. The warranty from Malling contained a limitation clause, reading as follows: "notwithstanding the date hereof no proceedings shall be commenced against the contractor after the expiry of twelve years. . ." (the last works having been carried out in 2000). Since C was out of time as against Malling, it issued claims against D and Buro Happold. D then, in turn, brought a claim against Malling pursuant to the Civil Liability (Contribution) Act 1978. Malling relied upon the wording in its warranty clause which read "no proceedings" and insisted that this included proceedings sought to be commenced by any other party. *Held*, by Fraser J: that the wording only related to C; the judge noted that the overall effect of Malling's argument would be, if granted, that the parties could contract out of the operation of the Act: *Bloomberg LP v Sandberg* (2015).[5]

3 [2015] EWHC 2624 (TCC).
4 [2016] EWHC 76 (TCC).
5 [2015] EWHC 2858 (TCC).

2–065 Add the following Illustrations:

(1) *Facts*: C was a building contractor. D was the owner of two properties in the Royal Borough of Kensington and Chelsea (RBKC). The parties entered into a contract for C to carry out demolition, refurbishment and reconstruction works at the properties to form a single residence. Whilst work was underway, RBKC wrote to C and D stating that it considered the extent of proposed demolition to amount to "substantial demolition" and that conservation area consent was required. The critical demolition works were suspended by C and did not resume until about a year later. C claimed an EoT, submitting that consent had not been obtained by D for the demolition works necessary to execute the works. One issue was whether there was an implied term in the contract that D was responsible for ensuring that all required consents were obtained prior to the commencement of the works. *Held*: that a reasonable developer would know that he was likely to need conservation area consent in advance. However, this was not a case where it could be implied that the parties could have intended that nothing should happen about planning permission. It would be obvious to an informed bystander that the party best placed to obtain planning permission was the employer, not least because he knew in advance what he wanted to do. Any reasonable person would know that a failure to make a timely application could result in a delay. However, the essential point was whether a term should be implied that the employer would ensure that planning permission was obtained, or whether there should be a limited obligation to exercise reasonable diligence. There was nothing inequitable about leaving the loss caused by the unreasonable actions of a third party to lie where they fell. Commercial necessity did not require the employer to undertake the entire risk of obtaining planning permission. Imposing such an obligation was not necessary to make the contract work, because it could not prevent the local authority from acting unreasonably. If the necessary planning permission had not been obtained at the time when the contractor submitted its tender, he should decide whether he wanted to take on the risk and could protect himself accordingly by inserting a clause into the building contract: *Walter Lilly and Co Limited v Clin* (2016).[6]

(2) *Facts*: On 16 November 2006, shipbuilder A concluded a diesel engine sales contract with manufacturer B at a price of RMB7.36 million, with the diesel engine to be delivered by 15 February 2008. On 25 November 2008, A concluded a contract with C to rent C's building berth to build an 18,000DWT bulk vessel with a price of RMB118,000 per month and a rental period (provisionally agreed) from April 2007 to 28 February 2008. On 27 June 2007, A concluded a vessel sales contract with D to sell the 18,000 DWT vessel to D at a price of RMB71.78 million, with the delivery date being 15 March 2008. B failed to deliver the vessel engine to A as scheduled and, as a consequence, A failed to deliver the vessel to D. D terminated the contract and A sub-sold the vessel to E at a reduced price of RMB53 million. A then commenced proceedings against B for delayed

6 [2016] EWHC 357 (TCC).

delivery of the diesel engine. B defended on the basis that its delay of delivery was caused by force majeure (snow storms and an earthquake) and that its liability could be exempted. *Held*, by the Zheijing High People's Court, PRC: that the amount of RMB14 million (including RMB11.28 million price difference) should be reimbursed in favour of A, because: (1) under art. 113 of the PRC *Contract Law*, where either party fails to perform its obligations under the contract, the amount of compensation for the loss should equal to loss actually caused by the breach of contract and should include the profit obtainable after the performance of the contract, but should not exceed the total loss that might be caused by the breach of contract and had, or ought to have, been anticipated by the party in breach at the time of making the contract; (2) as a major provider of vessel engines in the Taizhou area, B was entirely familiar with the business of shipbuilding in Taizhou and B sent representatives there many times for contract negotiations, testing of the facility and after-sales service. B should have been able to know that A would sell the vessel for profit and, as a very important part of the vessel, the shipbuilding could not be completed if there was no main engine. In the diesel engine sales contract, it was also agreed that B should send engineers to attend the sea trials for free. As such, B could foresee A's loss caused by delay. At the time of this case, the 2008 world economic crisis happened and the vessel price dropped substantially. Although this market price fall was not foreseeable by B, A's loss was caused by B's breach of contract; (3) in terms of the snow storm, the south of China suffered very severe snow storms at the beginning of 2008. However, B was located in the north-west of China and it was quite normal to see snow storms in that area. In terms of the Wenchuan earthquake, this happened on 12 May 2008 and, at that time, B was already late for delivery by three months. B sent a letter to A regarding the alleged force majeure as late as 23 August 2008, and, even if force majeure could be admitted, B failed to notify A timeously to find a substitute diesel engine and to reduce its loss. In addition, during January to December 2008, according to data from the Zheijang Ship Survey Bureaux, 12 main engines were delivered by B to the Taizhou area. B therefore had the ability to manufacture the diesel engine during the alleged force majeure period and this defeated its allegation regarding force majeure: *ZHZZ No 113* (2014).[7]

2–066 Add at the end of footnote 78:
See also J Charlson and C Odouza, "Construction industry legal risk identification for SMEs" (2016) 32 Const LJ 630.

Add the following Illustration:

Facts: a dispute arose out of a car component purchase agreement which (at art. 6.3) provided as follows: "Entire Agreement; Amendment: This Agreement, which includes the Appendices hereto, is the only agreement between the Parties relating to

---

7 [2014] Zheijang High People's Court, PRC.

the subject matter hereof. It can only be amended by a written document which (i) specifically refers to the provision of this Agreement to be amended and (ii) is signed by both Parties." The issue was whether, or not, a company known as Porto became a party to the agreement, even though there had been no formal amendment, as required by art. 6.3. The judge at first instance decided that, whilst it was possible for parties to agree to vary or waive a requirement such as that in art. 6.3, whether they have done so was fact-sensitive. *Held*: that the general principle of the English law of contract is that parties have the freedom to agree whatever terms they choose, and can do so in a document, by word of mouth, or by conduct. The consequence in this context was that in principle the fact that the parties' contract contained a clause such as art. 6.3 did not prevent them from later making a new contract varying the contract by an oral agreement or by conduct. An oral agreement or the conduct of the parties to a contract containing such a clause may give rise to a separate and independent contract, which has the effect of varying the written contract. The conduct of the parties was sufficient to mean that the agreement had been varied by conduct. On the basis of "open, obvious and consistent" dealings over a long period, there was no other explanation but that the parties intended to add Porto as a party to the agreement: *Globe Motors Inc v TRW Lucas Variety Electric Steering Limited* (2016).[8]

2–068 **Add at the end of footnote 80:**

See also S Jackson, "Good Faith Revisited" (2014) 30 Const LJ 379: and J van Dunné, "On a clear day, you can see the continent: the shrouded acceptance of good faith as a general rule of contract law on the British Isles" (2015) 31 Const LJ 3.

2–073 **Add the following further Illustration:**

(2) *Facts*: This case concerned a contract under which BHA was engaged to drill several oil production wells in Iraqi oil fields. An on-demand performance bond was issued by D on behalf of BHA worth 5% of the contract value of $142.3 million. It provided that D was responsible for the payment of $7.1 million if BHA failed to fulfill their contractual provisions. This was subject to a condition in paragraph 4, namely that no amendment had been made to the contract, which impacted upon the timely performance of the work. C made a written demand to D, requesting payment, and stating that BHA was in breach of contract. D rejected the validity of the demand and refused to make the payment. They claimed that to comply with paragraph 4, C should have expressly stated in their request that no amendment had been made to the contract, which impacted upon the timely performance of the work. *Held*: that the bond should be interpreted as a whole and any individual words, or clauses, should be interpreted in context. It would also not endorse an interpretation, which was commercially absurd. D's submission lacked "commercial or principled legal justification". There was no express requirement in the bond, which

---

8 [2016] EWCA Civ 396.

required C to make a statement that no amendment had been made to the contract which impacted upon the timely performance of the works under it. It was "almost inconceivable" that, in the course of such a huge contract, there would be no changes to the scope of the works which would impact on timely performance. D's interpretation would have meant that C would essentially never have been able to make the statement required for a valid demand, in effect thereby rendering the bond "virtually useless": *Lukoil Mid-East Limited v Barclays Bank plc* (2016).[9]

2–074 Add the following Illustration:

Facts: C and D entered into a JCT *Design and Build Contract, 2011 Edition* with bespoke amendments, which had been made to the standard form payment provisions that resulted in the parties opting for staged payments; this resulted in agreement of a payment schedule comprising 23 interim payment applications. The works did not reach practical completion on the date set out in the contract. The parties had, therefore, in advance of the expiry of the payment schedule, sought to reach agreement on a revised schedule, but were unable to do so in time. D issued interim payment application 24, despite no agreement having been made as to the mechanism for making future payments beyond the 23 interim payment applications provided for under the contract. *Held*: that D had no contractual right to make, or be paid for, any interim payment application beyond the 23rd application. Such a future payment provision could not be implied into the contract, because the possibility of providing for further interim payments as a consequence of a delay in reaching practical completion, was something the parties could have negotiated prior to agreeing to the original payment schedule. Further, the payment procedures set out in the Scheme for Construction Contracts 1998 could not apply to future payments due to the parties having already agreed a schedule pursuant to which payments would be made. Further interim payment to the contractor was subject to the parties agreeing the terms upon which they would be made, which they had already been unable to do: *Grove Developments Limited v Balfour Beatty Regional Construction Limited* (2016).[10]

2–076 Add at the end of footnote 94:
See also N A Brown, "Industry standard terms: another fly in the ointment of contractual intent?" (2013) 29 Const LJ 259.

2–090 Add the following Illustrations:

(1) *Facts*: Arnold (R) leased a group of chalets at Oxwich Leisure Park on the Gower Peninsula to Britton and others (A). Various covenants were included in clause 3 of the lease and, in particular, cl. 3(2) thereof, which contained an annual service

9 [2016] EWHC 166 (TCC).
10 [2016] EWHC 168 (TCC).

charge. This was fixed for the first year at £90 per annum, with an increase of 10% for each ensuing year. A appealed with regard to R's correct interpretation of cl. 3(2) in 25 leases. R contended that the service charge provisions in cl. 3(2) in the above 25 leases provided for a fixed annual change of £90 for the first year of the term, increasing each subsequent year by 10% on a compound basis. A argued that such a construction of cl. 3(2) led to an increasingly absurdly high annual service charge in the last years and that the correct interpretation was, therefore, that A was required to pay a fair proportion of R's costs of providing the services, subject to a maximum of £90 in the first year of the term, increasing every year by 10% on a compound basis. *Held*, by Neuberger LJ, that: (1) despite one, or two, very small errors in the drafting, there was nothing significantly wrong with the wording of cl. 3(2); (2) this was one of the rare forms of residential lease that fall outside any of the protections provided by the law; (3) the court did not have any power to remedy long-term contracts in order to preserve the essential nature of the service charge in changed economic circumstances, which did not mean that A's predicament was acceptable; (4) whenever the parties could not agree an amendment of the leases on a fair basis, A would have to seek parliamentary intervention and, as a consequence, the appeal should be dismissed: *Arnold v Britton* (2015).[11]

(2) *Facts*: Marks and Spencer plc (A) subleased different floors in a building in Paddington, London from BNP Paribas Securities Services Trust Company (Jersey) Limited and another (R). The lease ran from 25 January 2006 to 2 February 2018, including a break clause of six months' prior written notice. A served a break notice to R on 7 July 2011, determining the lease on 24 January 2012. R invoiced A for its share of the insurance rent premium plus VAT, which was paid by A. Clause 8.3 of the lease stated that a break notice would only be valid if on the break date there were no arrears of basic rent, or VAT on the basic rent, whilst cl. 4 thereof stated that a break notice would only be valid on the first break date if on or prior to the first break date, the tenant paid to the landlord the sum of £919,800 plus VAT. A paid R the rent due on 25 December 2011, regarding the quarter from that date up to and including 24 March 2012, in compliance with cl. 8.3 above. Payment included the basic rent plus VAT and the car park licence fee. Later, on 18 January 2012, A paid R £919,800 plus VAT in compliance with cl. 8.4. On 3 September 2012, R served A a service charge certificate regarding those services provided in the calendar year 2011, showing that the cost of the services had been less than the estimate and thus crediting A for the excess payment. C appealed, contending that there should be an implied term into the lease that if the tenant exercises the right to break under cl. 8 and subsequently the lease determines on 24 January, the landlords ought to pay back a proportion of the basic rent paid by the tenant due on the immediately preceding 25 December, being apportioned in respect of the period 24 January up to an including the ensuing 24 March 2012. Likewise, A claimed the same implied term should exist in regard to the car park licence fee and the insurance rent. *Held*, by

---

11 [2015] UKSC 36.

Neuberger LJ, that: (1) neither the common law, nor statute, apportions rent in advance on a time basis; (2) this position was generally understood and accepted when the deed and the lease were negotiated and executed; (3) it was reasonable for R to have insured the building for the whole of the ensuring year and, as a consequence, the appeal was dismissed: *Marks and Spencer plc v BNP Paribas Securities Services Trust Company Limited* (2015).[12]

(3) *Facts*: Transformers and Rectifiers Limited (C) had been in a commercial relationship with Needs Limited (D) for over 20 years, placing orders for nitrile gaskets and other components. The top copy of C's purchase order was printed on white paper, on the reverse of which were the terms and conditions in small and light-coloured lettering. There was no reference to such terms and conditions on the face of the purchase order. C did not always follow the same pattern when placing such orders, sometimes posting them, or using facsimile, or email, and, when using the last two methods, C did not transmit a copy of the reverse side of the purchase order. When acknowledging purchase orders, D replied that the prices and deliveries were subject to their normal terms and conditions of sale. C argued that the gaskets supplied by D were unsuitable and not in accordance with the contract. C claimed that its terms and conditions applied, because they were printed on the back of the purchase orders, whilst D argued that their terms and conditions applied because they were written on its acknowledgements of orders. This was a preliminary issue to determine the terms of the contracts made between the parties. *Held*: *by* Edwards-Stuart J, that: (1) where A makes an offer on its conditions and B accepts that offer on its conditions and, without more, performance follows, it was correct to assume, provided that each party's conditions have been reasonably drawn to the attention of each other, that there was a contract on B's conditions; (2) where there is reliance upon a previous course of dealing, three, or four, occasions may suffice; (3) a consistent and unequivocal course of dealing needs to be followed by the party contending that its terms and conditions are incorporated; (4) whenever there exist standard trade, or industry, terms, it will be easier for a party contending for those conditions, to persuade the court that they should be incorporated, as long as reasonable notice of the application of the terms has been given; (5) a party's standard terms and conditions would not, however, be incorporated, unless that party has given the other party reasonable notice of those terms and conditions; (6) if the terms and conditions are referred to in subsequent invoices, it is not necessary for a party to include, or refer to, these in the documents forming the contract; (7) an invoice following a concluded contract effected by a clear offer upon standard terms, which are accepted, even if only by delivery, would, or might be, too late; (8) since D did not print its terms and conditions on the reverse of the acknowledgment of order, or provide C with a copy of such terms and conditions, it did not do enough to bring these to C's attention and hence turned the acknowledgment of order into a

---

12 [2015] UKSC 72.

counter-offer. As a consequence, neither party's terms and conditions were incorporated into the two relevant purchase orders: *Transformers and Rectifiers Limited v Needs Limited* (2015).[13]

2–142 Add the following further Illustrations:

(4) *Facts*: Caterpillar Motoren GmbH & Co KG (C) entered into two sub-contracts for construction services for two power plants; each sub-contract required the sub-contractor to procure an advanced payment bond (APB) and a performance bond (PB), described as instruments that guaranteed the due performance by the sub-contractor for an advance payment made by C to the sub-contractor and effects that guarantee for due performance of all the work by the sub-contractor, respectively. Once dispute arose, C demanded the return of advance payments and LADs. *Held*, by Teare J: that APBs with such wording as "guarantees", "forthwith on demand" and "without reference to" met the *Wuhan* requirements for an on-demand bond, since (1) it relates to an underlying transaction between parties in different jurisdictions, (2) it is issued by a bank, (3) it contains an undertaking to pay on demand, and (4) it does not contain clauses excluding, or limiting, the defences that are available to a guarantor. The PBs were also qualified as on-demand bonds, instead of guarantees, since any demand was expressed as being conclusive as regards the amount that was due from the bondsman and also because of the fact that the bondsman was to pay unconditionally the amount of damages claimed by C, which was inconsistent with the concept of lawful claims and payment guarantees: *Caterpillar Motoren GmbH & Co KG v Mutual Benefits Assurance Company* (2015).[14]

(5) *Facts*: Lloyds Bank plc (C) sued McBains Cooper Consulting Limited (D) for breach of its retainer with regard to a redevelopment. Part of the property was run by a trust, that funded the development with the money borrowed from C. The sum did not include allowances on contingencies and understated the professional fees and interest. Late in the project, D advised that there was not enough money available to complete the development and C subsequently called in the loan, which the borrower was unable to pay. As a result, the property was sold, leading to a loss of £1.4m for C. The latter sought to claim this from D. *Held*, by Edwards-Stuart J: that D was in breach of its duty in failing to advise that there was not enough money to complete the works; however, since the insufficiency of the facility to cover the development was known to the relevant individuals at C and the latter also failed to share information, or properly to respond to reports, C had to bear one-third of the losses: *Lloyds Bank plc v McBains Cooper Consulting Limited* (2015).[15]

---

13 [2015] EWHC 269 (TCC).

14 [2015] EWHC 2304 (Comm). See also, Alex Bevan, "Independent guarantees in international construction projects: a note of caution" (2012) 28 Const LJ 200 and Lauren Adams, "New clots in the lifeblood of international construction projects: enjoying employers calls on performance bonds" (2014) 30 Const LJ 325.

15 [2015] EWHC 2372 (TCC).

2–165 Add the following Illustrations:

(4) *Facts*: This case concerned the tortious duties of care owed by a construction professional when providing services free of charge in the course of a long-running friendship. C had previously been good friends with D, but relationships had turned sour. The key questions was did D owe C a duty of care in tort and, if so, what was the content of that duty? *Held*, by Mr Recorder Alexander Nissen QC, that: D owed duties to C in respect of project management services she had gratuitously provided the C. The relationship was more akin to a professional one and so there was no danger of imposing legal duties onto what had been merely a social and informal arrangement. This was a significant project and was being approached in a professional way. It was not a piece of brief ad hoc advice of the type occasionally proffered by professional people in a less formal context. Instead, the services were provided over a relatively lengthy period of time and involved considerable input and commitment on both sides. They also involved significant commercial expenditure on the part of C: *Burgess v Lejonvarn* (2016).[16]

(5) *Facts*: Trebor Basset and Cadbury (A) had an agreement for the operation of a popcorn production area in Pontefract, known as New Manufacturing Unit (NMU). ADT (R) concluded a contract with A to design, supply install and commission a fire suspension system, intended to extinguish fires in the oil pop production area, the elevator and the hopper arrangements. On 8 June 2005, a fire in the oil pop production area, destroyed the entire NMU. Both parties agreed that, if the fire suppression system had discharged CO^2 into the hopper at the right time, the fire would have been extinguished. A sued R for the loss suffered as a result of the fire: damage to the building, damage to machinery, increased costs of working and business interruption. The first instance judge found that R owed C a contractual duty to exercise reasonable skill and care in carrying out the design of the system and that R had a tortious duty of care to A, as well as finding that A shared in the responsibility for the damage for being negligent and reckless in its failure to segregate the oil pop production area from the rest of the building and to install sprinklers, hence reducing A's damages to 75%. On appeal, R contended that certain actions by A's employees in the immediate aftermath of the discovery of fire should be considered the proximate cause of its subsequent spread: they released some of the burning popcorn from the bottom of the hopper (180 litres altogether), which was then stamped out on the factory floor. When the fire alarm went off, A's employees thought that the fire had been put out and left the oil pop production area, went into the next-door packaging hall and exited the NMU, as identified by the judge concluding that the fire spread as a result of the discharge from the hopper onto the floor of a large quantify of burning popcorn, which has been displaced when stamping. A argued that R's obligation was beyond the use of reasonable skill and care in the design of the system, as R was in breach of a contractual term to the effect that the system was designed to suit the risk. Likewise, R had failed to comply generally with the

---

16 [2016] EWHC 40 (TCC).

requirements of BS5306 Part 4 distinction between surface and deep-seated fires and CO^2, and similarly R had failed to supply good quality services pursuant to s 4(2) of the Supply of Good and Services Act 1982. *Held*, by Tomlinson LJ, that: (1) R had primarily agreed to supply design skills and reasonable care in exercising them; (2) the shortcomings in the system were matters of design, not the inherent quality of goods that were also supplied and that were of good quality. In consequence, the appeal should be dismissed and damage recoverable by A must be reduced to reflect its responsibility for the damage caused by the fire: *Trebor Bassett Holdings Limited v ADT Fire and Security plc* (2012).[17]

2–166 Add a new footnote 215A at the end of the paragraph:

See also D Pliener, "Outflanking *Murphy v Brentwood*: claiming in tort for pure economic loss" (2010) 26 Const LJ 270 and A Gunawansa, "Pure economic loss relating to construction defects – A comparative analysis" (2010) 26 Const LJ 439.

2–183 Add the following Illustration:

Facts: C brought proceedings in private nuisance against D, after the slippage of clay from their land into a nearby stream removed support from their garden, leading to fears that the landslip would eventually cause subsidence. C argued D had abandoned significant lengths of sewer in the area, which were leaking sewage and rainwater into the clay hill and saturating it, causing a series of rotational shears to the hill. D were under a statutory duty pursuant to s 94(1) of the Water Industry Act 1991 (the Act) to maintain the pipes and ensure that the area around them was effectively drained, and the Act already provided a statutory scheme for enforcement that was inconsistent with common law liability in nuisance: *Marcic v Thames Water Utilities Limited* (2003).[18] However, in *Dobson v Thames Utilities Limited* (2007),[19] Ramsey J determined that a similar statutory scheme would not protect D against common law liability if the nuisance resulted from a negligent failure at an operational level rather than resulting from broader strategic decisions made by the authority. Whether a particular failure fell on one side of the line or the other was a matter of fact and degree, and Ramsey J contrasted an allegation that a particular filter should be cleaned against one which would require a major plant to be renewed in order to illustrate the difference. *Held*: that this was the former type of case and an action in nuisance could therefore lie. D failed to maintain the pipe, or adequately repair defects in it. Those were operational in nature rather than "strategic". They were more akin to cleaning a filter than major plant renewal: *Bell v Northumbrian Water Limited* (2016).[20]

2–183 Add a new footnote 242A at the end of the sentence:

See also P Singh, "Rethinking nuisance in the 21st century: a critical analysis of *Coventry v Lawrence*" (2016) 32 Const LJ 606.

---

17 [2012] EWCA Civ 1158.
18 [2003] UKHL 66.
19 [2007] EWHC 2021 (TCC).
20 [2016] EWHC 133 (TCC).

CHAPTER 3

Project procurement

Introduction

"When a man is buying a basket of strawberries it can profit him to know that the bottom half of it is rotten."[1]

3–022 Add the following Illustration:

(1) *Facts*: D engaged C to carry out building works. Work started under a letter of intent. Although the parties proposed to enter into a JCT *Intermediate Form of Building Contract* (the IFC), no contract was ever concluded. S later terminated C's employment. D started the first adjudication seeking a declaration that a valid construction contract existed between the parties, and the terms of that contract include the provisions of the JCT form. The adjudicator decided there was a valid construction contract, but the terms were in the letter of intent and not the *IFC*. D served a notice of adjudication claiming money under the letter of intent. C applied to the court for declarations that the first adjudicator's decision was enforceable and the second adjudicator did not have jurisdiction to decide the matters set out in D's notice, because the first adjudicator had already decided those matters.

---

1 SC Langhorne, M Johnson (eds), *More Maxims of Mark* (1927), p. 941.

17

Held, by Coulson J, granting declaratory relief: that the parties were bound by the first adjudicator's decision regarding the letter of intent. However, the judge declined to make the declaration with regard to the alleged lack of jurisdiction in any future adjudication. It would not have been possible for the adjudicator in the first adjudication to "decide whether or not there was a valid contract without deciding whether basic terms had been agreed and, if so, what precisely those terms were", because a valid contract can only come into existence if there is agreement between the parties on certain basic matters: *Penten Group Limited v Spartafield Limited* (2016).[2]

3–056   Add at the end of footnote 50:
See also D W M Chan; A R C Chan; P T I Lam and J H L Chan, "Exploring the key risks and risk mitigation measures for guaranteed maximum price and target cost contracts in construction" (2010) 26 Const LJ 364.

3–057   Add a new footnote 50A at the end of the paragraph:
See also J H C Chan; D W M Chan and W Lord, "Key risk factors and risk mitigation measures for target cost contracts in construction – A comparison between the West and the East" (2011) 27 Const LJ 441.

3–060   Add at the end of footnote 52:
See also J Mason, "The views and experiences of specialist contractors on partnering in the United Kingdom" (2009) 25 Const LJ 206.

---

2 [2016] EWHC 317 (TCC).

CHAPTER 4

Standard form provisions for time and cost

Introduction

"Words differently arranged have a different meaning, and meanings differently arranged have different effects."[1]

4–053   Add at the end of footnote 150:
See also E Kratochvilova and M Mendelblat, "'*Force majeure*' clauses" (2012) 28 Const LJ 12.

Add the following Illustration:

> *Facts*: Sato Kogyo Pte Limited (R) contracted with Alliance Concrete Singapore Pte Limited (A) for the supply of ready-mix concrete (RMC) for three projects in Singapore. Soon after, the Indonesian government banned the export of sand to Singapore. In order to reduce the impact of this ban, the Singaporean government provided sand from its own stockpile to ongoing Singaporean projects. A was unwilling to pay for the increased price of RMC and a dispute arose, with R arguing that the original price of the RMC applied, whilst A argued that the contract had been frustrated and a new price should therefore apply. The court had to establish whether the "sand ban" was a supervening event, which frustrated the contract. The first instance judge did not consider that the sand ban was a supervening event, because there was no term which stipulated that the sand was required to come from Indonesia and, as a consequence, found that the contracts had not been frustrated. R appealed. *Held, by* the Singapore Court of Appeal: that the contracts had been frustrated, since both parties contemplated the use of Indonesian sand and so the ban was a supervening event beyond the parties' reasonable control: *Alliance Concrete Singapore Pte Limited v Sato Kogyo Pte Limited* (2014).[2]

4–123   Add at the end of footnote 414:
See also D Bordoli, "Weather claims in the United Kingdom construction industry" (2009) 25 Const LJ 18.

4–256   Add at the end of footnote 885:
See also R Davis, "Remedial security and construction contracts" (2011) 27 Const LJ 480.

4–257   Add a new footnote 885A:
See, in particular, the new chapter 26 below.

4–365   Add footnote 1141A at the end of the paragraph:
See also N Lane and K Pickavance, "Cost and time management in the Joint Contracts Tribunal Major Projects Contract and the Chartered Institute of Building Complex Projects Contract – a comparative analysis" (2015) 31 Cost LJ 295.

---

1 B Pascal, *Pensées, No 23* (1670) (translated by London: J M Dent & Sons, 1931).
2 [2014] SGCA 35.

Add the following additional paragraphs after paragraph 4–366:

4–367 *The Time and Cost Management Contract 2015 [TCMI5]*

In 2015, the CPC was renamed and reissued by the CIOB (perhaps in response to a possible perception in the industry that anything characterised as "complex" might be something of a disincentive to potential users!), as explained in more detail (in the introduction thereto), as follows:

> "The Time and Cost Management Contract (the Contract) is a revised edition of what was previously the Complex Projects Contract, published in 2013. The name has been changed to reflect more clearly the core strengths of the Contract. The Time and Cost Management Contract is written for use with the Time and Cost Management Contract suite's Subcontract and Consultancy Appointment to provide a uniform approach to time cost and risk management from initiation to completion of building and engineering projects."

The introduction continues as follows:

"Naming

The Contract is formally called the 'CIOB Time and Cost Management Contract', 2015 Edition. However, it may also be referred to as 'The Time and Cost Management Contract' or simply 'TCM15'. It is referred to within this document as the 'Contract'.

The use of the contract

The Contract is most suitable for those projects that cannot be effectively managed intuitively and that require for their success a more scientific approach to time and cost risk management than is usual on more simple projects. The Contract can be used by companies, public authorities and private individuals in the UK and in any other country. The Contract can be used for

- build only of a design prepared under the direction of the employer
- build only of a design prepared under the direction of the employer, but with the contractor's design of parts
- design and build or turnkey projects in which the contractor is responsible for both the design and construction of the works
- construction management and management contracting (with some changes in terms required by special conditions).

Pricing

The Contract can be used with any method of pricing. Commonly, these include fixed price, target cost, measured term, fixed fee, cost reimbursement, partnering and alliancing. The required method of pricing is to be described in the Special Conditions.

   (. . .)

Time management

The Contract requires competence in critical path network modelling, resource allocation and productivity analysis. The working schedule is required to be in differing densities updated and revised on the rolling wave principle that constantly predicts the currently attainable completion date, sectional completion dates and key dates.

Cost management

Cost management is by reference to the values attributed to the activities in the working schedule with progress updated from databased progress records. The updated working schedule constantly predicts the out-turn cost of the works and the value of work done to date.

Risk management

The Contract is a collaborative contract requiring the contractor, its sub-contractors and the design consultants to work with the time manager, cost manager, contract administrator and the employer to constantly appraise risk, and to confer in taking practical action to overcome and avoid their unnecessary consequences. The Contract contains power to instruct acceleration both to overcome the effects of a delay to progress and bring forward completion dates where practical.

Collaboration

The Contract requires a collaborative approach to design in conformity with British Standards Institution's BS 1192:2007, but goes further in expressly requiring the Contractor and all sub-contractors and consultants having a continuing rôle in design, administration or quality control during the works to participate in decision-making, quality control, time management, cost management and risk management.

Building Information Modelling

The Contract is suitable for Level 2 Projects and the collaborative production of information throughout the project life cycle. It is compatible with the requirements of the British Standards Institution's PAS 1192: Part 2, 2013 'Specification for information management for the capital/delivery phase of construction projects using building information modelling' and it may be used with any desired Building Information Modelling protocol.

Information transfer

The Contract requires information to be transferred electronically either by readable file or in native file format and in accordance with a file transfer protocol compatible with the British Standards Institution's PAS 1192:4 2014 COBie."

4–368 It is, perhaps (particularly now following the 2016 US presidential election!), something of a pity that a solidly British industry body should persist in characterising a "programme" as a "schedule"! Whatever, *TCM15* contains the following numbered clauses relating to the subject-matter of this book:

"(. . .)
5. Commencement and completion
(. . .)
11. Information
12. Contractor's Requests for Supply
13. Contractor's Submissions
(. . .)
17. Building Information Modelling
(. . .)
34. Early Warning
35. Risk Management
36. Failure to Provide Risk Management Information
37. Working Schedule
38. Incorporation of Contractor's Pricing Document
39. Progress Records
40. Updated Working Schedule
41. Revised Working Schedule
42. Schedule Quality Assurance
43. Calculation of Effect of Event on Time

44. Calculation of Effect of Event on Cost
45. Float and Time Contingencies
46. Contractor's Improvements of Progress
47. Employer's Improvement of Progress
48. Instructed Recovery
49. Instructed Acceleration
50. Failure to Comply with an Instruction to Recover or Accelerate
51. Extension of Time
52. Concurrency
53. Partial Possession and Use of the Works
54. Substantial Completion
55. Making Good Defects
56. Failure to Achieve Substantial Completion
5. Liquidated Delay Damages
(. . .)
64. Contract Administrator's Notice of Payment Due
65. Contractor's Notice of Payment Due
66. Payment
(. . .)
73. Issue Resolution
74. Dispute Resolution."

4-369 It is extremely refreshing at last to see a standard form construction contract dealing head-on with BIM, updating and revising the working "programme", float, recovery, acceleration, concurrency and "pre-dispute issue resolution" and the CIOB is warmly to be congratulated upon this initiative; it remains to be seen whether users will be persuaded by the "emperor's new clothes"!

4-370 *The JCT 2016 suite*
The 2016 edition of the *Design and Build Contract* family [*DB16*] is now available from *jctld.co.uk* and JCT stocklists, the following contracts being available:

- JCT *Design and Build Contract 2016 (DB)*
- JCT *Design and Build Contract Guide 2016 (DB/G)*
- JCT *Design and Build Sub-Contract Agreement 2016 (DBSub/A)*
- JCT *Design and Build Sub-Contract Conditions 2016 (DBSub/C)*
- JCT *Design and Build Sub-Contract Guide 2016 (DBSub/G)*
- JCT *Design and Build Contract Tracked Change Document 2016*
- JCT *Design and Build Sub-Contract*

4-371 The following new features are included in DB16 it:

- The provisions of the JCT *Public Sector Supplement 2011* relating to Fair Payment, Transparency and BIM are incorporated;
- Adjustments to reflect the *Construction (Design and Management) Regulations 2015 and the Public Contracts Regulations 2015*;
- The works and existing structures insurance provisions are more flexible;
- The section 4 payment provisions are revised and simplified including:
- Establishing (for fair payment purposes) interim valuation dates that applying to main contract, sub-contract and sub-sub-contract levels;
- increased flexibility in relation to fluctuations provisions;

- Consolidating the notice requirements of the Housing Grants, Construction and Regeneration Act 1996;
- Provisions for the grant of performance bonds and parent company guarantees;
- Extension of the optional provisions for collateral warranties from sub-contractors to include third party rights;
- Changes to the way the requirements for collateral warranties and/or third party rights are set out.

4–372 JCT *Minor Works 2016* suite published

The JCT has also launched its much-awaited new suite of building contracts(with options for contractor design, or not) and a form of sub-contract which can be used in conjunction with the main form (also making provision for sub-contractor design) together these constitute the first three agreements in the JCT's new 2016 edition (*JCT16*). The 2016 editions of the remaining agreements were rolled out during the second half of the year and into 2017 (although these are also labelled "2016"). As yet, the Scottish Building Contract Committee has not released details of its planned dates for publishing its Scots Law versions of the JCT building contracts, but it has confirmed that the SBCC contracts will be issued in the same order as the JCT new forms.

4–373 The *JCT16* it suite is the JCT's third edition in little more than decade. Ten years ago, a wholesale revamp of the entire family of contracts coincided with the JCT's 75th anniversary. Six years ago, the *JCT 2011* edition made changes to its agreements to make them compliant with the updated *Construction Act*. Looking at the *JCT Minor Works* agreements and anticipated changes to the suite as a whole (based upon press statements released by the JCT), the new edition incorporates some interesting new features and noteworthy changes, as follows:

- *JCT16* reflects the *Public Contracts Regulations 2015* and includes provisions for use by public bodies, contractors and sub-contractors on public sector projects; the *2015 Regulations* replace the previous UK public sector procurement régime and aim to make public procurement more accessible to small businesses.
- It is almost 15 months since the *CDM Regulations 2015* came into force; the new forms incorporate the JCT's own 2015 amendments (previously published as *Amendment 1*) to make the building contracts CDM-compliant.
- In 2011, the JCT published a 45-page document entitled *Public Sector Supplement*. Aimed primarily at public sector clients and their contract administrators (although the amendments proposed could also be used by private sector clients to ensure that the principles covered apply in their agreements and supply chain too), the document dealt with three issues, namely, BIM, "Fair Payment" and "Transparency"; the *JCT16* it suite incorporates into the new suite certain provisions from this supplement:
- BIM: The UK government mandate was that all centrally-procured public sector projects should be undertaken implementing BIM, Level 2 by April 2016 (with Scottish public sector projects adopting BIM, Level 2 by April 2017); JCT 2016 now makes express provision for BIM (or other communications protocols), to be included in the contract documents.
- Transparency: In 2013, the government published a policy paper *2010 to 2015 Government Policy: Government Transparency and Accountability*. The JCT *Public*

Sector Supplement includes a model clause authorising disclosures by public sector clients in accordance with the *Freedom of Information Act 2000*. JCT 2016 now includes this clause within its supplemental provisions schedule.

- Fair payment: In 2007, the OGC launched its *Guide to Best Fair Payment Practices* (which included a *Model Fair Payment Charter*, intended to apply to government contracts entered into on, or after, 1 January 2008). The publication was supported by both government and industry. In 2013, *Construction 2025*, the government's long-term vision for the construction industry, cited equitable financial arrangements and certainty of payment as critical to success for the industry. In 2014, the government launched a *Construction Supply Chain Payment Charter* to build upon the payment provisions of the *Construction Act* (as amended), the *Late Payment of Commercial Debts Regulations*, the *Fair Payment Charter and Prompt Payment Code*. JCT 2016 incorporates a number of changes designed to reflect these principles, including interim valuation dates, which will operate at main contract, sub-contract and sub-sub-contract levels.

- The revised payment provisions have also been simplified more generally with clearer *Construction Act* notice requirements, a procedure for prompt assessment of loss and expense claims and flexibility in relation to fluctuations provisions.

- Under the interim payment due date provisions, the monthly cycle of payment due dates continues to apply after practical completion, up to the due date for the final payment; this is consistent both with the new loss and expense ascertainment procedure and Fair Payment principles.

- In the new JCT building contracts for larger works, there is be an extension of insurance option C (insurance by the employer of existing structures and works in, or extensions to, them) to allow for alternative solutions to the problems typically encountered by tenants (and domestic homeowners) in obtaining existing structures cover for contractors. This approach is reflected within section 5 of the new Minor Works forms. In addition; *JCT16* consolidates (within the conditions) general provisions applying to insurance options A, B and C (evidence of insurance, insurance claims and reinstatement work).

- In the new JCT building contracts for larger works, *JCT16* also includes provisions for the grant of performance bonds and parent company guarantees and extend the optional provisions for obtaining collateral warranties from sub-contractors to include (as an alternative) the granting of third party rights by sub-contractors. Finally, the new suite includes sundry changes to make the contracts more user friendly and improve functionality. JCT 2016 aims to be fit for the future and provide greater clarity and flexibility.

4–375 The main new features of *JCT16* edition are as follows:

- In summary, incorporation of the provisions of the JCT *Public Sector Supplement 2011*, which relate to Fair Payment, Transparency and BIM.
- Adjustments to reflect the *Construction (Design and Management) Regulations 2015*.
- Incorporation of the provisions of the *JCT 2012 Named Specialist Update*.
- Extension of works insurance option C to allow alternative solutions for tenants and domestic homeowners to obtain existing structures cover for

contractors. In addition, the main text consolidates some of the general provisions relating to evidence of insurance, insurance claims and reinstatement work previously in each of insurance options A, B and C.

4–376 The JCT has revised and simplified the section 4 payment provisions, including:

- Introducing a procedure for prompt assessment of loss and expense claims.
- Establishing (for Fair Payments purposes) interim valuation dates that apply to main contract, sub-contract levels.
- Increased flexibility in relation to fluctuation provisions.
- Introducing a subsection to consolidate the notice requirements of the *Housing Grants, Construction and Regeneration Act 1996.*
- Provisions for the grant of performance bonds and parent company guarantees.
- Extending the optional provisions for collateral warranties from sub-contractors to include third party rights; changes are made to the way the requirements for collateral warranties and/or third party rights are set out, removing part 2 of the contract particulars and replacing it with a separate document, the rights particulars.

CHAPTER 5

Notices, claims and early warnings

Introduction

> *"Thus in the beginning the world was so made that certain signs come before certain events."*[1]

5–012 Add the following Illustration:

Held, by Coulson J: that a valid application for payment must: (1) set out the total sum said to be due, (2) set out the basis upon which that sum has been calculated and (3) be clear and free from ambiguity: *Severfield (UK) Limited v Duro Felguera UK Limited* (2015).[2]

5–023 Add the following Illustration:

Facts: NH International (Caribbean) Limited (C) suspended work, following disagreements between the parties, and purported to terminate the agreement. Subsequently, a number of issues were referred to arbitration. C requested evidence from National

---

1 Cicero, *De divinatione*, 1.118.
2 [2015] EWHC 2975 (TCC).

Insurance Property Development Company Limited (Trinidad and Tobago) (D) that the latter had made arrangements to pay the contract price (under cl. 2.4 of FIDIC Red Book). Unsatisfied with the answers, C suspended, and then terminated, the work; D disputed that the contract has been validly terminated. *Held*: by the Privy Council, that the contract had been validly terminated, since cl. 2.4 goes beyond merely showing that the employer is able to pay. With regard to cl. 2.5 (employer's right to set off); any claim by the employer must be notified promptly and particularised, failure of which invalidates the claim: *NH International (Caribbean) Limited v National Insurance Property Development Company (Trinidad and Tobago) Limited* (2015).[3]

5-024 Add the following Illustrations:

(1) *Facts*: The number and valuation date of an interim application indicated that it related to April, but it was served too late for April's due date. *Held*, by Akenhead J, that: it was not a valid application for May (the employer could not reasonably have understood to which month it related, since it was too late for April and too early for May); the court held that "the document relied upon as an interim application must be in substance, form and intent an interim application stating the sum considered by the contractor as due at the relevant due date and it must be free from ambiguity": *Henia Investments v Beck Interiors Limited* (2015).[4]

(2) *Held*, by Coulson J: that an interim application issued was invalid, since the documents (namely the "final account application summary" and supporting documents) did not identify themselves as a new application for payment; moreover, the application was two weeks early. The court ruled that "interim application must be clear that it is what it purports to be so that the parties know what to do about it and when": *Caledonian Modular Limited v Mar City Developments Limited* (2015).[5]

(3) *Held*, by Edwards-Stuart J: that, although applications for payment had to be made on the dates set out in the contract, the parties had established (through their conduct) that applications made a few days later would also be processed. However, that cannot be said with regard to any applications made earlier, since the applications must state the financial position as at the date stated in the contract. An earlier application is hence invalid and paying it once does not establish a waiver: *Leeds City Council v Waco UK Limited* (2015).[6]

5-055 Add the following Illustrations:

(1) *Facts*: Kingwood Electrical Services Limited (D) engaged CSK Electrical Contractors Limited (C) to carry out electrical works at Twickenham Stadium. Two adjudications arose out of the contracts concluded between the

---

3 [2015] UKPC 37.
4 [2015] EWHC 2433 (TCC).
5 [2015] EWHC 1855 (TCC).
6 [2015] EWHC 1400 (TCC).

parties. In both, D was ordered to pay C, which brought an application for summary judgment to enforce both of the decisions. D disputed the enforcement proceedings on the grounds that, first, a dispute had not crystallised, and, secondly, that the sentence "it is strongly preferred that any of the adjudicators in the attached list are not appointed" (included by C in its application for appointment of an adjudicator) constituted a fraudulent misrepresentation (relying upon *Eurocom Ltd v Siemens Plc* (2014)[7]), and, thirdly, that the timetable was too tight. *Held,* by Coulson J: that a dispute had crystallised, D having stated before the adjudication was referred, that the claims were unfounded and would be strenuously defended; that including the sentence "it is preferred that any of the adjudicators in the attached list are not appointed" did not invalidate the adjudicator's appointment; the wording was included in error and no list of adjudicators to avoid was actually attached; that the timetable set down by the adjudicator made the best use of the 28 days available; D had been in possession of the relevant invoices for a month before the adjudication; there was nothing too complex about the disputes and the matter could have been easily determined within that time and D did not request more time. In any event, the challenges had been waived by D, by its failure to raise objections at the outset and, afterwards, by performing clear and unequivocal acts to show that the alleged breaches had been waived: *CSK Electrical Contractors Limited v Kingwood Electrical Services Limited* (2015).[8]

(2)   *Held,* by the Singapore Court of Appeal: that the Singapore Mediation Centre (SMC) has powers under the Building and Construction Industry Security of Payment Act (SOPA) to enact adjudication procedural rules restricting the lodging of documents, on a particular day, to certain hours, and that the de minimis rule is excluded from applying (a document lodged two minutes late therefore being considered out of time): *Citiwall Safety Glass Pte Limited v Mansource Interior Pte Limited* (2015).[9]

---

7 [2014] EWHC 3710 (TCC).
8 [2015] EWHC 667 (TCC).
9 [2015] 5 SLR 482 (SGCA).

CHAPTER 6

Extensions of time and time at large

Extensions of time

Introduction

> *"Time for you and time for me, And time yet for a hundred indecisions, And for a hundred visions and revisions, Before the taking of a toast and tea."*[1]

6–001 Add a new footnote 1A at the end of the paragraph:
See also M Nardin, "Programmes, delay and extensions of time: a practical approach" (2014) 30 Const LJ 159.

---

1 TS Eliot, "The Love Song of J Alfred Prufrock", *The Norton Anthology of Poetry* 3rd edn (New York: WW Norton & Company, 1983) (l. 31–34).

6–014 Add the following Illustration:

Facts: Under a JCT *Standard Form of Building Contract (Without Quantities)*, the contractor issued an ineffective payment application. The contractor (Beck) had previously (in April 2015) applied for £2.9m (against a gross value of £6.5m), which included a sizeable claim for preliminaries in respect of an EoT that had yet to be awarded. The response to that application was interim payment certificate no 18, giving a gross value of £3.9m and a sum payable of £226,000. In May 2015, no interim application was issued; however, the CA issued an interim payment certificate no 19, giving a gross value of £4m and a sum payable of £18,000. The employer (Henia) then issued a payless notice, stating that £0 was due to Beck under certificates 18 and 19 because it had an entitlement to LADs for 40 weeks' delay, amounting to £373,000. Beck referred the matter to adjudication and the adjudicator issued a decision largely in Henia's favour. In the meantime, Henia issued CPP Part 8 proceeding, seeking decisions: (1) on the effectiveness of Beck's April application as a payment notice for the May payment date; (2) the validity of Henia's payless notice; and (3) whether the failure by the CA to provide a decision on the EoT prevented Henia from claiming LADs. *Held*, by Akenhead J, that: (1) application was not an effective for May; (2) the payless notice was valid; and (3) Henia was entitled to claim LADs, even where the CA had not awarded an EoT. This part of the judgment was obiter (because the adjudicator had decided Beck had not made an application for an EoT) and so assumed that an effective EoT claim had been submitted and that the CA had failed to reach a decision on it. The judge concluded that cl. 2.32 was not drafted in such a way that the CA's proper operation of the EoT provisions was a condition precedent to the entitlement to deduct LADs, although he found that the non-completion certificate and employer's notice were conditions precedent: *Henia Investments Inc v Beck Interiors Limited* (2015).[2]

6–037 Add at the end of footnote 56:
See also R Gibson, "'Time' in the Noughties" (2011) 27 Const LJ 376.

6–078 Add the following Illustration after the existing Illustration (which should be numbered (1)):

---

(2) *Facts*: C entered into a JCT *Standard Form of Building with Contractor's Design*, 1998 edition with R as the employer. This had provisions relating to LADs and extensions of time upon the occurrence of a "relevant event". The works were delayed. C and R subsequently entered into a supplemental agreement, agreeing that C had no claims for an EoT and agreeing a new contract sum, which included C's liability for LADs. C had entered into sub-contracts with D for the provision of mechanical and electrical services. C commenced proceedings against D for the delay in which it claimed its own costs as well as those it was liable for under its contract with R. D argued for an entitlement to an EoT and that they should not be held liable for LADs because C had no liability to R for such damages, and/or had not paid such sums to R and/or that such sums had not been deducted from sums otherwise payable by R to C. *Held*: that (1) D was entitled to an EoT under the

---

2 [2015] EWHC 2433 (TCC).

sub-contract, which should be added contiguously to the end of the date for completion of the sub-contract works. Any EoT due to D under the sub-contract could be added to the end of the existing period for completion of their works, allowing a single extended period for completion. C was therefore unsuccessful in arguing that the sub-contract permitted the main contractor to grant EoTs that did not necessarily run contiguously with the existing period for completion; (2) C's liability to R for LADs was not extinguished by any further supplemental agreement, as D contended, which would have enabled the repayment of LADs applied before this date. The further supplemental agreement did not have the same effect as agreeing a new completion date under the contract, through application of its EoT provisions: *Carillion Construction Limited v Woods Bagot Europe Limited* (2016).[3]

6–107 Add the following Illustrations:

(1) *Facts*: C engaged D to carry out shell and core works at a house. The contract was the JCT SBC without quantities 2011. Completion of the works was delayed. C claimed LADs. D did not pay, so C referred its claims to adjudication. The adjudicator decided time for completion had been set at large and no LADs were due. C maintained the decision was unenforceable as a result of a breach of natural justice; D had not argued that time for completion of the works was at large and the adjudicator had not given the parties a fair opportunity to comment on this. The adjudicator then went on to decide that a reasonable date for completion was 5 March 2016. C said neither party had asked for a decision on the reasonable date for completion, nor had the parties' submissions addressed the issue. Therefore, the decision as to a reasonable date for completion was also outside the adjudicator's jurisdiction and/or in breach of natural justice. *Held*: that (1) there was no breach of natural justice; the issue of whether time was at large was obviously "in play between the parties". The parties were each aware of the relevant material and the issues had been canvassed fairly before the adjudicator. The adjudicator had decided the case, not by accepting the precise submissions of one party or another, but rather by reaching a decision on a point of importance on the material before him; (2) the notice of intention to refer did not confer jurisdiction on the adjudicator to consider alternative claims that did not affect the sums that might be due to C in LADs. The words "or such other amount that the Adjudicator deems appropriate" could not be stretched to encompass a claim for unliquidated damages. Whilst D had raised a claim for EoTs by way of defence to C's claim for LADs, the question of whether or not D was entitled to an EoT was quite separate and distinct from the question of what would be a reasonable date for completion in the event that time was at large: *Satellite Construction Limited v Vascroft Contractors Limited* (2016).[4]

(2) *Facts*: The Marine Corps Research, Development and Acquisition Command (R) employed Essex Electro Engineer Inc (A) to manufacture, test and deliver a number of skid-mounted floodlights. R notified A that the drawings for

---

3 [2016] EWHC 905 (TCC).
4 [2016] EWHC 792 (TCC).

the floodlights contained errors and omissions and stopped work on that day. Some of the concerns were addressed. Among other claims, R argued that it was entitled to delay and disruption costs in relation to the approval processes and the defective generating equipment. A appealed to the Armed Services Board of Contract Appeals, which determined that much of A's claim was barred by its own delays, which concurrently delayed the project. A appealed. *Held*, by the Court of Appeals, that: the delay events were sequential and not concurrent, thus reversing the Board's decision: *Essex Electro Engineer, Inc v Danzig* (2000).[5]

(3) *Facts*: this was an application for enforcement of an adjudicator's decision by C resisted by D on the grounds that there had been a breach of natural justice or wrongful delegation of the adjudicator's decision-making function. The dispute arose out of a contract to carry out civils works at a combined cycle power plant worth some £36m, of which the adjudicator had awarded Sisk £10m. D identified three matters in support of their position: (1) there was a real danger that the adjudicator had approached issues with a closed mind; (2) the adjudicator delegated certain parts of his decision-making rôle to a third party without notifying the parties of this, or seeking their consent to that course; and (3) he purported to rectify, or to amend, the contract, in circumstances where neither party had submitted that it should be rectified and without giving the parties any notice of his intention to take that approach. *Held*, that: (1) the adjudicator described conclusions that he reached as being a "non-binding opinion"; the purpose of reaching those conclusions was for him to determine whether, or not, he had jurisdiction to continue the referral. He decided that he did; at no stage did he indicate that he would not entertain further submissions on the same points; (2) there was "no basis whatever" for doubting the adjudicator's explanation; indeed, the adjudicator's task would have been "almost insuperable" without the assistance of someone who could assemble and manipulate the data in a manner which made the figures manageable and the portion of the work completed by Mr Hutchinson amounted to no more than copying and pasting; (3) it was clear that the adjudicator was merely adopting C's view as the correct approach and so there was no breach of natural justice: *John Sisk and Son Limited v Duro Felguera UK Limited* (2016).[6]

6–125 **Add at the end of footnote 202:**
See also D Hrustanpasic, "Time-bars and the prevention principle: using fair extensions of time and common-sense causation" (2012) 28 Const LJ 379.

6–126 **Add at the end of footnote 203:**
See also M Ross, "The status of the preventive principle: good from far, but far from good?" (2011) 27 Const LJ 15.

6–133 **Add at the end of footnote 224:**
See also E H W Chan and M C Y Au, "Enforceability considerations for deleting the extension of time provisions in building contracts" (2010) 26 Const LJ 249.

---

5 [2000] 224 F 3d 1283 (Fed Cir 2000).
6 [2016] EWHC 81 (TCC).

CHAPTER 7

Planning and programming

Introduction

"A schedule defends from chaos and whim. It is a net for catching days. It is a scaffolding on which a worker can stand and labour with both hands at sections of time."[1]

Throughout: It is very much regretted that this entire chapter remains littered with references to the Americanised forms "schedule" (both as a noun and as a verb), "schedules", "scheduled", "scheduling" and "scheduler", both in the main body of the text and in footnotes, to the extent that square brackets were adopted replace such terms where the original phraseology adopted the Queen's English version, namely "programme", or its derivations of the above. Save for various examples where a direct quotation (or a specific publication title) is concerned, or the context quite clearly refers to practice in the United States (whether pre-, or post-, Trump!), every effort will be made to ensure that the sixth edition of this publication reverts solidly to the Anglican canon.

7–093 Add a new footnote 85A at the end of the first sentence:

See also J G Zack Jr, "Early completion schedules: a form of contingency bidding – Revisited" (2016) 32 Const LJ 620 and A Stephenson, "Early completion and its effect on the contractor" (201) 32 Const LJ 591.

7–195A Add the following additional paragraphs under paragraph 7–195:

NRMI and *NRM*

Mark Blackmore[215A] has helpfully summarised the key differences between *SMM7* and its successors in a short article,[215B] as follows:

> "[SMM7] was published in a new format to *SMM6* and now uses the *Common Arrangement of Work Sections* for *Building Works* [*CAWS*] as a basis to achieve completion.
> *Co-ordinated Project Information* [*CPI*] for the construction industry.
> Although this gave guidance for the creation of bills of quantities, there was still a large divergence between different surveying practices and even quantity surveyors in the preparation and presentation of cost estimates and cost plans for the earlier stages of a project.
> Recognising this problem, the Royal Institute of Chartered Surveyors (RCS) developed the *New Rules of Measurement (NRM)*.
> A standard set of measurement rules and essential guidance for the cost management of construction projects and maintenance works contained within three volumes.
> *NRM1 (Order of Cost Estimating and Cost Planning for Capital Building Works)* was first published in March 2009. This was subsequently revised and the second edition was issued in 2012, becoming operative on 1 January 2013.
> *NRM1* details the rules of measurement for the production of cost estimates and cost plans, and also provides guidance in respect of cost terms not included within the measured works, such as preliminaries, overheads and profit, design fees, etc.
> The guidance is aligned with the RIBA *Plan of Work* and/or the OGC *Gateway Process* dependent on the project being undertaken, and provides the user with explanations of the different methods of cost planning and estimating, appropriate to the current stage of the project.

---

1 A Dillard, *The Writing Life*, Ch.2 (San Francisco: Harper & Row, 1989).
215A Senior Consultant, Driver Trett.
215B See the article *New Rules of Measurement vs Standard Method of Management* published in *Trett Digest*.

NRM1 is in essence a new guidance document, prepared and sued in response to the need for some regularly to the estimating and cost planning of projects at the early stages of either the RIBA *Plan of Work*, or OGC *Gateway*.

The second volume in the *NRM* set is *NRM2* entitled 'Detailed Measurement for Building Works was published in April 2012 and became operative on 1 January 2013. This guidance replaced *SMM7* for best practice in measurement on 1 July 2013. From the end of July 2013 the RICS were recommending that *NRM2* was used in place of *SMM7*.

NRM2 is basically enhanced version of *SMM7* hence its replacement by the RICS as the best practice guidance and, in common with *NRM1*, is aligned with the RIBA *Plan of Work* and OGC *Gateway Process*.

When comparing *NRM2* to *SMM7* the major change is the document layout. There are no longer any references to *CPI*, and where lettering was used within *SMM7*, which was correlated to the *National Building Specification (NBS)* categories, this has been replaced by numbers.

Aside from the formatting of the new guidance, there are some fundamental changes to the 'ancillary' works that no longer need to be measured. An example of this could be that detail items, such as a brick on end head detail to a window opening would no longer need to be measured.

There are also items which require a different method of measurement, for example:

- Glazing supplied with windows and doors. The glazing panes are now enumerated and size given rather than being measured by m² as per the *SMM7*. Any engraving or etching, which was previously measured as m² or design work enumerated is now measured as an extra over item and numbered.
- Below ground drainage has also changed, the excavation, bed, and surround is included within the drain run length as a composite item.
- Natural and reconstituted stonework is now measured under the same element.
- The weight categories for steelwork has varied significantly.

These changes will obviously have an impact on the preparation and style of the bills of quantities or schedule of quantities which contractors will be required to price. When pricing a project which has been measured under the *NRM* scheme, estimators will need to be fully conversant with the new measurement rules to ensure that their pricing includes suitable allowances for all works which are now deemed included within the measured quantities so as to avoid any potential financial difficulties later in the project.

The final volume within the *NRM* suite is *NRM3* entitled *Order of Cost Estimating and Cost Planning for Building Maintenance Works*. This was published February 2014, and became operative on 1 January 2015. These measurement rules mirror those upon which *NRM1* is based, but give further detail on the methodology to be used in calculating maintenance costs through the life of the building."

7–221 Add the following to footnote 236:

In section 1 of his occasional paper entitled *The Use of the Primavera Software for the Management of Infrastructure Projects in Romania,* Giovanni Di Falco (Giovanni.difalco@ technology.ro)) helpfully records as follows:

"European contractors operating in Romania during the years 2002 to date have made use of the Primavera software (either P3, or P5, versions) at one stage, or another, of their projects as their favoured planning software during the development of the following projects:

i. Bucharest – Constanta Motorway – Sub-section 3 Lehliu-Draina
ii. Bucharest – Constanta Motorway – Sub-section 1 Bucharest – Fundulea
iii. Contract 4R12. Rehabilitation of the DN 6 road section Craiova – Drobeta Tumu Severin km 268+390 – km 298+000
iv. Road Rehabilitation IV Project EIB FI 20.781 Contract 4R2 km 154+000 – km 179+917, Baru – Hateg.
v. Rehabilitation of the DN 17 County Limit Cluj/Bistita Nassaud-Bistrita, km 6+500-km 58+900 Contract 4R6

vi. Road improvement Project for National Road No 6 Contract No 93/9502:JO2 – Improvement of Existing Road between Timisoara and Lugoj

vii. Road Improvement Project for National Road No 6 Contract No 93/501: JO1-Construction of Timisoara Bypass

viii. Rehabilitation of DN1C Livada – Dej km 38+000–61+528, Rehabilitation of DN17 Dej-Cluj km 0+000–6+500 Contract No 4R5

ix. Sibiu Urban Transport Pre-accession Project Rehabilitation of Station Square and Selected Roads

x. Contract 4R13, Rehabilitation of DN6 Road Section Craiova – Drobeta Turnu Severin, km 298+000-km 332+150

xi. Bucharest Wastewater Treatment Plant Rehabilitation – Stage 1

xii. Contract 5RB Rehabilitation of DN 1 (E68) Sercaia – County Limit Brasov – Sibiu km 220+000 – km 261+130

xiii. Contract 5R9 Rehabilitation of DN 1 (E68) County Limit Brasov/Sibiu-Vestem km 261+130 – km 296+293

xiv. Rehabilitation of the Railway Line Bucharest – Brasov, Section Campina – Predeal – Lot 1: Railway embankments and superstructure works

xv. Road sector restricting and Pitesti Bypass – EBRD Loan 13.119 construction of Pitesti Bypass

xvi. Contract A02/04 Construction of Section 4 of the Motorway Bucharest – Constant from Drajna to Fetesti to Cernavoda km 133+900–151–480

xvii. Contract BP 02 Construction of Sibiu Motorway Bypass

xviii. Lot 2 'Rehabilitation of DN6 road section Drobeta Turnu Severin – Bahna, km 332–150 – km 358+000, including Drobeta Turnu Severing Bypass'

xix. Lot 3 'Rehabilitation of DNS road section Bahna – Mehadia, km 358+000 – km 388+000 including Mehadia Bypass'

xx. Traffic Fluidization on DN1 – Widening of DN1 section from Baneasa Airport (km 7+535) to Otopeni Overpass (km 11+938)

xxi. Completion and Rehabilitation of Bacau Wastewater Treatment Plant 2002/RO/16/P/PE/018

xxii. Timisoara Waste Treatment Plant Rehabilitation 2000RO/16/P/PE/004–02."

CHAPTER 8

Presentation and approval of programmes

Introduction

> *"Most of our occupations are low comedy. We must play our part duly, but as the part of a borrowed character. Of the mask and appearance we must not make a real essence, nor of what is foreign what is our very own."*[1]

8–068 Add at the end of footnote 62:

See also E Maclean, "The programme under NEC3: the unacceptable truth" (2013) 29 Const LJ 205.

8–092 Add the following paragraphs after paragraph 8–091

The rôle of the programme in assessing contractor applications for EoTs (whether under the contract, or via dispute resolution methods)

---

1 M De Montaigne, "Of Husbanding Your Will", *The Essays (Les Essais)*, Vol. III, Ch. 10 (Paris: Abel Langier, 1588).

It is difficult to state the position more elegantly and succinctly than did Will Cooper[2] (in his 2016 article[3]), as follows:

"The relevant drafting of a building contract should address three distinct points.

First, the contract should seek to establish the agreed methodology for the programme. This can be achieved in a number of ways, but perhaps the most straightforward is for the drafting to make provision for an agreed initial form of master programme which incorporates all packages and work items to a prescribed level of detail. In addition, the contract should set out what information all future iterations of the programme should include and in what manner this should be presented. The question of key dates, logic links and float within the programme should be dealt with, perhaps with reference to the approach adopted by the initial master programme. This should ensure that the scope for disagreement between the employer and contractor as to what programme information is required to be provided is much reduced.

The second consideration with any drafting relating to programme is the frequency with which an updated programme should be prepared and issued to the employer. In particular, care should be taken to ensure that the contractual régime for updating and issuing the programme is not overly onerous as this can add unnecessary cost, and increase the administrative burden on both the employer's and contractor's administrative staff. Worse still, an update requirement that is too onerous might ultimately become unworkable and have to be abandoned, leading to uncertainty as to what the parties are in fact required to do once the contractual régime has been discarded.

It is essential to ensure that the requirements dealing with the use of programme information for assessment of extension of time applications and resolving disputes are addressed in the building contract. The contractor may feel that the terms outlined above represent and intrusive attempt to look into his underlying management of the works, but the benefits to both parties in fully transparent programme information must ultimately come to be regarded as outweighing this concern.

In light of this, the mechanisms provided for in the two JCT contracts considered [below] provide pragmatic and unfussy drafting approaches to this point, although they will only be of real benefit to the parties if the relevant technical parts of the contract document provide the detail required and dovetail with the drafting of the conditions."

8–093 He continues as follows, by reference to two of the *JCT 2011* suite of standard form contracts:

"The *JCT Standard Building Contract 2011*

Viewed from the perspective of the proposals above, the *JCT Standard Building Contract 2011* adopts a notably pragmatic approach, which is married to an admirable economy of drafting. Clause 2.9.2 requires the contractor to produce the master programme at its own cost as soon as possible after the Contract is entered into. Moreover, the Conditions deal with the form that this master programme should take by leaving the detail to be set out in what is presumably meant to be the technical sections of the Contract Documents. Given the technical nature of the information involved, this approach is undoubtedly the most appropriate.

On first reading, the drafting perhaps leaves open the question as to the frequency with which the programme should be provided to the employer and does not seem to address any question of resolving the non-provision of the programme. That said, both of these points could be easily dealt with in the technical sections of the Contract Documents, providing care is taken to be these requirements back into the relevant contractual terms. On this point, the draftsmen of the relevant part of the Contract Documents should look closely at clause 2.9.2 and 2.27 (the latter clause dealing with the notices on delay that the contractor is to provide).

2 Senior Associate, Clyde & Co LLP.
3 *A quantum of programme, JCT News,* February 2016, page 4.

The *JCT Design and Build Contract 2011*

In contrast to its sister contract, the *JCT Design and Build Contract 2011* does not expressly deal with the question of programme information. This approach is largely appropriate, given the nature of works carried out by way of design and build and the flexibility as to programming allowed for as a result. However, the employer may still need access to programme information to assess extension of time, and contractual requirements should therefore be included to address the points set out above. Furthermore, in the event of a disagreement arising between the parties, joint access to the contractor's programmes may, as discussed above, be the most expeditious and forensic way of resolving this.

As with the *JCT Standard Building Contract* though many of these requirements can be (and arguably, should be, given the nature of the information involved) incorporated in the technical parts of the Contract Documents (with the most appropriate location being in the Employer's Requirements) without any amendment to the terms of the Conditions being required."

CHAPTER 9

Revising, updating, monitoring and reporting

There are no updates to this chapter.

Introduction

"The road to hell is paved with work-in-progress."[1]

---

1 Philip Roth, *New York Times* (15 July 1979), Book Review.

CHAPTER 10

Project control

There are no updates to this chapter.

Introduction

> " 'Would you tell me, please, which way I ought to go from here?' 'That depends a good deal on where you want to get to,' said the Cat. 'I don't much care where – 'said Alice. 'Then it doesn't matter which way you go,' said the Cat. '– so long as I get somewhere,' Alice added as an explanation. 'Oh, you are sure to do that,' said the Cat, 'if you only walk long enough'."[1]

---

* As regards *Rider 1* to and the *second edition* of the SCL *Protocol*, please see the note regarding appendix 3 below.

1 L Carroll, *Alice's Adventures in Wonderland* (London: Macmillan, 1897), Ch. 6, "Pig and Pepper".

CHAPTER 11

Mitigation, recovery and acceleration

Introduction

"Nothing bothers the trier-of-fact more than an otherwise valid damages proof which has been inflated by the failure of the entitled party to mitigate the event of the damage. In most construction situations, damages can be mitigated. Therefore, mitigation is a third major proof rôle for the construction process/damages expert. Was there demonstrable effort? Actual success of mitigation is not essential, but can reduce necessary additional proof of mitigation effort. Generally a recognition of the need to mitigate and demonstrable follow through can be sufficient. Failure to see reasonably obvious mitigation options, even with other effort, may be held the responsible party. The expert can demonstrate such effort from the factual evidence available. . . ."[1]

---

1 K Nielsen and P Galloway, *Journal of Trial Advocacy* (1984).

11-010   Add the following Illustration:

(1)   *Facts*: Leander Construction Limited (C) was employed by Mulalley and Company Limited (D) to carry out groundworks and other associated works at a development in Lewisham. Clause 12.1 of the contract set out the terms for the implied term to carry out the works regularly and diligently, breach of which would lead to the termination of the contract. Clause 14 set out C's duty to notify D in writing of any delay and its consequences. The activity schedule contained some dates and periods that were later accepted by both parties as non-contractually binding. By May 2011, C was behind schedule. On 29 June 2011, D issued a notice of withholding for £131,078.12 for C's delay. A second notice of withholding was issued on 17 June 2011, with D looking to withhold the remainder of the £131,078.12 against the new sum, although the remaining sums were paid. C brought court proceedings under CPR Part 8, challenging the validity of the withholding notices. The court had to decide whether C owed D any interim obligation as to progress and performance that would entitle the latter to a claim for damages. *Held*, by Coulson J: that it cannot be inferred from cl. 12.12 that failure to proceed regularly and diligently (as one of the circumstances requiring a notice) amounts to a freestanding contractual obligation to that effect; actually, it points away from an implied term and, as a consequence, D was not entitled to withhold the sum of £131,078.14 due to C: *Leander Construction Limited v Mulalley and Company Limited* (2011).[2]

11-016   Add at the end of footnote 22:
See also A Whaley, "Accelerating construction works: pitfalls and perils in reducing delay" (2016) 32 Cost LJ 476.

---

2 [2011] EWHC 3449 (TCC).

CHAPTER 12

Variation and change

Introduction

"Change is not made without inconvenience, even from worse to better."[1]

12–004 Add a footnote 2A at the end of the first bullet point:
See also C Fischer, "Unilateral variations in construction contracts" (2013) 29 Const LJ 211.

12–005 Add at the end of footnote 4:
See also M Sergeant, "No EOT provisions for variations: why the rights to LADs should not be lost, (2016) 32 Const LJ 352.

12–043 Add at the end of footnote 52:
See also C Ennis, "Prospective claims for variations under FIDIC: evidential and protocol issues and comparison with the NEC3 régime" (2016) 32 Const LJ 303.

---

1 R Hooker, quoted in Samuel Johnson, *Dictionary of the English Language* (1755) preface.

CHAPTER 13

Construction records

Introduction

"When you believe you have a claim under a construction contract, thorough and comprehensive records are needed for proving that you are entitled to damages, and the amount of damages you should recover. Too often, contractors are able to show that something went wrong on a project, but because they lack records are unable to identify the exact causes of the problem, or prove that claimed costs are attributable to the problem."[1]

13–088   Add at the end of footnote 88:

See also D Tyerman, "Building information modelling and change management: a single version of the truth" (2013) 29 Const LJ 295, M Winfield, "Building information modelling: the legal frontier – overcoming legal and contracted obstacles" (April 2015) SCL paper D178.

See also D-J Gibbs, W Lord S Emitt and K Ruikar, "Building information modelling" (2015) 31 Const LJ 167 and C Rogers, M Reza Hosseini, N Chilehe and R Rameezdeen, "Building information modelling (BIM) within the Australian construction-related small and medium-sized enterprises (SMEs): awareness, practices and drivers" (2016) 32 Const LJ 257.

13–105   Add the following footnote 107A at the end of footnote 107, as follows:

Please refer to paragraphs 4–366 to 4–368 inclusive above, with regard to the "re-christening" of *"CPC 2013"* as *"TCM 15"*.

13–188   Add at the end of footnote 175:

See also D-J Gibbs; S Emmitt, K Ruikar and W Lord, "Recommendations on the creation of computer general exhibits for construction delay claims" (2014) 30 Const LJ 236.

---

1 "Construction Project Records Basic Principles and Guidelines", Federal Publications No 79–6, November 1979.

13–253   Add the following Illustration:

Illustration

Facts: Bilfinger Berger (C) was engaged to build two large tunnels for Metro Vancouver (D) with a contract value of some C$100 million. Worked stopped part way through the works, following the discovery of unexpected rock conditions which were allegedly dangerous, together with a flawed design on the part of D's engineer. D alleged that C was in breach of contract and had ceased work for differing reasons, ie C had underbid and the contract had become uneconomical.

D engaged a replacement contractor to complete the works and commenced proceedings to recover damages in the region of C$200 million from C. A previous application had been accepted by the court, ordering D to produce any and all site documents related to the completion of the works.

In this application, C was seeking to secure the release of all documents relevant to its defence after August 2010. C understood that D had only agreed to produce electronic correspondence up until that date. D argued that it would be too onerous to produce all the ongoing email correspondence relating to the ongoing works. C argued that "email correspondence tends to be the most revealing, rather than written project reports. . ." and would provide a true indication of site conditions. C sought information relating first to the actual ongoing site conditions and secondly, to the costs of the ongoing works.

Held: That the documents sought by C did relate to the matter in question; however, the court placed restrictions reducing the required subject fields. The court did not accept D's argument on the grounds of quantum involved in the alleged breach of contract action: *Bilfinger Berger (Canada) Inc. v Greater Vancouver Water District* (2013).[2]

13–259   Add at the end of footnote 231:

See also Dr R Champion, "Electronic documents in construction litigation: lessons from experience" (2011) 27 Const LJ 227.

---

2 [2013] BCSC 2305.

CHAPTER 14

Cause and effect

Introduction

"Even after one instance or experiment, where we have observed a particular event to follow upon another, we are not entitled to form a general rule, or foretell what will happen in like cases; it being justly esteemed an unpardonable temerity to judge of the whole course of nature from one single experiment, however accurate or certain. But when one particular species of event has always, in all instances, been conjoined with another, we make no longer any scruple of foretelling one upon the appearance of the other, and of employing that reasoning, which can alone assume us of any matter of fact or existence. We then call the one object, Cause; the other, Effect."[1]

14–097   Add a new footnote 80A at the end of the paragraph:

See also Rick Shaw and Nick Lane, "Statutory suspension – a commentary on section 112 of the Housing Grants, Construction and Regeneration Act 1996 (as amended)" (2012) 29 Const LJ 414.

---

1 D Hume, *An Enquiry Concerning Human Understanding* (London, 1777).

CHAPTER 15

Forensic programme analysis

Introduction

" 'Forensic' is defined as 'belonging to, used in, or suitable to courts of judicature or to public discussion and debate'. Thus, forensic schedule analysis is that form of schedule delay analysis intended for use in delay claim situations in negotiation, mediation, arbitration, or litigation. As a result, the RP/FSA focuses primarily on the Critical Path Method (CPM) of scheduling. As defined in the RP/FSA, forensic scheduling is the study and investigation of events on a project using CPM or other recognized schedule calculation methods, for potential use in a legal proceeding. Forensic schedule analysis is the study of how actual events on a project interacted in the context of a complex scheduling model for the purpose of understanding the significance of those events on the following activities within the scheduling model."[1]

---

1 J Zack, Jr, *Delay and delay analysis – isn't it simple?* a paper presented to 1st ICEC and IPMA Global Congress on Project Management Ljubljana (Slovenia, April 2006).

Windows and watersheds

15–164   Add the following Illustration:

Illustration

Facts: In 1997, La Caille Developments Inc (D) entered into a contract with Graham Construction Limited (C) for the construction of a 17-storey high-rise condominium project. D had engaged a professional team, led by Gibbs Gage Partnership (Gibbs) as architects and contract administrators to prepare tender specifications and drawings for the project.

In April and May 1997, D and C entered into two contracts for the construction of the condominiums and additional work for the La Caille on the Bow restaurant (a second company owned and managed by D's owner). Both contracts were in the form of the (Canadian) *Standard Construction Document – CCDC 2 – 1994 edition.* Substantial performance of the contract was required by 15 August 1998.

As part of the main works, Gibbs had detailed an exterior cement stucco finish system. C (through its sub-contractor) proposed to install an exterior insulation and finish system (EIFS) in place of the stucco system; work on the exterior cladding ultimately did not start until 6 May 1988.

Construction began on 22 May 1997, but issues soon arose. By 27 June 1997, C had been instructed by D to stop work upon the foundation construction, following soil test results, pending possible revisions to the structural design. Following a site meeting on 8 July 1997, D advised C that the foundations would need a complete redesign.

On 21 July 1997, C received an instruction to recommence excavation work for a revised structural foundation design. This was subsequently issued on 22 July 1997. The revised main floor foundation and slab of the foundation was cast on 9 August 1997.

As part of the proposed exterior cladding package, revisions to the building permit were sent to the City of Calgary by C on 6 November 1997; following a number of revisions, installation of the modified EIFS package commenced on 6 May 1998.

During the EIFS approval period, work on-site continued with the interior elements which were not susceptible to the weather. It had been C's intention to complete the interiors starting at the base and working in an orderly fashion up the building, completing the floors as work progressed. Ultimately, this was not possible.

As part of the contract administration to deal with change, D had put in place two systems to manage the instructed changes to the structure itself (base building change orders **[BBCOs]**) and a separate system to manage the condominium homeowner changes (Homeowner Change Orders **[HCOs]**). Gibbs administered the BBCOs, but had virtually no involvement in the HCOs.

Schedule B to the contract provided for HCOs. It placed an obligation upon C only to "coordinate interior design modifications requested by purchasers" and it required D to "provide homeowner design modification information, proposed and approved, in a timely fashion to C".

At a site meeting, C advised D that the scheduled completion date would be 1 December 1998. Further delays occurred and C requested substantial completion

---

to be certified on 8 January 1999, which was rejected by Gibbs. Substantial completion was eventually certified by Gibbs on 1 March 1999.

During the project, extensions of time [EoTs] totalling 23 days were awarded by Gibbs. This resulted in a substantial completion date being extended to 23 September 1998.

The foundation redesign was never being covered by a BBCO, although both parties agreed that it had caused a delay. C claimed 36 days and D acknowledged an entitlement of 28 days and advocated a revised substantial completion date of 2 November 1998.

By the time of project completion, a total of 253 BBCOs had been instructed, with a further 516 HCOs also having been issued.

Both D and C relied upon expert opinion testimony on the issue of the delay quantification. D's expert concluded that C was responsible for 71 days of the 137 days from 15 August 1998 to substantial completion on 1 March 1999.

D's expert then contended that both D and C had contributed to the delay from substantial performance to final completion. By its written argument D submitted that the delay was due to C and the poor performance of its sub-contractors and the change to the exterior stucco. D's expert acknowledged that the numerous change orders, (many relating to home owner improvements), delayed certain aspects of the interior work; however, he contended that the delay to the building exterior works were the controlling factor.

C's expert chose to examine eight events and review the manner in which they impacted upon the project schedule and, if so, to assess the magnitude of that impact in terms of delay. Following this review, C's expert found that, by 27 April 1998, C had been responsible for five days of delay. He submitted, however, that, due to the internal building and HCOs (which were the responsibility of D), that the project would not have been completed any earlier than it was.

In the litigation, C claimed that delays to the project were fully (or for the most part) the responsibility of D and sought damages from D.

D's primary claim in response was that responsibility for the delay in completion lay with C by reason breach of contract and its failure to achieve substantial completion by 2 November 1998, for which it also sought damages.

Further side claims were brought, both by the main parties and by third parties to the main contract. The court was faced with eight principal issues, the primary issue being ownership of the project delay.

Held, following detailed review of both experts' reports and other evidence adduced, that: C's expert evidence was to be preferred over that of D's expert and, where opinions differed, the court preferred C's expert evidence in its entirety.

The court first examined the approaches to the delay analysis methodology employed; both experts initially used "snapshot (windows) methodology" for delay analysis, although using differing approaches to the identification of milestone events and window durations.

Following a review of the standard procedure used to carry out a snapshot analysis, the court detailed the key differences between the findings of the experts. D's expert established his first two windows as running from the start of the project to the completion of the redesign of the foundation, with the second running to the termination by C of its concrete sub-contractor; the latter sub-contract was terminated due to breach of contract owing to poor performance.

By comparison, C's expert commenced his first window from the start of the project to the pouring of the main slab. The second window covered the period from the pouring of the main slab to the completion of the concrete structure. C's expert used what D's expert in his report, called the "usual time" periods. That is, time periods determined by significant milestones on the project; the court questioned the milestone selection by D's expert.

C's expert (in defending his milestone selection) "chose to look at the major issues and do a detailed analysis of each one and construct the history of what happened, rather than try and create a milestone that really didn't mean much". C's expert continued to defend his milestone selection, stating that the clearly-defined milestone of pouring the slab offered a logical point against which to determine the effects of the late drawings, the performance of the concrete sub-contract or/and any other events which occurred on the project up to the main floor, with which the court agreed.

The court noted that C's expert had employed the "snapshot" approach, using two periods to cover the entire project. However, D's expert chose to break the project into four periods and to utilise a collapsing analysis methodology for periods 3 and 4. The court again questioned the selection by D's expert of key milestones and his failure to assess what the court felt to be key events and factual errors, lending further support to C's expert evidence. By way of example, D's expert assessed the final water tightness as being achieved on 6 November 1998, releasing the start of the internal work. However, based upon C's site diary evidence, the court agreed with C's expert assessment of 7 September 1998 as the final date of window installation.

The court felt that further questions arose with the approach of D's expert in his failure to provide any material discussion concerning the structural steel, the volume of interior revisions, or the late issue of internal packages for framing and finishing, all being items which C's expert had assessed.

Secondly, the court proceeded to review the available programme information so as to establish C's planned intention and to identify a baseline programme and subsequent project critical path.

In June 1997, C produced a programme dated 30 May 1997, in which 33 activities were listed and described by C as "an overview", prepared to satisfy its contractual commitment. This programme was further developed by C's site management, with a paper copy dated 24 June 1997 listing some 102 activities.

C's expert relied upon an electronic version of the 24 June 1997 programme (dated 2 July 1997), detailing 145 activities, as his baseline programme, since it most closely aligned with the 24 June 1997 programme and accurately reflected C's construction plan of about 24 June 1997. D's expert chose to rely upon the 30 May 1997 programme, which C's expert attacked for its obvious errors and lack of detail.

C produced further programmes as the project continued and were reviewed in turn by C's expert. C's expert was able to identify a second baseline programme dated 26 August 1997, which detailed the works above the main floor. The nearest paper copy, dated 2 September 1997, listed some 341 activities.

The court stated that he was satisfied that the two programmes used by C's expert, namely those dated 2 July and 26 August 1997, best represented C's planned intention, even if not issued to D or Gibbs.

As part of the court's assessment of the true project critical path (despite D's expert contention that the revised exterior works and the resulting delay in achieving water tightness was the controlling work activity), the court again agreed with C's expert that the considerable time between the point of water tightness and commencement of the internal finishing work indicated that the former was not the cause of any significant delay.

Rather, the court again agreed with C's expert in assessing that the project critical path started with the foundations, continued through the below-grade structure, ran up through the lower portion of the superstructure (where it switched to the interior finishes) and continued through the entire interior finishing of the building and the suites.

Thirdly, the court found that C's expert evidence showed a greater attention to detail than that offered by D's expert. Five examples were relied upon by the court: by way of example, C's expert had noted that D's expert gave completion of the concrete structure as being 13 April 1998, whereas contemporaneous evidence indicated that it was actually completed by 27 April 1998 (as correctly identified by C's expert).

As a fourth issue, the court found D's expert report "regarding the installation of the windows less than forthright, albeit, on close reading, not misleading"; a number of authorities were provided by the court.

The fifth and final reason again turned upon the available evidence; the court agreed with C's expert assessment, which he set out in his rebuttal report, namely "that the considerable time between completion of the building exterior to the point of water tightness and the commencement of the bulk of the building's interior finishing work indicated the former was not the cause of delay", which was again supported by the site diary evidence.

The court further accepted C's expert evidence on the delay quantification "in its entirety" and held that D was responsible for 59 days delay, with C responsible for five days of project delay. Nevertheless, the project would not have been completed any sooner than it was, by reason of delay caused by the change orders, all of which were attributable to D. D was, therefore, held to be ultimately responsible for the delay in completing the project. The court went on to decide various further quantum issues, based upon the ownership of the project delay, finding that D had no accrued entitlement to damages: *Graham Construction and Engineering (1985) Limited v La Caille Developments Inc* (2006).[2]

---

2 [2006] ABQB 898.

CHAPTER 16

Float and time contingencies

Introduction

> *"If every activity is a problem, then nothing is really a problem. If all blends into the overall morass of project difficulties, and the most appropriate target of management attention and available resources fades into the mist."*[1]

There are no updates to this chapter.

---

1 M Harfield, *PM Network* (2001).

CHAPTER 17

Disruption to progress and lost productivity

This chapter is replaced in its entirety.

Introduction

> *"All too often in construction, the terms 'productivity' and 'production' are used interchangeably. This is, however, incorrect. Production is the measure of output (ie, things produced) whereas productivity is the measurement of the production."*[1]

17–001 Productivity is the measure of work which can be performed by a given resource. Where the works are planned by reference to the resources and productivity they are planned to achieve, identifying lost productivity (that is, where productivity has fallen below that which was planned) is relatively simple. In the absence of a fully resourced schedule, however, identifying lost productivity caused by disruption to the resources and work in progress can be far from straightforward.

17–002 As with the word "delay", "disruption" is a comparative term, which has no intrinsic meaning, except by reference to a standard of performance, against which it can be measured. In construction and engineering contracts, disruption is really no more than the difference between an intention and reality as to productivity, where the reality is a derogation from the intent. Disruption is not delay. Although disruption may cause delay and it may be caused by delay, delay is not a precondition of disruption and, indeed, disruption may occur when the progress of the works is not only not delayed, but when the effect of an earlier delay is being mitigated, or recovered, or when the work is accelerated. In recognising this distinction, in *Bell v US*,[2] the court said:

> "There is a distinction between (1) a 'delay' claim; and (2) a 'disruption', or 'cumulative impact' claim. Although the two claim types often arise together in the same project, a 'delay' claim captures the time and cost of not being able to work, while a *'disruption' claim captures the cost of working less efficiently than planned.*" (Emphasis added).

17–003 The SCL *Protocol* puts it as follows:

> "Disruption is often treated by the construction industry as if it were the same thing as delay. It is commonly spoken of together with delay, as in 'delay and disruption'. Delay and disruption are two separate things. They have their normal everyday meanings. Delay is lateness (eg delayed completion equals late completion). Disruption is loss of productivity, disturbance, hindrance or interruption of progress. In the construction context, disrupted work is often work that is carried out less efficiently than it would have been had it not been for the cause of disruption.
>
> Disruption to construction work may lead to late completion of the work, but not necessarily so. It is possible for work to be disrupted and for the contract still to finish by the contract completion date. In this situation, [C] will not have a claim for an EOT, but it may have a claim for the cost of the reduced efficiency of its workforce."[3]

17–004 In order to make good a claim for compensation arising out of lost productivity, C must prove no more and no less than it needs to prove with any other claim for reimbursement:

1. liability;
2. causation; and
3. loss or expense suffered.

---

1 American Association of Cost Engineers International, *Estimating Lost Labour Productivity in Construction Claims, Recommended Practice No 25R-03* (2004).

2 *Bell BCI Company v United States*, Fed Cl No 03–1613C (filed 14 July 2006).

3 At paras.1.19.2 and 1.19.3. As regards *Rider 1* to and the *second edition* of the SCL *Protocol*, please see the note regarding appendix 3 below.

17–005 In *Lisbon v US*,[4] the US Federal Court of Claims stated the principle thus:

"[C] bears the burden of proving the fact of loss with certainty, as well as the burden of proving the amount of loss with sufficient certainty so that the determination of the amount of damages will be more than speculation."

17–006 In *Ascon*,[5] the Court declined to entertain a claim by the sub-contractor against C for lost productivity in a period over which an extension of time had been granted, which had been insufficiently particularised, saying:

"[The SC's expert witness's] first item is for labour. He calculates it by assessing the full cost of the labour employed during the period of extension. [Counsel for C] submits that that is wrong in principle. I agree; the labour content of the contract works is not necessarily increased at all, let alone proportionately, by an extension of time. There may indeed be labour-related losses by reason of delay, for example because of down time, loss of productivity, repetition of tasks or other uneconomic working, but it is for [the SC] to establish and quantify specific claims for losses of that kind, if they have been suffered."

17–007 In the urgency to arrive at a figure to be claimed, the need to prove liability and causation is sometimes forgotten. Whereas it is usually possible to find some way of calculating the reasonable cost of an event, which is at D's risk, and which can be demonstrated to have adversely affected C's progress, a calculation of costs that cannot be demonstrated to have been caused by D is useless. In the US case of *Bay Construction*[6] for instance, C's expert had produced an estimate of C's losses, without demonstrating a causal nexus between the occurrence of D's risk item and lost productivity alleged to have been suffered. His estimate of lost productivity also relied upon references taken from "Means Estimating Guide"[7] and to a type of analysis which he had wrongly referred to as the "measured mile" method. His evidence was rejected by the Board, which said:

"[C] has the fundamental responsibility to prove by a preponderance of the evidence that [D's] action caused its labour to be less efficient than planned as well as the extent of that impact. [C] wholly failed to present probative evidence of lost productivity. Again, [C's expert's] charts and summary conclusions that [C] had lost productivity because work was in some instance done out of sequence and piecemeal in some areas fall far short of the proof we expect for such cases. His attempt at quantification, applying two methods to price [C's] alleged damages for what he said was [C's] lost productivity was not compelling for many of the same reasons we articulated in our earlier discussions of his delay and suspension analysis. [C's] lack of contemporaneous project documentation of the impact of the delays and its failure to proffer credible testimony, impeached the overall reliability of its evidence. While [C's expert] was very willing to assume [D]-caused delay and interference, there was very little evidence in the record to back up his assumptions. He had even less professional experience analysing lost productivity than he had in delay and suspension analysis.

Given the size and complexity of this project, the number and nature of changes reflected in the SAs were not so momentous as to impact the project in the significant and serious ways that [C] claims. As we recently stated in *Clark Construction*,[8] '[t]he after-the-fact, conclusory

---

4 *Lisbon Contractors, Inc. v United States*, (1987) 828 F 2d 759, 767.
5 *Ascon Contracting Ltd v Alfred McAlpine Construction Isle of Man Ltd* (1999) 66 Con LR 119; (2000) 16 Const LJ 316, at para.39.
6 *Bay Construction Co* (2002) VABCA Nos 5,594, 5,625–5,626, 5,628, 5,831.
7 RSMeans is a US supplier of construction cost information. A product line of Reed Construction Data.
8 *Clark Construction Group Inc* (2000) VABCA No 5674, 00–1 BCA 30,870, in which the court relied on the decisions made in *Fru-Con Construction Corporation v The United States* (1999) 43 Fed Cl 306, affirmed (2000) 250 F 3d 762 (Fed Cir); *Centex Bateson Construction Co* (1998) VABCA Nos 4,613, 5,162–5,165, LEXIS 14, 99–1 BCA (CCH) 30,153, affirmed, *Centex Bateson Construction Co v Togo D West, Jr, Secretary of Veterans Affairs* (2000) 250 F 3d 761 (Fed Cir) and *Triple "A" South* (1994) 94–3 BCA 27,194.

assessments of the [CA] or the opinions of its experts are not sufficient substitutes for [C's] underlying obligation to contemporaneously document the severe adverse impact on labour efficiency it now claims resulted from the changes and RFIs'.

We conclude that [C's] evidence failed to provide proof of change to working conditions or loss of productivity. To the extent [C] or [D] raised other issues or arguments related to these appeals, we have fully reviewed and considered them and found them unpersuasive."

17–008 The third factor, the loss and expense suffered, is the difference between the cost of performance of the work without any impact for which D is liable and the cost of the performance when affected by the effects of D's cost risk event. In the US case of *Centex Benson*,[9] the relationship was put as follows:

"Impact costs are additional costs occurring as a result of the loss of productivity; loss of productivity is also termed inefficiency. Thus, impact costs are simply increased labour costs that stem from the disruption to labour productivity resulting from a change in working conditions caused by a contract change. Productivity is inversely proportional to the man-hours necessary to produce a given unit of product. As is self-evident, if productivity declines the number of man-hours of labour to produce a given task will increase. If the number of man-hours increases, labour costs obviously increase."

17–009 In *Luria v US*,[10] the Federal Court of Claims set out the principles upon which a calculation of loss could reasonably be acceptable, stating:

"[T]he mere expression of an estimate as to the amount of productivity loss by an expert witness with nothing to support it will not establish the fundamental fact of resultant injury nor provide a sufficient basis for making a reasonably correct approximation of damages.

Even if [C] has proved that its loss of efficiency was attributable largely to [D], its increased costs are subject to reduction if they include elements for which [D] is not responsible. Such elements could include inadequate supervision, incompetent personnel, non-availability of materials, and other similar factors."

Productivity

17–010 Disruption will result in enhanced costs and may also cause delay when it causes a reduction in the rate of productivity that otherwise could have been achieved. Productivity in this context may be defined as "productive efficiency" and can be related to any measure of produced output (or "production") per unit input. Economists[11] have identified convenient measures of productivity as being:

1. labour productivity;
2. capital productivity;
3. time productivity;
4. total factor productivity; and
5. value added total factor productivity.

17–011 These five indices can be calculated as follows:
[Please refer to Figure 17.1]
17–012 It is significant to note that, of these indices, it is the value added total factor productivity (VATFP) which provides the truest measure of the particular worth of a

---

9 *Centex Bateson Construction Co* (1998) VABCA Nos 4,613, 5,162–5,165, LEXIS 14, 99–1 BCA (CCH) 30,153, affirmed, *Centex Bateson Construction Co v Togo D. West, Jr, Secretary of Veterans Affairs* (2000) 250 F 3d 761 (Fed Cir).

10 *Luria Brothers & Co v United States* (1996) 369 F 2d 701, 713 (Ct Cl).

11 JG Lowe, "The measurement of productivity in the construction industry", 1987 *Construction Management and Economics*, Vol. 5, at pp. 101–113.

process, and is analogous to the percentage return on an investment. Conversely, the other indices can be regarded as simplifications, or approximations of VATFP. As Figure 17.1 illustrates, the output of the first four indices is measured in job-specific units (such as the number of beams, or segments produced), or quantities (such as the mass of steelwork, or volume of concrete). Input, on the other hand, is measured by the number of man hours, machine hours, or hours, or by the cost of labour, or capital employed.

17–013 Whilst VATFP is the measurement with the greatest theoretical legitimacy, productivity is most frequently represented by labour, or plant productivity. This is understandable because man hours, plant hours and quantities are obtainable from site records, are practical and are easy to understand. It can be argued, moreover, that in many construction projects, save for the effect of intervening events,[12] machinery and equipment ("capital") will generally tend to perform at a consistent rate. Thus it is likely to be only the human resources whose efficiency fluctuates to any significant extent. Accordingly, it will often be appropriate to take labour productivity as an approximation of true productivity. On the other hand, where there are capital-intensive processes involving significant machine hours, for instance in earth movement, pile driving, or tunnelling, plant usage is likely to be a more relevant input measure than man hours.

17–014 Unproductive working may occur as a result of a variety of circumstances for which C may bear the risk as to time and cost, or D may bear the risk as to time only, or as to both time and cost. For example, whereas (depending upon the terms of the contract) the cost of lost productivity caused by weather may normally be at C's risk, it may come to be at D's risk if, as a result of an event at D's risk as to cost, C has to work in adverse weather, which renders its work more difficult and time consuming. Sometimes, as a result of failing to update its schedule, or as a result of variations imposed upon it, the lost productivity can result from C, or its sub-contractors becoming confused about how the works should be sequenced.

Illustration

Facts: Collins/Snoops Associates Inc (CSA) agreed to perform $2.69m worth of plumbing, heating, and air conditioning mechanical work as part of the renovations at three Baltimore County school buildings. From the beginning, CSA's progress was delayed, because the county failed timeously to reply to CSA's requests for information, the county hindered CSA's work by allowing public access to the schools during potential work hours and CSA's unexpected discovery of asbestos in the school required CSA to suspend work until the asbestos was removed. On the other hand, there was also evidence that CSA was unduly slow in performing its work, largely because it failed to provide enough qualified manpower and to secure necessary equipment and materials. Furthermore, CSA's own sub-contractors caused multiple delays. After CSA had completed only a portion of the specified mechanical work, the contractor (CJF) asserted that strict deadlines were required by the county. CJF terminated CSA and engaged a replacement firm to take over

---

12 In the majority of cases, machinery breakdown (at C's risk) is likely to cause a complete cessation of work by that item of plant, or equipment and thus can relatively easily be separated from the effects of disruption caused by other events (at D's risk).

the mechanical work. Subsequently, CJF itself was terminated by the county, because the county was not satisfied with CJF's progress. The trial court concluded that neither CJF had proved that CSA had failed to perform, nor had CSA proved that it was wrongfully terminated. *Held*: that there should be judgment in favour of CJF for all claims brought against CSA and judgment in favour of CSA for all claims brought against CJF. The trial court further found that CSA performed at a much slower pace than another electrical sub-contractor on the same project. During the same periods that CSA claimed it could not work because of interference by school activities, that other electrical sub-contractor was able to complete 78% of its work at one school, 58% at a second school, and 37% at the third. By contrast, CSA claimed it had only completed 15.2% of total work under its sub-contract. The trial court found that the county considered CSA's rate of progress unsatisfactory and that county officials had advised that staffing levels for mechanical activities were inadequate. Delays by CSA were not insignificant. To the contrary, the county was so dissatisfied with the lack of progress that the county terminated CJF's employed. But CSA was only required to complete by the project's completion date. According to the court, there was still time for CSA to complete within the project completion date: *Collins/Snoops Associates Limited v CJF LLC* (2010).[12A]

17–015 In calculating lost productivity, the way in which time is measured will be an important factor. For any worker, or piece of equipment, for instance, the time that it spends can be categorised in several ways:[13]

1. total time;
2. working time and non-working time; and
3. productive (working) time and unproductive (working) time.

17–016 This can be illustrated as in Figure 17.2 in which total time is split between working time (where the resource is ordinarily available for working) and non-working time, and working time can then be further divided into value-adding, or "productive" time and non-value-adding, or "unproductive" time.

[Please refer to Figure 17.2]

17–017 For a crane driver, for instance, hoisting beams into position would be an example of productive time. Climbing up to the crane's cockpit would be an example of working, but unproductive, time and taking a refreshment break would be classified as not-working time.

17–018 The measurement of lost productivity can be difficult for a number of reasons, amongst which are:

1. absence of defined planned productivity by reference to resources and intended production rate;
2. failure to record contemporaneously the resources used and productivity actually achieved;
3. failure to calculate lost productivity contemporaneously;

12A 190 Md App 146, 988 A 2d49 (2010).
13 See Dr H Lal, *Quantifying and Managing Disruption Claims* (Thomas Telford, 2003) p. 95.

4.   lack of confidence in methods used to calculate lost productivity; and

5.   difficulty in establishing causation.

Resource-based planning

17–019 The primary problem with proof of disruption and consequent prolongation, or interruption of activity durations as a result of changed use of project resources is that, in order to demonstrate that there has been a detrimental change to the use of resources, it is necessary first to be able to show how the particular resource would have been utilised, but for the disruption.

17–020 Resource-based planning may well be an advantage in even the simplest of construction projects. However, in major land clearance, some civil engineering, pipe-work and similar projects it is an essential management tool. The *CIOB Guide* advises:[14]

> "Work which can be carried out in defined sequences, over brief periods, requires a different approach to time management than work containing activities which may take several months to complete. The former can be managed by reference to the activity start, work in progress and completion date. However, the latter can only be managed from day to day by reference to the applied resources and productivity achieved.
>
> Resource-based planning will thus be necessary wherever productivity is more likely to affect completion than logical sequence. Typically this can be applicable to such activities as earth moving in large-scale projects, piling on open sites, pipe welding on large process plants and other linear projects. In this form of time management, the unit productivity of each resource is interpolated as the works proceed to provide the data for calculating the time which the activity will take to complete."

17–021 In such projects, whilst there may be a logic to the sequence of activities, the activities themselves extend over large areas and, within broad limitations, can be carried out virtually anywhere, so long as they are carried out efficiently. The *CIOB Guide* advises:[15]

> "Although in building construction, work on site will generally follow activities of short duration in discrete areas which are, to a great extent, subject to a critical path and thus subject to critical path network, time-modelling of complex major projects will often include a number of other construction works, some of which will be in the nature of civil engineering and/or mechanical engineering and will not necessarily be subject to the same type of time control.
>
> For example, in major land clearance, or cut and fill of land profiles, work may continue over a long period and may usefully follow some sequence (land will be dug out before depressions are filled), but not necessarily a sequence which is cogently linked from beginning to end of the operation as a whole.
>
> Commonly, such a process may usefully be mapped out in what is referred to as a time-chainage diagram which illustrates, in linear terms, where work is intended to be carried out. Although such figures may be logically linked to some extent, because they are drawn rather than calculated from a database, they do not commonly function as a time-model and other methods must usually be used to manage time and predict the consequences of change.
>
> In such circumstances, where activities can be carried out over a long period in a multiplicity of areas, in any order (subject perhaps to limited sequences in any particular area), the time-model will commonly focus on the management of resources and productivity instead of critical path sequences within the particular activity and critical path sequences between sections of the activity and the interface with the remainder of the works."

---

14   Chartered Institute of Building, *Guide to Good Practice in the Management of Time in Complex Projects* (Chichester: Wiley Blackwell, 2010), para.3.7.2.

15   Chartered Institute of Building, *Guide to Good Practice in the Management of Time in Complex Projects* (Chichester: Wiley Blackwell, 2010), paras 3.5.2.3 to 3.5.2.6.

17–022 The rate at which a particular resource can produce work under normal conditions is called the productivity quotient of the resource. It can vary according to the size of the labour gang, or number of plant units in operation at any given time, together with the climatic conditions, space available, method of payment and numerous other factors. The productivity quotient of a particular resource can be determined in a number of ways, including:

1. published output rates;
2. historical data from other projects;
3. benchmarking by sample, or on the project;
4. advice from specialists; and
5. personal experience.

17–023 In regard to resource-based planning, the *CIOB Guide* advises that:[16]

"in most construction projects, labour will be the most common variable across most types of work, but in earthworks, for example, machine type and numbers as well as the production capability of the processing plant, will be more relevant.

At low and medium density there will often be insufficient data available to make precise computations of durations by reference to productivity and resource alone. At these densities, it is quite often the case that activities have a mixture of resources and other methods of estimation are therefore necessary. For example: estimation by reference to previous projects, experience, standard outputs and so on are acceptable at low and medium densities.

At high density, the planned duration of an activity is a function of the quantity of work, the productivity quotient and the quantity of the resource type to be deployed, in the formula:

Duration = {Quantity of Work × Productivity Quotient × Quantity of Resource}."

17–024 Wherever work is scheduled by reference to the resources to be used and the productivity to be expected, and where the work carried out is monitored and records kept of the resources actually used and the productivity actually achieved, the analysis of disruption to the resources and the effect of lost productivity can be calculated and the effects of disrupting events proved relatively easily.

The importance of records

17–025 The successful calculation of lost productivity caused by disruption is dependent upon records of how the work was actually performed. Without good quality as-built records, C will inevitably be faced with difficulties in establishing:

1. the productivity it could have achieved when not disrupted;
2. the productivity achieved when disrupted;
3. the resources affected;
4. the cost and time effect of the disruption; and
5. a causal relationship between an event at D's risk as to cost and the loss of productivity suffered.

17–026 Whereas in the United Kingdom courts and tribunals have sometimes been forgiving of contractors who have failed to keep records and, occasionally, have been willing to accept anecdotal evidence from those concerned with the project as proof of the cause

---

16 Chartered Institute of Building, *Guide to Good Practice in the Management of Time in Complex Projects* (Chichester: Wiley Blackwell, 2010), para.3.5.1.

of their alleged difficulties,[17] on the whole, the courts and Boards of Contract Appeals in the United States, whilst being prepared to adopt various methods of valuation, have tended to require more strict proof of liability and causation by reference to records.

17–027 *Clark Construction*,[18] for example, was a case concerning the construction of a hospital in West Palm Beach, Florida, in which the sub-contractors and principal sub-sub-contractor for the mechanical installations sought recovery from D in a name-borrowing[19] action for the costs of their alleged lost productivity in carrying out the plumbing and ductwork installations.

17–028 In this case, C had originally planned to construct the superstructure proceeding horizontally with each floor in all three blocks before proceeding to the next floor. However, shortly after commencement, D failed to apply for a licence for the approved site dewatering system and the work was stopped by the water authority. In order to get on, C re-sequenced the job from the planned horizontal sequence to a vertical sequence and commenced vertical construction of the west tower, where the foundation was complete while, at the same time, with a limited dewatering system, continuing east and centre wing foundation work.

17–029 Whilst the SCs were handicapped by the change in sequence caused by D, C also failed to forewarn them of the re-sequencing and, for the first year of their work on site, they were not provided with C's schedule. Both these failures also caused problems with materials, deliveries and sequencing. There were also various conflicts in the drawings, which became the subject of RFIs, inhibiting the sub-contractors from completing their co-ordination drawings.

17–030 The SC presented its claim using three separate methodologies based upon hypothetical data. Declining to accept the SC's calculations of what it thought it reasonably might have lost by way of productivity for which D, rather than C, or the SC itself was liable, the Board said:

"The fact that proving the amount of productivity losses is recognised as being notoriously difficult does not abrogate [the SC's] fundamental responsibility to prove by a preponderance of the evidence that [D's] action caused its labour to be less efficient than planned and the extent of that impact.

[The SC] primarily relies on the testimony of [the SC's and its sub-SC's] project managers and its expert to prove that a large portion of this overrun is due to [D]-caused labour productivity losses. We consider the testimony of the project managers to be candid and forthright. However, [the SC] made little, if any, effort as we would ordinarily expect, to cite us to contemporaneous project records in support of the testimony. The record in this appeal is one of the largest ever submitted to this Board. It contains all daily reports by [D] and [C] and its SCs, all CPM updates, voluminous correspondence, and all payment requests. Given this voluminous body of evidence, the parties were reminded of the importance of directing the Board's attention to the specific evidence that they believed supported their respective positions. The parties were instructed that it was their responsibility to provide proposed findings of all relevant facts specifically citing supporting appeal file or trial exhibits. [The SC] asserts here that [D] is liable for the loss of labour productivity resulting from it having to work in

17 See, for example, the discussion of the first instance decision of *McAlpine Humberoak v McDermott* (1992) 58 BLR 1 at 15–20; see also *Ascon Contracting Ltd* (1999) 66 Con L R 119; (2000) 16 Const LJ 316; *Kvaerner Construction Ltd v Egger (Barony) Ltd* (2000) QBD (TCC), Lawtel 8 September 2000, (unreported); *Skanska Construction UK Ltd v Egger (Barony) Ltd* [2002] EWHC 773 (TCC); *Skanska Construction UK Ltd v Egger (Barony) Ltd* [2004] EWHC 1748 (TCC); *Great Eastern Hotel Company Ltd v John Laing Construction Ltd* [2005] EWHC 181 (TCC); and *City Inn Ltd v Shepherd Construction Ltd* [2007] CSOH 190; [2008] BLR 269; (2008) 24 Const LJ 590, affirmed [2010] CSIH 68.
18 *Clark Construction Group Inc* (2000) VABCA No 5,674, 00–1 BCA 30,870.
19 Also known as a "pass-through" claim, a procedure whereby C agrees to permit a subcontractor to C to proceed in C's name against D for compensation for losses suffered by the subcontractor.

conditions where there was excessive water in the building and from [D's] failure to timely respond to RFIs. Given the labour overrun that [the SC] knew had begun very early in the project, we find it difficult to believe that the contemporaneous documentation contained in the record would not provide relevant evidence supporting both the fact that an impact on productivity occurred and the extent of that impact. Therefore, in this circumstance, we make the inference that the contemporaneous project records do not support [the SC's] position."

Conditions causing lost productivity

17–031 Various attempts have been made to list exhaustively the causes of productivity loss on construction projects. The Association for the Advancement of Cost Engineers International has identified the following factors as contributing to lost productivity in construction:[20]

1. absenteeism;
2. acceleration (directed, or constructive);
3. adverse, or unusually severe weather;
4. availability of skilled labour;
5. variations, ripple impact, cumulative impact of multiple changes and rework;
6. competition for labour;
7. labour turnover;
8. crowding of labour, or trade stacking;
9. defective engineering, engineering recycle, or rework;
10. dilution of supervision;
11. excessive overtime;
12. failure to coordinate trade contractors, sub-contractors, or vendors;
13. fatigue;
14. labour relations and labour management factors;
15. learning curve;
16. material, tools and equipment shortages;
17. over-manning;
18. poor morale of labour;
19. project management factors;
20. out-of-sequence work;
21. rework and errors;
22. schedule compression;
23. site, or work area access restrictions;
24. site conditions; and
25. untimely approvals or responses.

17–032 It should be noted that these causes are not mutually exclusive and are often overlapping, or interrelated. Furthermore, many of these factors will frequently arise as a secondary, or intermediate, cause rather than a primary cause. A CA might, for instance, exercise a contractual power to order C to accelerate, which, although intended to result in an increase in overall production per unit time, may well cause a decrease in C's average productivity when measured in units of work per man hour, or machine hour. The acceleration instruction can be considered a primary cause of the loss of productivity, the effects of which may entitle C to an extension of time or reimbursement of loss and/

20 American Association of Cost Engineers International, *Estimating Lost Labor Productivity in Construction Claims, Recommended Practice No 25R-03* (2004) pp. 4–7. See, in htis regard, chapter 16 of *Construction Schedule Delays: 2016 Edition*, by W Stephen Dale and Robert N D'Onofrio (Thomson Reuters).

or expense incurred. The instruction may also, however, be found to trigger several secondary causes: for instance, a dilution of supervision, an excess of overtime work, overmanning and fatigue. Furthermore, for the purposes of demonstrating its entitlement to an extension of time, or to reimbursement, C, naturally, will not only need to link any resultant instance of lost productivity to a primary, or secondary cause, but also to an event for which the contract gives the appropriate relief.

17–033 A more compendious classification of the causes of lost productivity is:

1. staffing;
2. variations;
3. recovery and acceleration;
4. errors and omissions;
5. partial possession;
6. adverse weather;
7. loss of morale;
8. extended working hours;
9. dilution of supervision;
10. learning curve;
11. logistics and site restrictions;
12. ripple effect; and
13. trade stacking.

17–034 Each of these factors will now be addressed in turn.

Staffing

17–035 There is a practical limit to the number of workmen and quantity of equipment that can be used effectively on a site at any one time. In order to achieve a given level of productivity, a certain amount of skilled craftsmen, together with supporting labour and trainee, or apprentice, labour will usually be assumed. However, if the mix should change so that, for example, there are insufficient labourers to support the craftsmen, or insufficient craftsmen to direct the labourers and apprentices, the productivity of the gang can be expected to diminish.

17–036 Where there is a high turnover of staff, a gang may not achieve its optimum productivity simply because of the learning curve of new additions, which can be expected to reduce the quantity of work performed in a given time unit. Absenteeism can be expected to have a similar effect because the optimum production rate will not be achievable with fewer resources, or a less efficient mix of skill and support. Labour added to existing work teams can also adversely affect labour rhythm and thereby reduce productivity.

17–037 Productivity can also be adversely affected when workers are indiscriminately added to work teams. Unplanned changes can create this situation by necessitating additional work within the same timescale. The AACE *Recommended Practice* expresses the problem with over-manning thus:[21]

> "Productivity losses may occur when [C] is required to or otherwise utilizes more personnel than originally planned or can be effectively managed. In these situations, productivity losses may occur because [C] may be forced to use unproductive labour due to a shortage of skilled

---

21 American Association of Cost Engineers International, *Estimating Lost Labour Productivity in Construction Claims, Recommended Practice No 25R-03* (2004).

labour; there may be a shortage of materials, tools, or equipment to support the additional labour; or [C] may not be able to effectively manage the labour due to a dilution of supervision."

Variations

17–038 The effect of variations is probably the most common cause of lost productivity. That is so notwithstanding that it is a term of all the standard forms of contract that D may vary the work in numerous ways.[22] Notwithstanding that C is to be paid a fair valuation of its costs and may be entitled to more time if a variation is (at its lowest) likely to cause a delay to completion of the works beyond the completion date, C has an obligation to manage the integration of change on site. In this regard, the AACE *Recommended Practice* recognises that:[23]

"All projects encounter some change during construction. This is to be expected. Some authors believe that 5–10% cost growth due to changes is the expected norm. However, major change (change well beyond the norm), change outside the anticipated scope of work (cardinal change), multiple changes, change's impact on unchanged work, or the cumulative impact of changes may all impact productivity. The need to tear out work already in place, the delays attendant to changes, the need to replan and resequence work, for example, may also cause productivity to decline." (Internal references omitted).

17–039 Although the quantification of loss caused by variations is more often than not dealt with by estimation rather than by calculation, generally, a valuation of a variation should take into account all the effects of the variation. Thus, depending upon the particular conditions of contract, where a variation can be expected to cause some disruption to progress, it will be appropriate to include the estimated effect of loss of efficiency in the valuation of the variation. In this regard, the SCL *Protocol* recommends that:

"Where practicable, the total likely effect of variations should be pre-agreed between [D, the CA and C], to arrive at if possible, a fixed price of a variation, to include not only the direct costs (labour, plant and materials) but also the time-related costs, and agreed extension of time and the necessary revisions to the [schedule].

It is not good practice to leave to be compensated separately at the end of the contract the prolongation and disruption element of a number of different variations or changes. This is likely to result in [C] presenting a global claim, which is a practice that is to be discouraged. Where it is not practicable to agree in advance the amounts for prolongation and disruption to be included in variations and sums for changed circumstances, then it is recommended that the parties to the contract do their best to agree the total amount payable as the consequence of the variations or changes separately as soon as possible after the variations are completed. Though some standard forms of contract have a provision that where a variation affects unvaried work, the affected unvaried work may be treated as varied, these provisions are rarely used. The use of these provisions is encouraged, in order to promote early agreement on the complete effect of the variation."[24]

17–040 This extract draws attention to a number of significant characteristics of disruption to progress:

"it is possible to evaluate the estimated loss of efficiency likely to arise due to the disruptive effect of variations in advance of implementation of the varied work;

1.   disruptive events often cause disruption to work activities other than those directly impacted by the event; and
2.   disruption often arises as a result of the interaction of a number of causes."

---

22 See Ch.4, "Standard Form Provisions for Time and Cost" at paras 4–103 to 4–120.

23 American Association of Cost Engineers International, *Estimating Lost Labour Productivity in Construction Claims, Recommended Practice No 25R-03* (2004).

24 Society of Construction Law, *Delay and Disruption Protocol* (2002).

17–041 In order to evaluate the estimated effects of variations in advance of implementation of varied work, it is first necessary to identify the planned activities that will be affected by the variation and the productivity of the resources required to complete these activities. In other words, it is necessary to determine a resourced, planned schedule for the work as envisaged immediately prior to receipt of the variation order. The activities and resources required for the varied work must also be ascertained, thus forming a revised schedule that will be implemented in response to the variation order. Comparison of the "before" and "after" scenarios can then be used to establish the proper valuation of the variation, including its consequential effects on resource efficiency and any potential loss of productivity. This approach is part of the procedure that should normally be undertaken in the valuation of varied works for most construction projects.[25]

17–042 Such a procedure, applied to the particular varied work, will normally enable identification of appropriate monetary compensation in respect of the changes to the varied work itself. However, if the full effect of the variation is to be evaluated, the activity and resource changes resulting from the variation should be considered, not in isolation, but as part of the schedule for the relevant work section, or the works as a whole. This requires the preparation of a fully resourced, planned schedule for the relevant work, into which the local changes arising from the variation can be impacted. Whilst this impacting is no different from the impacting of any other event upon the planned schedule, the inclusion of resource in the planned and revised schedule will enable evaluation of both the local and the wider, or "ripple", disruptive effects of the variation.

17–043 As to whether C is entitled to be compensated for the disruptive elements of a variation by reference to valuation, or cost, the SCL *Protocol* advises:

> "The tender allowances may be a useful reference point for the evaluation of prolongation and disruption caused by a variation, but only in those circumstances where the different conditions or circumstances under which the variations are carried out make it inappropriate to apply the contract rates or prices. Notwithstanding the advice of the Protocol, there is nothing to prevent the use of the tender allowances as a rough guide for the agreement of prolongation costs or for checking the recovery of prolongation costs through the value of varied work, if that is what the parties for convenience wish to do."[26]

17–044 Frequently, the effects of disruption are seen in changes to the execution of works not directly affected by the principal change. For example, a contractor engaged in the construction of a series of motorway bridge structures may experience significant productivity losses in use of labour, plant and temporary materials if, during construction, progress of one of the structures is deferred by instruction pending design changes. The redeployment of resources resulting from such an instruction is likely to have an effect upon productivity at many locations other than the deferred structure and the use of temporary materials may need to be substantially re-planned as a result of such a change, resulting in reduced efficiency of material usage. By maintaining an updated, resourced works schedule, into which the changes caused by the variation can be meaningfully impacted, the full effects of such changes, including reduced productivity and loss of efficiency caused by disruption, can be appraised and valued, along with the direct costs of the variation.

17–045 On large construction projects, it is very common for a large number of variations to arise in a relatively short period and for the effect of each variation to interact

---

25 See Ch.10, "Project Control".
26 At para.1.9.4.

with the effect of others. This interaction can be so complex that, without such resource-based planning and impacting, it can be virtually impossible to discern the individual disruptive effect of each individual change. Thus, although the changes to activities and resources caused by the variations must be impacted in such a way that the effects resulting from each variation remain discernible, it may be necessary to seek compensation in time and money in respect of appropriate groupings of causes where those effects interact.[27]

Recovery and acceleration

17–046 The AACE *Recommended Practice* advises that:[28]

> "The deliberate or unintentional speeding up of a project may result in lengthy periods of mandatory overtime, the addition of second shifts, or the addition of more labour beyond the saturation point of the site or that can be effectively managed or coordinated, all of which may have distinct impacts on productivity."

17–047 The need to carry out two activities over the same time-frame instead of sequentially can arise as a result of added operations to a planned sequence of operations. Unless gradual and controlled implementation of additional operations is effected, there can be an adverse effect on the remaining activities. However, whilst there appears to be a widespread assumption that, when work is speeded up, it will lead to increased costs, this may not always be true. Take, for example, Figure 17.3. This illustrates a construction period, in which the fixed costs are distributed over a 12-month construction period, in comparison to a reduced period of ten months. Whether the costs of the recovery, or acceleration, to achieve the latter, outweigh the fixed overheads which would have been incurred over the two months of the original extended construction period is not a matter of assumption, it is a matter of fact, which is to be proved in each particular case.

17–048 The amount of that increase in cost is not readily susceptible to quantification and the valuation of additional costs arising from accelerated working is often difficult. In this regard, the following three questions arise:

1. What combination of resources and outputs leads to minimum duration and costs?
2. If the duration of the contract is changed and costs increase, how much of the increase stems from the change in duration and how much from other causes?
3. To what degree does quicker working result in cost savings?

[Please refer to Figure 17.3]

17–049 Probably the greatest cause of increased unit costs due to shortened working periods is reduced labour productivity. There is a significant difference between the loss of productivity arising simply because big sites employ large workforces and that which arises because a compressed schedule demands over-manning. In the first case, a three-fold increase in the workforce causes a loss of productivity of some 15% and, in the second, the loss can be expected to be nearer 40%. These conclusions are supported by

---

27 See paras 17–088 to 17–162.

28 American Association of Cost Engineers International, *Estimating Lost Labour Productivity in Construction Claims, Recommended Practice No 25R-03* (2004).

the finding that a reduction of two-thirds in the "comfortable" working space results in a loss of productivity of more than 40%.[29]

17–050 As the size of the labour force increases, it may be necessary either to import from further afield, or to accept a reduction in quality. Whilst labour-only sub-contractors paid by the piece may cost more per man hour than directly employed labour, the increase in cost may be offset by an increase in productivity of between 10% and 40%.

17–051 The adverse effects on labour productivity resulting from delays to progress that are outside C's control are a common source of contention in retrospective delay analysis and the calculation of damages. However, whilst primarily a source of concern retrospectively, these considerations have great importance in the calculation of prospective allowances for the effect of change that is to be the subject of a collateral agreement[30] and, indeed, in the initial planning of a project.

17–052 Acceleration by re-sequencing, which is not properly thought out in advance, can have a deleterious effect on productivity; the AACE *Recommended Practice* advises that:[31]

> "When there are delays early on in the project, the compression of the overall timeframe for later activities is often looked to as the way to make up for delays and finish the project on time. From a strict scheduling perspective this may be possible to do without accelerating individual work activities by utilizing float in the project's overall schedule. However, on many projects, schedules are not fully resource loaded. As a consequence, a properly updated schedule reflecting the delays may show the project finishing on time, without shortening individual activities. It may result in overmanning of the work by [C] due to the shortening of the overall duration allowing [C] to complete the total remaining work. This is known as schedule compression. Schedule compression, when associated with overmanning often results in significant productivity losses due to dilution of supervision, shortages of materials, tools or equipment to support the additional labour, increased difficulty in planning and coordinating the work and shortages of skilled labour." (Internal references omitted).

Errors and omissions

17–053 Errors and omissions can adversely affect productivity, whether they are D's responsibility, the CA's, C's, or an SC's. For example, the AACE *Recommended Practice* advises that:[32]

> "Work that is not properly scheduled, shortage of critical construction equipment or labour, and incorrect mix of labour crews may result in decreased productivity because crews may not be able to work as efficiently as they would otherwise do. Improperly planned and implemented project initiation procedures may also lead to lost labour productivity. For example, mobilising labour prior to having access to site electrical power or prior to having adequate site parking can both impact early on labour productivity. Additionally, poor site layout can contribute to loss of productivity. If, for example, crews have to walk a long way to lunch rooms, tool cribs, laydown areas, washrooms, entrances and exits, etc., then productivity may suffer as a result. In design/build or EPC projects, mobilising to the field prematurely before

---

29 RMW Horner and BT Talhouni, *Effects of Accelerated Working, Delays and Disruption on Labour Productivity* (Chartered Institute of Building, 1995).

30 ECC2 and ECC3 cl.62; JCT98 cl.13A; JCT05 cl.5.3 and Sch.2, and GC/Works/1 and GC/Works/1/98.

31 American Association of Cost Engineers International, *Estimating Lost Labour Productivity in Construction Claims, Recommended Practice No 25R-03* (2004).

32 American Association of Cost Engineers International, *Estimating Lost Labour Productivity in Construction Claims, Recommended Practice No 25R-03* (2004).

engineering is sufficiently complete to support efficient work schedules may lead to rework and inefficiencies."

17–054 Defective work, which is condemned and which then has to be taken out and done again, affects productivity, not just because of the essential rework but often because of the growth of a concomitant blame culture and consequential loss of morale as a result of getting it wrong.

17–055 When additional work is required because, for instance, an urgent variation is required to account for a suddenly discovered error, or omission in a design, productivity may decline because the labour loses confidence and becomes uncertain of what work needs to be done. This may also occur as a result of approval of submittals, or responses to requests for information not being dealt with promptly.

Partial possession

17–056 An unplanned change that delays completion of the project could result in work having to be performed after the area is occupied by D's materials, plant, or equipment on an informal basis or, because of a more formal partial possession.[33] This can have adverse effects on productivity because of the need to work around D's usage, additional security requirements, restrictions from certain areas, noise, or working time limitations. Access to the project areas can also become congested, or restricted at the time the work is scheduled in that area. Time in gaining access can be more costly and the effect on additional visitors to the area can complicate work patterns.

17–057 In *Dubaldo v Montagno*,[34] on appeal from the court of first instance, Gruendel J held that Dubaldo as sub-contractor (SC) to Montagno, the contractor (C), suffered a 20% loss of productivity by D moving in to do its shop-fitting while the electrical installation works were still in progress. In this case, perhaps because it was also supported by other sub-contractors, notwithstanding that all the evidence was anecdotal, this was accepted by the Court, which stated:

> "[The SC's Director] testified that the fixturing created difficulties in completing the job. Specifically, he testified that much of the work performed by his company required the use of man lifts and that [D's] fixturing impeded the effectiveness of those lifts because he was forced to operate around the fixturing. [The SC's Director] further testified that such difficulties caused him to expend at least 1000 additional man hours and resulted in a 30 percent loss of efficiency, costing an extra $25,000 to $30,000. Zachary Welburn, an independent electrical contractor hired by [the SC] to work on the . . . project for two weeks in September, and owner of Welburn Electrical Contractors, LLC, testified that store fixturing was taking place the entire time he was on the job. That fixturing, Welburn testified, was in his way and required that he put more time into the job than he would have otherwise because he had to work around it. Finally, despite Globe's long-standing relationship with [D], Marotti testified that fixturing of the store hampered his company's performance by 30 percent to 50 percent. That fixturing, Marotti testified, made it difficult to maneuver in the store to do work. Marotti further testified that 'everything in the whole store that we did was an issue because they were stocking the store. When you get 200 to 300 people in there and there's truckloads coming in with pallets all over the place, [it makes working there difficult]' Based upon the testimony of [the SC], Welburn and Marotti, which it deemed credible, the court [of first instance] found

---

33 See, for example, JCT05 cl.2.33.
34 *Dubaldo Electric, LLC v Montagno Construction, Inc* [2010] AC 30063, *Connecticut Law Journal*, 23 February 2010.

that [the SC] suffered a 20 percent loss of efficiency as a result of the fact that [D] began fixturing unreasonably early."

17–058 Accordingly, where partial possession is required and C is likely to need access to adjacent areas, it would be prudent for C to make any agreement to partial possession conditional upon compensation for the loss of productivity likely to occur.

Adverse weather

17–059 The AACE *Recommended Practice* advises that:[35]

"Some bad weather is to be expected on almost every project. But, pushing weather sensitive work from good weather periods into periods of bad weather, or encountering unusually severe weather, may impact productivity (e.g., earth backfill and compaction operations pushed into wet weather periods)."

17–060 When disruption occurs through exceptionally adverse weather, under most standard forms of contract, an extension of time may be granted, but C will not be entitled to compensation.[36] On the other hand, once progress has been delayed as a result of a D's cost risk event, C may then become entitled to compensation for the effect of weather, as a result of lost productivity, irrespective of whether it is exceptionally adverse, so long as it is materially different from the weather conditions reasonably to be anticipated for that activity at the time of contract.[37] This is because, in this scenario, the lost productivity arises out of the consequential effects of a D's cost risk event. Take, by way of example, summer and winter working. If C is forced to carry out an activity during a period of poor weather, which would otherwise have been carried out in more hospitable conditions, it will reduce its productivity because:

1. there is not as much daylight in the winter;
2. excessively hot, or cold, conditions can induce lethargy and reduce morale; and/or
3. excessively wet, or windy, conditions can render external work more difficult.

17–061 Delayed work may result in C's having to perform work in the winter that was planned to be carried out in summer conditions, or *vice versa*, in high winds, high humidity, or other adverse weather conditions.[38] This will have the effect of reducing the efficiency of labour and add to the costs of operating and maintaining equipment. Furthermore, because of special problems that may arise in performing the work under adverse weather conditions, additional labour, material and equipment may be required in excess of that originally anticipated. Notwithstanding that most standard forms provide that the financial risk of adverse weather should be borne by C, those who find themselves delayed by seasonal weather may be entitled to recover the additional costs

---

35 American Association of Cost Engineers International, *Estimating Lost Labour Productivity in Construction Claims, Recommended Practice* No 25R-03 (2004).

36 But see the NEC family of contracts, which provide for compensation for every excusable event.

37 See, for example, *E H Cardy & Son Ltd v Anthony Edward Vye Taylor* (1994) 38 Con LR 79, per H H Judge Bowsher QC at 95.

38 In a case of the author's experience concerning development in the Arctic Circle, unusually, the adverse weather was marginally above freezing conditions. This melted the permafrost and rendered the ground too soft for efficient working.

as well as time if they are able to show that, had it not been for an earlier delay caused by D, they would not have been affected by the weather of that season. In *Cardy*, when considering periods of loss caused by faulty design of a public house, HH Judge Bowsher QC observed that:

> "There was some delay due to inclement weather. If the design had been done properly in the first place, the work would not have gone into the period of inclement weather, nor would there have been any intervention of a Christmas break. The delay due to inclement weather, Christmas break, and redrawing were all results of the original bad design of the third party."[39]

17–062 Again, in the US case of *Williams v Strait*,[40] by reason of the delay caused by collapse of a steel frame, C was forced to extend some of its work into the winter months and claimed all costs associated with protecting the structure during the 1985–1986 winter. C argued that the excessive costs incurred were the product of the delay to rendering the building weather-tight. D argued that, following the suspension of work, C had resumed in less than two weeks and that enclosing the structure was dependent upon the suspended precast erection, which could not have been completed before winter. The Court stated that:

> "The evidence presented, persuasively shows that costs arising from protecting the structure are valid. The steel frame erection was a critical path item; therefore any degree of delay directly affected the project schedule. The Court finds that the accident resulted solely from (the SC's) action in the steel frame erection. Winter protection costs were associated with the collapse."

17–063 In the Canadian case of *Ellis Don*,[41] the Court considered that the additional cost of pouring concrete in winter rather than during other seasons was allowable. In that case, where C contracted to construct a new car park in Toronto over a period of 52 weeks, but completion was delayed by 32 weeks, one of the causes of delay was D's failure to obtain an excavation permit, which delayed the site start. The initial period of delay was seven weeks, but C claimed the following consequential periods of delay to the works:

- Delay in obtaining the excavation permit: 7 weeks
- Consequent delay in commencing excavation: 1.5 weeks
- Consequent delay in obtaining crane: 6 weeks
- Consequent delay due to extension of work into a winter period: 3 weeks
- Total delay: 17.5 weeks

17–064 Relying upon the English decision in *Koufos v Czarnikow*,[42] in this case, the judge said:

> "In my view the parties to the contract at the time the contract was entered into contemplated or should have contemplated that if [D] did not have available the necessary excavation permit until 8 weeks after [C] had need of it [C] would be delayed in carrying out its work, and that such delay would throw the sub-contractors off [schedule] which would entail further delays and that such delays would cause [C] damages of the very type or nature it suffered."[43]

---

39 *E H Cardy & Son Ltd v Anthony Edward Vye Taylor* (1994) 38 Con LR 79, per Judge Bowsher, at 95.
40 *Williams Enterprise Inc v The Strait Manufacturing & Welding Inc* 728 F Supp. 12 (DDC 1990).
41 *Ellis Don Ltd v The Parking Authority of Toronto* (1978) 28 BLR 98.
42 *Koufos v Czarnikow Ltd, the Heron II* [1967] AC 350.
43 *Ellis Don v The Parking Authority of Toronto* (1978) 28 BLR 98 at 121, per O'Leary J.

Loss of morale

17–065 Workers who are happy and have pride in their work will be more motivated than those who are not and are thus more likely to work productively. Morale can have a profound effect upon the productivity of labour resources, and its loss can occur for a multitude of reasons. Uncertainty about how, or where, a job is to be performed, dissatisfaction, or lack of confidence about a job, the company, or the project itself, boredom, difficult relationships with co-workers, and extraneous factors personal to individual workers can all play a part in this regard. As it is entirely subjective and predominantly influenced by issues internal to C and its labour force, however, the effects of any morale loss will not only be difficult to quantify, but are also very likely to present problems in establishing that the losses were solely attributable to an event at the risk of D. Accordingly, any such claim would seem likely to succeed only in the most extraordinary circumstances.

Extended working hours

17–066 The AACE *Recommended Practice* advises that:[44]

> "Numerous studies over many years have consistently documented the fact that productivity typically declines as overtime work continues. The most commonly stated reasons for this result include fatigue, increased absenteeism, decreased morale, reduced supervision effectiveness, poor workmanship resulting in higher than normal rework, increased accidents, etc. One author has gone so far as to suggest that 'on the average, no matter how many hours a week you work, you will only achieve fifty hours of results.' The thought underlying this statement is that while overtime work will initially result in increased output, if it is continued for a prolonged period, the output may actually decline for the reasons stated earlier. Thus, long term overtime may lead to increased costs but decreased productivity. The effect of continued overtime work on labour productivity is, perhaps, one of the most studied productivity loss factors in the construction industry." (Internal references omitted.)

17–067 Overtime may be required to complete the original contract work within the contract period because of a variation, either as a result of an instruction to accelerate, or an implied instruction to accelerate as a result of the failure of the CA to award an extension of time.

17–068 Where overtime is required in one part of the project, men working on another part of the project, which does not require overtime, may be expected to compete for some part of it. Competition for overtime may contribute to poor morale and attitude, thereby reducing the ultimate productivity and lowering efficiency.

17–069 Overtime breaks the established rhythm of a project and lowers work output and efficiency through physical fatigue. Workers who are tired also tend to make mistakes, resulting in rework and loss of morale; they also suffer from an enhanced risk of injury. The inverse relationship of cost to benefit from increased working hours is illustrated by the example of acceleration by increased working hours given previously.[45] There it was demonstrated that, on a progressively decreasing productivity over the time during which extended hours were worked, the saving varied between approximately 6% and 20% on time against an additional cost of between approximately 33% and 35%, depending upon which hours and days were worked.

---

44 American Association of Cost Engineers International, *Estimating Lost Labour Productivity in Construction Claims, Recommended Practice* No 25R-03 (2004).

45 See Ch.11, "Mitigation, Recovery and Acceleration" at paras 11–177 to 11–188.

Reassignment of manpower

17–070 Reassignment of the workforce is generally required when changes to work in progress come unexpectedly, when changes are major, or when a demand is made to expedite, or re-schedule completion of certain phases of the work. Productivity can decrease if sufficient time is not allowed to plan an orderly effort to ensure work proceeds smoothly and efficiently.

17–071 Loss of productivity tends to occur with fluctuations in labour moving on and off a work-face because of unexpected changes, excessive changes, or demand to expedite, or re-schedule completion of work phases and when there is insufficient opportunity to plan for orderly change.

17–072 Apart from the question of reallocation of labour employed at the work-face, it is entirely possible that disruption may involve managerial and other staff having to carry out different tasks, or to relocate from what would ordinarily be their day-to-day tasks. Irrespective of whether it is D's, C's or a sub-contractor's claim, whether such management time can properly form a head of damages depends largely upon what was the management's ordinary work and in what way that was disrupted so as to cause a loss.[46]

17–073 In *Bridge v Abbey Pynford*,[47] in a contract under an exchange of letters, a 62 tonnes printing press was to be installed on new foundations in an empty factory over a tendered period of ten days. Work started on 19 August 2002, but on 4 September it was discovered that the existing floor was not level and a shuttered, raised base would be required. On attending site to inspect prior to the installation of the press on 13 September, it was discovered that the raised base would render the printing machine inoperable. It was agreed that remedial work would be completed by 20 September, and D would move in on 23 September. On 24 September, it was discovered that the printer base was defective and would move under the weight of the press. Further remedial work was completed by 4 October and the press was eventually commissioned and ready for use by 28 October. On 14 November 2002, D's "New Business Director", who was the manager in charge of the project, wrote to C to say that D had incurred costs and losses as a direct result of C's inability to complete the work on time and that he would be quantifying its losses. Negligence was ultimately admitted, but quantum and causation disputed in relation to D's claims for, amongst other things, D's manager's time allocated to seeing that the repair work was correctly carried out.

17–074 In this case, Ramsey J had no difficulty in holding C liable for the costs of D's management time as damages, notwithstanding that they had been no more than estimated, retrospectively, saying:[48]

> "At exhibit PR 33 to his witness statement [D's manager] has set out a schedule of the time spent from 31 August 2002 to 30 April 2003. He says that he calculated that he was engaged for 128 hours in dealing with the problems caused by [C]. As he explained in evidence the hours were based upon his assessment of the time he spent on various matters. That assessment was made retrospectively. He prepared it by looking through the various documents which record what happened.
>
> Such a method of retrospective assessment is, I consider, a valid method of calculation. I have been referred to the judgment of His Honour Judge Bowsher in *Holman Group v. Sherwood* (Unreported, 7 November 2001)[49] where he indicated that in the absence of records,

---

46 See Ch.21, "Damages", throughout.

47 *Bridge UK.com Ltd v Abbey Pynford Plc* [2007] EWHC 728 (TCC).

48 *Bridge UK.com Ltd v Abbey Pynford Plc* [2007] EWHC 728 (TCC) at [122]–[128].

49 Now reported at *Horace Holman Group Ltd v Sherwood International Group Ltd* [2001] All ER (D) 83 (Nov).

evidence in the form of a reconstruction from memory was acceptable. I respectfully agree. However, it must be borne in mind that such an assessment is an approximation of the hours spent and may over-estimate or under-estimate the actual time which would have been recorded at the time.

Some hours have been included for organising the outsourced work at [a sub-contractor]. In addition, I consider that a discount should be applied to allow for the inherent uncertainty in this retrospective method. Overall, I consider that a discount of about 20% would be appropriate to allow both for the hours wrongly included for outsourcing to [the sub-contractor] in August 2002 which I have disallowed for and for the uncertainty arising from the method. The relevant hours spent by [D's manager] were, therefore, I find 100 hours.

I accept that the appropriate approach to the question of recovery of such management time is that set out by Gloster J in *R+V Versicherung*[50] and I respectfully adopt the approach. At para 77 Gloster J said that:

> 'as a matter of principle, such head of loss (i.e. the costs of wasted staff time spent on the investigation and/or mitigation of the tort) is recoverable, notwithstanding that no additional expenditure "loss", or loss of revenue or profit can be shown. However, this is subject to the proviso that it has to be demonstrated with sufficient certainty that the wasted time was indeed spent on investigating and/or mitigating the relevant tort; i.e. that the expenditure was directly attributable to the tort – see per Roxburgh LJ in *British Motor Trades Association* at 569.[51] This is perhaps simply another way of putting what Potter LJ said in *Standard Chartered*[52] namely that to be able to recover one has to show some significant disruption to the business; in other words that staff have been significantly diverted form their usual activities. Otherwise the alleged wasted expenditure on wages cannot be said to be "directly attributable" to the tort.'

In this case [D's manager] states at paragraph 79 of his witness statement and I accept that [D] 'suffered losses due to lost opportunities since I was the New Business Development Director at the time, and I was unable to leave the premises in order to attend to other responsibilities such as selling and marketing [D's] business'.

> In his evidence [D's Finance Director] explained that [D's] turnover has increased from about £2 million in 2002 to an estimated £10 million this year. It is therefore clear, in my judgment that [D's manager's] time would have been spent in selling and marketing [D's] business rather than being occupied in dealing with the problems for which [C] has accepted liability.
>
> As a result, I am therefore satisfied from [D's manager's] evidence that he spent time dealing with, investigating and mitigating the effect of the problems caused by [C]. That time amounted to 100 hours. [D's manager] would otherwise have been selling and marketing [D's] business during that time. On that basis [D] is entitled to recover for 100 hours of [D's manager's] time."

Dilution of supervision

17–075 The AACE *Recommended Practice* describes the effect of dilution of supervision as:[53]

> "When crews are split up to perform base scope work and changed work in multiple locations or when work is continually changed or resequenced, field supervision is often unable to effectively perform their primary task – to see that crews work productively. Field supervision ends up spending more time planning and replanning than supervising. It is probable that productivity will decline because the right tools, materials and equipment may not be in the right place at the right time."

50 *R+V Versicherung AG v Risk Insurance and Reinsurance Solutions SA (No.3)* [2006] EWHC 42 (Comm).
51 *British Motor Trade Association v Salvadori* [1949] Ch.556; [1949] 1 All ER 208.
52 *Standard Chartered Bank v Pakistan National Shipping Corp* [2001] EWCA Civ 55; [2001] CLC 825.
53 American Association of Cost Engineers International, *Estimating Lost Labour Productivity in Construction Claims*, Recommended Practice No 25R-03 (2004).

17–076 It is foreseeable that, while the site agent is engaged in analysing a variation, organising and assigning labour, procuring additional materials and goods, equipment and tools, and so on, the productivity on the original works can adversely be affected. It is foreseeable that, for any given change, the site agent may have to:

1. analyse the content of the variation, stop and replan the affected work;
2. estimate quantities, order and expedite delivery of materials, goods and equipment;
3. incorporate changes into the as-planned schedule and method statement;
4. instruct the foreman and ganger;
5. supervise the work in progress; and
6. revise any snagging lists, testing and commissioning procedures.

17–077 Accordingly, if management resources are not adequately increased in order to deal with changes, the works can be expected to be adversely affected.

Learning curve

17–078 "Learning curve" is the description of a cumulative productivity graph that illustrates increased productivity over time attributed to experience and increased knowledge and familiarity with the work type. Productivity losses can also occur on recommencement following identifiable suspensions of progress. In such circumstances, it is often necessary for the labour force to re-familiarise itself with the state of the work previously achieved and to develop afresh an efficient working method for the remainder. During this process, less work can be expected to be carried out than would otherwise be the case. The AACE *Recommended Practice* advises that:[54]

> "At the outset of any project, there is a typical learning curve while the labour crews become familiar with the project, its location, the quality standards imposed, laydown area locations, etc. This is to be expected and is typically included in as-bid costs. However, if the work of the project is shut down for some period of time and labour crews laid off, then when work recommences the labour crews brought back to the project may have to go through another learning curve. This is probably an unanticipated impact to labour productivity. If this happens more than once, then each time a work stoppage occurs another learning curve productivity loss impact may occur."

17–079 According to scientific theory at least, a learning curve is a decaying exponential function, where every doubling of accumulated production is accompanied by a decrease in the time taken by a constant percentage.[55] For example, if a process with a 90% learning curve takes 100 minutes to produce a first unit, then the learning curve will predict that the second unit should take 90 minutes, the fourth unit should take 81 minutes (= 90% × 90), the eighth should take 73 minutes and so on. Thus, whilst rapidly diminishing until it becomes increasingly indiscernible, the potential for learning curve improvements will in theory never reduce to zero, and there will always be at least some scope for additional learning, however small. Empirical studies,[56] furthermore, have shown that learning curve rates between 75% and 95% occur in most applications

---

54 American Association of Cost Engineers International, *Estimating Lost Labour Productivity in Construction Claims, Recommended Practice* No 25R-03 (2004).

55 See, for example, A Belkaoui, *The learning curve – a management accounting tool* (Quorum Books, 1991) p. 6.

56 GM Peck, *The Principles of Learning and Forgetting and Their Influence on Productivity and Cost* (Australia: The Institution of Engineers, 1984).

in the world at large, with this value being influenced by the relative proportions of human and machine labour, and the complexity of the tasks.

17–080 Whilst of great importance to the high-volume and highly repetitive processes of the manufacturing industry, in construction work, unless the work has an unusually high degree of repetition and uniformity,[57] learning curve effects are likely only to be of any significance in the initial stages of any activity, when the new workmen initially become oriented to the job, and its drawings, specifications, tool locations, work procedures and so on. As Thomas puts it:

> "Construction activities like masonry construction, reinforcement installation, steel erection, formwork installation, conduit installation, duct erection, and most other activities are simple enough that skilled craftsmen have little to learn. Improvements in productivity are [therefore] not the norm and for most construction task-level activities, one would expect to see little or no improvement through repetition."[58]

Logistics and site restrictions

17–081 Difficult ground conditions such as saturated soil, or those with a multitude of services to be avoided, necessarily reduce productivity. Restricted working hours, short possessions and inhospitable working hours all go to produce lower productivity than could normally be expected. The AACE *Recommended Practice* also recognises that:[59]

> "If a work site is remote, difficult to get to, or has inefficient or limited access then productivity may suffer because labour, equipment and materials may not be on site when and as needed to support efficient prosecution of the work. In addition, productivity losses may occur when access to work areas are delayed or late and [C] is required to do more work in a shorter period of time, which may result in overmanning, dilution of supervision and lack of coordination of the trades.
>
> If the project management team fails to get sub-contractors, material or equipment to the right place at the right time, then productivity may decline as crews will not have the necessary resources to accomplish their work, various trades interfere with others or work is not available to the crews to perform.
>
> If material, tools or construction equipment are not available to a crew at the right location and time, then the crew's productivity will probably suffer as they may be unable to proceed in an orderly, consistent manner. Similarly, if the wrong tools or improperly sized equipment is provided, productivity may also suffer."

17–082 However, disruption can also occur because of problems in procurement and delivery of labour, materials and plant arising out of a variation. When access routes to the work-face are changed, there may also be additional travelling distances to be accommodated, resulting in lost working time.

Ripple

17–083 A variation issued to one works contractor, or sub-contractor can have an adverse effect on the work of other contractors. The other contractors may find themselves

57 Such exceptions may occur in civil engineering projects, when there are many similar components to be manufactured, for instance, the production of concrete roadway segments, or components of a railway.

58 Dr HR Thomas, "Construction learning curves: factual, or imagined?" Construction Claims Online (7 March 2005) *www.constructionclaims.com* (accessed July 2010).

59 American Association of Cost Engineers International, *Estimating Lost Labour Productivity in Construction Claims, Recommended Practice No 25R-03* (2004).

faced with additional costs simply because they have to change the schedule, or sequence of operations, or it interrupts their work flow.

17–084 Ripple effect works both ways. Where C, or C's sub-contractors, are in delay, D's consultants may reasonably be expected to be put to additional work which, in the event of a liquidated damages clause, must be taken into consideration in the calculation of the appropriate rate. However, where there is no such agreement, then it would appear that whether or not the consultants' costs are recoverable may depend upon whether there are adequate records illustrating what work was done, by whom and when. For example, in *Tate and Lyle v GLC*,[60] in the process of constructing two piers, heavy deposits of silt formed, preventing access to the moorings of Tate and Lyle (C), which attempted to set off its costs against liability to pay corporation tax to D. Forbes J held that, although C could properly recover damages for the managerial and supervisory expenses directly attributable to D's failure to dredge the silt once it had become deposited, C had kept no records of the time expended and, in those circumstances, C's claim failed.

17–085 On the other hand, it seems plain that in both UK and US[61] jurisdictions, in appropriate circumstances, provided that the facts are made out and liability and causation proved, the courts will be prepared to accept ex post facto estimates of the time lost and its cost. In *Holman v Sherwood*, Judge Bowsher made the position plain in saying:[62]

> "The case before me differs from the case before Forbes J in that while he had no evidence of the amount of time spent, there is before me evidence in the form of a reconstruction from memory of events from the past. I cannot and do not say, in the absence of records there is to be no recovery."

Trade stacking

17–086 A change, if not properly integrated in the schedule, can transform an orderly, well-sequenced schedule into one in which many operations must be performed concurrently. The workmen of several trades could be crowded, or "stacked" in a limited work area, creating a situation in which the work cannot be carried out in the most efficient sequence and thus cannot be done efficiently. A contractor that planned work in accordance with optimal outlays of cost and time, moreover, may find that, as a result of such poor sequencing, its ability to complete the project in such an optimal manner is severely compromised. In this regard, the AACE *Recommended Practice* recognises that:[63]

> "To achieve good productivity each member of a crew must have sufficient working space to perform their work without being interfered with by other craftsmen. When more labour is assigned to work in a fixed amount of space it is probable that interference may occur, thus decreasing productivity. Additionally, when multiple trades are assigned to work in the same area, the probability of interference rises and productivity may decline."

17–087 Various empirical studies have been done in the United States to measure the likely effects of crowding and trade stacking, considering such variables as workforce size, area per worker, type of contract and ratio of actual to planned manpower.[64]

---

60 *Tate & Lyle Distribution v Greater London Council* [1982] 1 W.L.R. 149.

61 See the decision in *Dubaldo Electric, LLC* (2010) AC 30063, *Connecticut Law Journal*, 23 February 2010, referred to above at para.17–057.

62 *Horace Holman Group Ltd v Sherwood International Group Ltd* [2001] All ER (D) 83 (Nov) at [73].

63 American Association of Cost Engineers International, *Estimating Lost Labour Productivity in Construction Claims, Recommended Practice No 25R-03* (2004).

64 See, for example the US Army Corps of Engineers, *Modification Impact Evaluation Guide* (1979).

The analysis of lost productivity

17–088 Loss of productivity is a relative concept and calculation of lost productivity as a result of disruption must be based upon two measurements: namely the productivity that would have been, *but for* the disruption (that is, the "baseline") and the productivity achieved *as a result of* the disruption (that is, the measure of achieved productivity against the baseline). In principle, unless a global approach is adopted,[65] the effect of events on productivity can be established by reference to either of the following baselines:

1. planned productivity on the project;
2. productivity expected to be achieved from a project-specific benchmark study;
3. productivity actually achieved when not disrupted by events at D's risk; or
4. productivity expected to be capable of being achieved according to data from other projects.

17–089 These alternatives give rise to the following alternative techniques for obtaining such a comparison:

1. planned (undisrupted) versus actual (disrupted);
2. historic (undisrupted – on other projects) versus actual (disrupted);
3. industry productivity norms (undisrupted) versus actual (disrupted);
4. benchmark study (undisrupted) versus actual (disrupted); and
5. actual (undisrupted) versus actual (disrupted) – the "measured mile" approach.

17–090 Whenever proof is advanced on the basis of an impact on the planned level of productivity, the starting point is usually what productivity C reasonably planned to achieve. This should be a matter of fact and not a matter of opinion. When the claim is based upon what actually happened by reference to the as-built schedule, then this should also be a matter of fact.[66] It is only in the event that there is a lack of factual authority for the claim that opinion evidence is at all necessary. If it is absolutely necessary to use expert opinion to establish this, then, as a check, productivity rates established by the expert should be compared to rates actually experienced in an unimpacted period, or to productivity rates established on another similar project.

17–091 Whilst comparison with other projects of like kind may be accepted in certain circumstances, comparison with the productivity of another contractor on the site is not, however, appropriate. In *Southern Comfort Builders*,[67] the court rejected the measured mile analysis of lost productivity costs as not being an acceptable comparison where the expert, who had been unable to find an unimpacted period, had posed as its baseline the production achieved by another contractor on the same project performing similar work.

A worked example

17–092 Whereas a delay analysis essentially determines the additional time that C remained on site, a disruption analysis may not only have to make that calculation, but also

---

65 For which see Ch.19, "Total Time, Total Loss and Claims", throughout.

66 In the Supreme Court of British Columbia, in rejecting expert opinion on the as-built record in *The Foundation Co of Canada Ltd v United Grain Growers* (1995) 25 CLR (2d) 1 (BC SC); (1996) 62 ACWS 3d 29, Brenner J said "I am of the view that the evidence of the people who actually did the job can be more compelling. These people were on the job each day and could, particularly with the assistance of their notes made at the time, explain what was happening."

67 *Southern Comfort Builders v United States* (2005) 67 Fed Cl 124 at 150.

a calculation of the loss of efficiency caused by disruption for the purposes of compensation. An idea of the likely effect of lost productivity on the cost and time of a project can be gleaned from a simple example of suspension of working time by the change in the siting of C's site administration accommodation. For the purpose of this example, C is required to move its site administration huts from the position it is entitled to use to a position at the rear of the site camp. The effect of this is that, by benchmark measurement, it can be calculated that it takes an additional five minutes walking time from the site administration huts to the work-face than was the case with the original site establishment.[68]

17–093 For the purpose of the calculation, suppose that the workforce travels from the huts to the work-face and back three times per day, that is six journeys at five minutes each, thereby giving a time loss of 0.5 hours of productive time per day.

17–094 Using, for the purposes of this example, the road construction project to which reference has previously been made,[69] we can assume that during the final three weeks of work, the schedule of work to be achieved is as shown at Figure 17.4 below.

17–095 The loss of time is 0.5 hours per working day up until completion, not 0.5 hours per day for each man, or plant item on site. On the other hand, the cost that will be incurred for which no productivity will be achieved is 0.5 hours for each person, or item of plant on site on any working day the resource in question was actually working. Suppose that the workforce usually work 10 hours per day and there are 17 working days left to complete the work. An extra 0.5 hours per day will thus add:

17 6 × 0.5 hours = 8.5 hours = (say) 1 day.

17–096 Accordingly, therefore, C has a prima facie entitlement to one working day's prolongation costs, which is what it would be entitled to if the next consecutive day was a working day. However, because the work was scheduled to finish on Friday 17 June 2005, the additional day's work cannot be achieved until the following Monday, and it will thus cause three days' prolongation of overheads.

17–097 The cost of the lost productivity, on the other hand, amounts to the cost of 0.5 hours per day for each of the different labour and plant categories employed on the activities carried out on each day. For the purpose of this exercise, the notional labour resources for these activities are as set out in the table at Figure 17.5.

[Please refer to Figures 17.4 and 17.5]

17–098 To calculate the reimbursable loss, it is necessary to apply the hours lost in relation to each grade of labour, or plant in use to the corresponding cost rates on the relevant working days. For the purpose of this example, assume that the cost rate of all grades of labour, across the board, is £15 per hour. If that were to be adopted, it would result in a labour cost of:

896 hours × £15 = £13,440.

---

68 In practice, studies have suggested that when work in progress is interrupted for less than 15 minutes at a time, the resultant time effects can be regarded as statistically insignificant and inseparable from the fluctuations in productivity which can normally be expected. (See, for example H Lal, *Quantifying and managing disruption claims* (Thomas Telford, 2003); R D Logcher and WW Collins, "Management impacts on labor productivity", *Proceedings of the ASCE Journal of Construction Division* (1978), Vol 104 at pp. 447–461; GR Smith, HR Thomas and SC Thrun, "Pavement Operation Performance Management", *Proceedings of the 20th Annual Meeting of the Project Management Institute* (Atlanta, 1989) at pp. 425–430.

69 See Ch.11, "Mitigation, Recovery and Acceleration", paras 11–154 to 11–157 and Ch.16, "Float and Time Contingencies", paras 16–013 to 16–030.

17–099 In addition, there will be lost plant usage time which, in the event of no machine operator overlap, will accrue at the rate of 0.5 hours per day per item of plant in use in relation to each day affected.

17–100 Finally, there will be the prolongation of overheads which, as previously identified, will amount to three days' overheads (including the additional weekend).

17–101 This simple example demonstrates the additional complexity that lost productivity calculations bring to claims in respect of time and cost. Although this example is predicated on an instructed change in working conditions, a similar calculation will be required for any event that affects the workforce so as to interfere with the length of the working day, rather than the activities being carried out during the day. Restrictions imposed on the duration of the working day because of noise, or other contingencies, for example, could also be calculated in this manner.

Planned versus actual

17–102 The first port of call for a productivity baseline is often the planned schedule of work. The reasoning behind this is that, in the simplest analysis, if "A" days is the period of time planned for the activity and "B" days is the amount of time that has actually been expended upon that activity, then the effect of the claimed disruption is $B - A$ days. Thus, when disruption occurs, the reasonableness, or otherwise of the as-planned schedule is often the starting point for consideration of how the proposed methodology has been affected by the disrupting event.

17–103 The planned versus actual analysis relies fundamentally on whether the durations of activities and quantities of resources as planned were reasonable at the time that the event happened. It is no use, for example, claiming that an activity that is scheduled to take ten weeks has taken 15 weeks to complete as a result of some alleged disruption if, when the projected ten-week period for the activity's duration is calculated objectively, giving consideration to the resource requirements of the activity tasks, it can be demonstrated that, instead of being planned to take ten weeks as shown on the schedule, on the basis of the resources allocated to it at the time of tender it should reasonably have been planned to take 15 weeks. Accordingly, both for the purposes of project planning and for retrospective delay analysis, evidence of a credible and logical approach to the calculation of activity durations relative to the resource demands and constraints can be vitally important.

17–104 This is particularly the case where change occurs. This can be illustrated by considering the example of a contract in which the foundations were originally designed to be shallow strip footings and, as a result of bad ground, were redesigned as deep trench fill, thereby requiring a shift from a labour-intensive to a plant-intensive method of working. C claimed that, instead of taking the 7.5 weeks to complete the excavation and concrete laying, it actually took 10.5 weeks. The analysis of this activity requires a calculation of the time it would reasonably take to carry out each process of work as follows:

1. As-planned;
   1.1. excavate the shallow trench;
   1.2. lay the thin strip of concrete foundation; and
   1.3. build 12 courses of brickwork to damp-proof course level.

This had to be compared with the time it would take to:

2. As-built;
   2.1. dig a deep trench;

91

2.2. fill with mass concrete; and

2.3. build two courses of brickwork to damp-proof course level.

17–105 The labour content in the as-planned scheme is likely to be the higher of the two, but the cost of the as-built scheme is likely to be higher than that of the as-planned simply because of the amount of concrete required for the deep trench fill. Similarly, whilst the timing of the as-planned is likely to be driven by the allocation of labour resources and the speed at which those resources work, that of the as-built is more likely to be driven by considerations of plant availability.

17–106 At the time of tender, C may have based its tender prices and its project schedule on the durations and rates from several different sources of reference. In the event of a change for which C claims relief from, or entitlement to reimbursement of loss or expense, it has to demonstrate that what it has done is different from that for which it tendered and that the durations and costs have changed as a result of the imposed change and not from the myriad other circumstances for which it is entitled neither to relief nor compensation. In this context, probative evidence is:

1. proof that the durations and costs included in the original tender are reasonable, or are otherwise comparable with the norm;
2. proof that the durations and costs included in the short-term, high density resourced schedule planned before the event occurred were not substantially different from those on which the tender was based;
3. proof that the basis of those durations, productivity and costs have been properly calculated; and
4. the source of the data upon which the calculation has been based.

17–107 C may be reluctant to disclose its in-house productivity guides on the basis that they are proprietary information upon which its success over its competitors is reliant. There may also be a reluctance to provide information about the make-up of tendered activity durations; however, if C wishes to make good its claim on this basis, it must show that it can properly justify its planned baseline productivity from which it claims the departure therefrom has been caused solely as a result of a D's cost risk event.

Industry productivity norms versus actual

17–108 In the absence of basic planned resource and productivity data, evidence of standard industry productivity rates, or "norms", might be adduced in support of estimates of lost productivity for the purposes of collateral agreements. However, in support of retrospective claims, proof that there were periods during which C met its planned productivity and resource utilisation rates, or a breakdown of the tender schedule indicating how durations have been derived from priced rates and schedule resources, will invariably be required. In the event that there are discrepancies between these rates and any corresponding "norms", then it may be helpful to seek disclosure of the guides from which the data has been accumulated and an explanation as to how and where the difference lies between the basic standards and the durations stated in the tender schedule.

17–109 So, for example, if a standard productivity guide indicates that two plasterers and a labourer can execute $150m^2$ of plaster in a week and, for the purpose of the tender duration, C has included $200m^2$ per week and is claiming that, as a result of change, it can only manage $150m^2$ per week, it would be entirely proper to seek some clarification and proof of the reasonableness of the $200m^2$ per week upon which its tender was based.

If the best rate of work that could reasonably have been achieved was never greater than 150m² and that is the rate that has actually been achieved, then the effect of whatever the change was will be nil, instead of the 50m² alleged by C.[70] Clearly, the extrapolation of the time effects of change must be related to a reasonable calculable basis and, if the basis upon which the claim is founded is at fault, then the result will also be at fault.

17–110 However, where C's schedule was compiled without reference to resources and productivity data, or when, notwithstanding that activity durations were planned according to resources and productivity coefficients, the work carried out was so materially different from that planned that the planned data is no longer relevant, then other methods of establishing a baseline have to be explored.

17–111 Industry standards of the percentage loss that can reasonably be expected as a result of particular conditions in representative circumstances do not prove that the event alleged to have caused the lost productivity has occurred, nor that the event has caused the type or degree of lost productivity of the type described in the standards.

17–112 Research carried out predominantly by industry bodies in the United States, but also in the United Kingdom, has produced some guidelines as to what can be expected to be the effect of various contingencies on productivity.[71] The table from one such set of guidelines that is produced by the Mechanical Contractors Association of America (MCAA), is set out at **Figure 17.6**.[72] Guides such as these are generally satisfactory for planning purposes and for gauging appropriate contingency periods for maturation of foreseeable risks and can also be useful in the process of estimating the likely effect of a variation, or other event for the purposes of early warnings, or collateral agreements.

17–113 However, it should be recognised that, when used in connection with the retrospective calculation of the cost of lost productivity, these figures are for guidance only. Individual cases will vary from the guide and will vary according to the particular contractor, trade, personnel and the particular type of activity concerned. The table covers a number of the most common conditions (in outline) that may be experienced. The values are a percentage to add on to labour costs for variations, or original, or estimated further contract durations for job activities.

17–114 Particular care should be exercised in using standard guides to make sure that the comparison is appropriate. Interestingly, in *Clark Construction*,[73] evidence on the source of the MCAA figures reproduced at **Figure 17.6** was received from the MCAA Executive Vice President. The record shows that his evidence was that:

> "the productivity factors contained in the MCAA manual were developed by MCAA's Management Methods Committee but are not based upon any empirical study determining the specific factors or the percentages of loss associated with the individual factors. [The witness] stated that these factors are intended to be used in conjunction with the experience of the particular contractor seeking to use them because percentage of increased costs could well vary from contractor to contractor, crew to crew and job to job. The MCAA factors are widely used in the industry for estimating and productivity valuation purposes. In assessing

---

70 The delaying effect will then be deduced to be caused by the loss of productivity as a result of matters within C's control, for which it may not receive relief, or compensation.

71 RMW Horner and BT Talhouni, *Effects of Accelerated Working Delays and Disruption on Labour Productivity* (Chartered Institute of Building, 1995); MCAA, *Change Orders, Overtime and Productivity* (1994).

72 MCAA *Labor Estimating Manual: Appendix B, Factors Affecting Productivity*. Other US studies include National Electrical Contractors Association (NECA) *Manual of Labour Units* (2003) and US Army Corps of Engineers, *Modification Impact Evaluation Guide* (Department of the Army, 1979).

73 *Clark Construction Group Inc* (2000) VABCA No 5674, 00–1 BCA 30,870.

productivity loss, the MCAA factors are generally used as a guideline as interpreted by experienced project personnel familiar with the specific circumstances of a particular job and contractor."

17–115 In this case, the Board declined to accept the sub-contractor's calculations of lost productivity, which it remarked amounted to "an approximate overrun of bid labour hours of 42%, an extraordinary amount". However, having discounted a number of claims because of concurrency, in which the SC had failed to separate the effect of D's risks from those borne by the SC, or C and failed to provide any records identifying lost productivity, the Board observed:

> "The adverse impact on the productivity of [the SC's and its sub-SC's] labour stemming from the two conditions for which [D] is liable, the change in construction sequence and wet exterior site conditions, is clear from the record. In those circumstances, common sense tells us the causation is proven by [D's] liability."

17–116 In applying common sense to the analysis of lost productivity caused by what had been acknowledged to be D's responsibility, and having declined to accept the calculation based upon the MCAA guide, the Board was then in the position of having to find some measure of the SC's loss. The Board used what it considered to be the appropriate measure by MCAA standards to calculate C's loss saying:

> "We have found that the change from a horizontal to vertical construction sequence caused by [D] would result in reduced productivity because of more difficult internal communication within the building and more difficult control of labour forces arrayed over different floors. We conclude that the applicable MCAA Factors are 'Dilution of Supervision' and 'Site Access'. Reviewing the description of these factors in the MCAA manual we find them to be descriptive of the conditions resulting from the change in sequence, including the inability to prefabricate pipe and duct. Because the sequence change occurred early in the project permitting [the SC] and [its sub-SC] to adjust to the condition we will class the percentage of loss for both of these conditions as 'Minor'. MCAA attributes a 10% loss of efficiency for a minor Dilution of Supervision Condition and a 5% loss of efficiency for a minor Site Access problem. Thus the productivity of [the SC and its sub-SC] installation labour was adversely impacted by a factor of 15%."

17–117 There does not appear to be any comparable set of figures in the United Kingdom, or Commonwealth jurisdictions, let alone any record of their being considered judicially.

Historic versus actual

17–118 Because of the complexity of large construction projects and the interrelationship of scheduled activities, there is generally a high probability that disruption to a particular activity will have an effect on several other activities.

17–119 If the entire project has been impacted by a series of disruptive events, it is not uncommon to find that it is impossible to find a period of time in which the works were not affected by one intervening event, or another. Where there is no such period of unimpacted productivity to use as a baseline, and C or D have not kept adequate records of progress achieved and resources used, it has been accepted by the US courts[74] that comparison of the productivity experienced on other similar projects may be used as a

---

74 *Maryland Sanitary Manufacturing Corp v The United States* (1951) 119 Ct Cl 100.

gauge. The cases suggest that, when comparing work periods from different projects, there is a greater chance of the data being accepted as comparable if:

1. the type of work closely resembles the disrupted work;
2. the weather conditions are similar over the period in question;
3. the geographical area of construction is comparable;[75] and
4. the labour mix is comparable.[76]

17–120 In using such a comparison of other projects, whether for a single activity, or for durations over multiple trades and activities, it is also extremely important to examine in detail the history of the project in order to establish the effect, if any, on the project of extraordinary impacts, such as work stoppages, as these can lead to distortion.

17–121 In *Clark Construction*[77] for example, the factual background of which has been referred to above, there were no records of undisrupted underground pipework and the SC's work had been severely disrupted by C's inability adequately to dewater the site. The SC attempted a proof by comparing the underground piping work for the hospital with the underground work for an adjacent nursing home, which had been constructed by the same contractor and sub-contractor ten years earlier because the nursing home underground piping installation had not been impacted by the dewatering problems it had suffered on the hospital and the nursing home was immediately adjacent to the main hospital building. However, the Board rejected the method of quantifying the disruption, saying:

> "Given the labour overrun that [the SC] knew had begun very early in the project, we find it difficult to believe that the contemporaneous documentation contained in the record would not provide relevant evidence supporting both the fact that an impact on productivity occurred and the extent of that impact. Therefore, in this circumstance, we make the inference that the contemporaneous project records do not support [the SC's] position."

Benchmark data versus actual

17–122 Benchmarking is a method for determining the amount of time model activities should reasonably take to accomplish in like conditions based upon an analyst making sample observations as to how work is to be performed in sample, or actually performed on site. It is a method of time allocation that which has been used primarily in the manufacturing industries and was common in the middle of the last century. It is not widely used in construction, however, and has been severely criticised by some commentators.[78]

17–123 Notwithstanding the reservations expressed by some commentators, it is strongly recommended by the *CIOB* in its Guide:[79]

> "in order to identify the normal productivity rate for given work types the process will normally follow the following procedure:

---

75 Rural should be compared with rural, as urban should with urban.

76 In the United States, it has also been held to be important to ensure that union projects are not compared with non-union projects, without making allowances for the different skill and productivity levels, see *Clark Baridon Inc v Merritt Chapman and Scott Corp* (1962) 311 F 2d 389 (4th Cir).

77 *Clark Construction Group Inc* (2000) VABCA No 5674, 00–1 BCA 30,870.

78 See Dr R. Thomas, "Using productive time to calculate labour inefficiencies", Construction Claims Online (10 January 2005), *www.constructionclaims.com* (accessed 19 July 2010).

79 Chartered Institute of Building, *Guide to Good Practice in the Management of Time in Complex Projects* (Chichester: Wiley Blackwell, 2010), paras 5.4.4.2–5.4.4.3.

Identify the various activities comprised in the work and examine the relationship between them. If there was a reasonable degree of continuity between relevant activities, then the data can be taken together to represent the performance of that work type from beginning to end. If not, then the analysis will also provide information on the degree of productivity lost as a result of intermittent working (if any) by comparison between the best continuity achieved and that achieved during broken periods, absent any other affecting events.

Identify the resources used throughout the various activities and establish whether there is any significant fluctuation between them in continuous and discontinuous operative conditions. If the resources were constant, then whatever fluctuation is apparent in productivity will have been caused by something other than resources. The effect of any known event, such as the effect of a learning curve, or an intervening event, can then be isolated and filtered out and the remainder will represent the average normal achieved productivity for that work type. Where there are remaining fluctuations, the best achievable productivity and average productivity can be established relatively easily.

Where there are fluctuating resources, then a separate analysis of achievable productivity should be made against each combination of resources in order to establish the effect of the different combinations on the average and best productivity in normal conditions.

Where commonly occurring events have interfered with productivity, data for the effect of those on the selected work type can also be established on differing combinations of resources.

The effect of different conditions on performance and the circumstances under which the work was carried out, are essential to the usefulness of the analysis of past performance on future planning, and for the best use of such records the data should be kept in a database, which can be searched, organised and filtered for future use. Typically, in relation to any search, the data retrievable should consist of values in at least the following data fields:

1. job name;
2. job type;
3. country and region;
4. date started, completed and construction period;
5. design team;
6. project-management team;
7. construction-management team;
8. activity type and whether it is a common activity, or with project-specific difficulties;
9. activity duration of which data is measured;
10. best working conditions, characteristics;
11. best working weather conditions;
12. best productivity achieved;
13. average uninterrupted productivity achieved;
14. average working conditions, characteristics;
15. most productive resource combination;
16. average resource combination; and
17. effect on productivity of specific events (by type, e.g. multiple reissues of drawings)."

Actual impacted versus actual unimpacted

17-124 Whilst a comparison with planned data may frequently be the easiest approach for parties to adopt, the most widely accepted method for analysing productivity is that which is referred to as the "measured mile", or "measured productivity"[80] approach. As the *SCL Protocol* puts it:[81]

"The most appropriate way to establish disruption is to apply a technique known as the 'measured mile'. This compares the productivity on an un-impacted part of the contract with that

---

80 JM Wickwire, I J Driscoll and S B Hurlbut, *Construction Scheduling: Preparation, Liability and Claims* (John Wiley & Sons, 1991) pp. 301–302.
81 Society of Construction Law, *Delay and Disruption Protocol*, p. 31.

achieved on the impacted part. Such a comparison factors out issues concerning unrealistic schedules and inefficient working. The comparison can be made on the man-hours expended, or the units of work performed."

17–125 In the words of Schwartzkopf:

"The measured mile calculation is favoured because it considers only the actual effect of the alleged impact and thereby eliminates disputes over the validity of cost estimates, or factors that may have impacted productivity due to no fault of [D]."[82]

17–126 The nature of the approach was elaborated upon in the US cases of *Clark Construction*,[83] in which the Board described the method of analysis as follows:

"A measured mile analysis compares work performed in one period not impacted by events causing a loss of productivity with the same, or comparable work performed in another period that was impacted by productivity-affecting events."

17–127 In *Lamb Engineering*,[84] the Board highlighted that the measured mile approach is most effective when the comparison periods are close in time, involve very similar types of work, and occur in the same contract so that like is compared with like:

"As we understand it, a measured mile employs the rate of production achieved in a representative sample of actual operations to estimate the amount of effort which would have been required to perform work which cannot be directly measured. Its probative value necessarily depends upon the comparability of the circumstances surrounding the sample to the circumstances which would have prevailed for the work which could not be directly measured. In our opinion, its use is limited to circumstances where, as here, proof of actual costs of the work as contracted is not feasible."

17–128 The measured mile tends to be particularly suited to situations in which the process to be analysed has a degree of continuity arising from a cyclical, or repetitive working pattern. Where an identifiable pattern is repeated, it is usually possible to apply such an approach involving the identification of the time taken to complete one, or more cycles in undisrupted conditions as a baseline against which can be compared the productivity of identical work cycles in disrupted conditions. Typically, this will be applicable to such cyclical work as piling, multi-storey concrete frame construction, pipeline construction, tunnelling and road laying, mechanical and electrical installations and furniture fit-out, amongst others.

The basic approach

17–129 At its most basic, the measured mile approach entails the comparison, for a given productivity measurement, of productivity in a representative period of time where progress is undisrupted, with that in a comparative period where progress is disrupted by a known event. **Figure 17.7**, for instance, illustrates an undisrupted period "A" and a disrupted period "B" where a volume of excavation per unit time has been, during the latter period, adversely affected by a period of exceptionally wet weather. The inference might then be drawn that the additional time, or cost to C, that the water causes is proportionate to the reduction in average productivity during period "B". Where an isolated

---

82 W. Schwartzkopf, *Calculating Lost Labor Productivity in Construction Claims* (1995, Aspen).
83 *Clark Construction Group Inc* (2000) VABCA No 5674, 00–1 BCA 30,870.
84 *Lamb Engineering & Construction Company* (1997) EBCA 97–2 BCA 29207.

activity is considered in this manner, it is important to recognise that productivity will normally vary throughout its duration as a result of any number of factors.

17–130 One of the attractive features of the measured mile approach is that it relies upon actual performance rather than planned performance. This also means, however, that the quality of C's record keeping becomes of paramount importance. In the absence of good quality data from which inferences legitimately can be drawn, the measured mile can be little better than speculation.[85] In *Southern Comfort Builders*[86] for example, the expert's measured mile analysis was dismissed as being fundamentally flawed where, apart from other things, the value of the calculated lost productivity exceeded the total loss claimed to have been suffered.

17–131 Other limitations to the approach arise from the assumptions that need to be made in order to draw the necessary inferences. Such assumptions include:

- that there actually exists a representative period that can be used as a baseline and that that period is itself actually undisrupted;
- that there actually exists a single period that has been consistently disrupted by the event being analysed; and
- that the relative lack of productivity in the disrupted period is solely attributable to the event being analysed and not to other events.

17–132 If these standard requirements cannot easily be met then, in certain circumstances, it may be possible to undertake a modified measured mile approach by abstracting the effect of known disruptions to achieve a modified baseline. This method is discussed below.

Modified measured mile approach

17–133 When there is no single undisrupted and representative period of time to use as a baseline, what is sometimes referred to as the "modified measured mile", or "baseline productivity" method might be used in place of a basic measured mile approach.[87]

17–134 In this method of analysis, instead of selecting a baseline comprised of a continuous set of data points, a baseline is achieved by isolating a non-continuous array of data points that are statistically most likely to represent undisrupted progress. Thomas, for instance, opines that "on all except the worst projects, one can generally find 10% of the reporting periods that are generally free from major disruptions".[88] Accordingly, he suggests that an appropriate baseline can be generated by averaging productivity in the 10% of reporting periods with the highest unit output, and that a measured mile analysis be run from that.[89]

17–135 Such a technique is most likely to find application where there exists a highly repetitive process and where entitlement to extension of time, or reimbursement can be

---

85 See for example, *Centex Bateson Construction Co* (1998) VABCA Nos 4,613, 5,162–5,165, LEXIS 14, 99–1 BCA (CCH) 30,153, affirmed, *Centex Bateson Construction Co v Togo D. West, Jr, Secretary of Veterans Affairs* (2000) 250 F 3d 761 (Fed Cir); *Adams Construction Company* (1997) VABCA No 4669, 97–1 BCA 28801; *Fire Security Systems Inc* (1991) VABCA Nos 2,107 et al, 91–2 BCA 23743.

86 *Southern Comfort Builders v The United States* (2005) 67 Fed Cl 124.

87 See, eg Dr H Thomas, "The baseline analysis", Construction Claims Online (7 February 2005) *www.constructionclaims.com* (accessed 19 July 2010).

88 Dr H Thomas, "The baseline analysis", Construction Claims Online (7 February 2005) *www.constructionclaims.com* (accessed 19 July 2010).

89 Dr H Thomas, "The baseline analysis", Construction Claims Online (7 February 2005) *www.constructionclaims.com* (accessed 19 July 2010).

correlated to fall outside the realms of "reasonable foreseeability". As was stated in the US case of *Bat v Pike-Paschan*,[90] for instance:

> "There is a range of reasonably expected adverse conditions in the performance of a construction contract within which there is no breach. It is only to the extent that [D's] lack of diligence as a general contractor caused these adverse conditions to move outside that expected range that [C] is entitled to recovery."

17–136 In certain circumstances, then, all data points falling outside a certain statistical range may be assignable to a single cause for which D bears the risk, for instance unforeseeable ground conditions encountered during oil platform caisson drilling.[91] This array of data then forms the "disrupted" measurements for the purposes of applying the measured mile approach.

Accounting for the effects of separate events

17–137 When a number of events influence the rate of productivity within the baseline period, it may be possible to isolate some of the effects of those events and consider them separately by filtering the data. Filtering thus provides another means by which the basic measured mile approach might be modified.

17–138 Take, for example, the disruption that might occur in the boring of a tunnel in rock. In the absence of external factors, the productivity of a tunnel boring machine (TBM) is largely a function of the diameter of the tunnel it bores and the material through which it has to bore. For example, it might be established that, for the purpose of tender, four different types of rock are to be taken into account in proportions of 40% good, 30% very good, 20% poor and 10% very poor, each one likely to give a different rate of advance. It may be expected that there will be some water leakage that can be coped with by tunnelling up hill and allowing the water to drain by gravity, or it might be pumped. For the purpose of calculating the period of boring, it can be assumed that two gangs will work two 12-hour shifts on six days per week and that maintenance will be carried out on the seventh day. All this will be important in arriving at an average rate of advance that can be used to give an overall duration for the bore in relation to its length.

17–139 In fact, when the bore is executed, the ratio of the four differing grades of rock will never be the same as anticipated and may change from metre to metre through the tunnel, but may not be so substantially different, when taken in the round, as to be capable of being described as "unforeseeable ground conditions", conditions which, for the purpose of this example, would be at D's risk as to both time and cost.

17–140 On the other hand, if the proportion of soft, weak and blocky rock to hard rock is so substantially different as to amount to conditions that were not reasonably foreseeable, it can be expected to cause additional maintenance to be required, interruptions for propping and insertion of rock anchors, and there may be increased water to a level significantly higher than was expected, which in some rock conditions makes no substantial difference to progress but, in others, binds with the soft rock to jam the cutters. At the same time, there may be plant breakdowns caused by insufficient maintenance, which

---

90 *Bat Masonry Co Inc v Pike-Paschan Joint Venture IT*, 842 F Supp 174, 182 (D Md 1993).

91 See F Samelian, "The disruption and productivity baseline", an occasional paper presented to the King's College Construction Law Association Annual Conference (King's College London, 2004). Referring to process control theories used in the manufacturing industry, Samelian suggests that data falling outside three standard deviations from the mean (or "six-sigma" spread) in such circumstances can be assigned to unforeseeable ground conditions.

may, or may not, be associated with the ground conditions, together with absenteeism, strikes and accidents that prevent C from achieving its planned productivity.

17–141 In this example, there are likely to be multiple overlapping causes influencing the rate of productivity and so the calculation of lost productivity resulting from an event for which D takes the risk independently of the lost productivity for which C takes the risk is by no means easy, and will always to some degree be subjective. However, there are some basic procedures that can be adopted to identify the appropriate periods for measurement and to provide a logical and methodical analysis of cause and effect. For instance, the analyst can prepare a database of the boring records, identifying:

1. the date and time of each shift;
2. rock conditions encountered;
3. water conditions encountered;
4. other conditions encountered;
5. the starting and finishing chainage of the drive;
6. the labour force and plant on site;
7. the periods during which the TBM was inoperable;
8. the reason for suspension of the drive;
9. maintenance carried out on each item of plant; and
10. the occurrence of suspensions due to events and other non-working days.

17–142 C's cumulative production (measured in metres advancement of the TBM), is plotted vertically against total time elapsed. Other relevant variables that have the potential to influence this measurement are the rock type encountered and the ingress of water; these are also plotted.

[Please refer to Figure 17.8]

17–143 In this example, plotting the total work sequence allows periods of no advance to be assigned to five individual events that deprived C of working time. Once identified, these events can be separately analysed and, if they are at the contractual risk of D, appropriate claims made.

17–144 The next stage of the process is to identify stoppages within actual working time that are assignable to discrete events. This can be done first by "filtering out" non-working time; that is, changing the horizontal axis from total time to working time. Accordingly, the effect of such stoppages can then be ascertained.

[Please refer to Figure 17.9]

The steps involved are:

1. identifying all discrete suspensions of work, or shifts when no advance was made;
2. identifying the proximate and root causes of the stoppages; and
3. identifying the alleged root cause of the lost advancement.

17–145 The discrete events shown in **Figure 17.9** can then be filtered out again. **[Please refer to Figure 17.9]**. When this has been done, all that should be left is the data indicating the differing degrees of progress achieved when there were no identifiable stoppages, or suspensions attributable to other discrete events. A basic measured mile analysis can then be undertaken on this remaining data, which will facilitate the identification of the following:

1. the periods of time of high, average and low productivity;
2. the prevailing conditions in the tunnel during each period; and

3.   a benchmark degree of progress achieved in conditions representative of those expected at the time of tender.[92]

17–146 In other words, having established the degree of progress per shift that could have been achieved in representative conditions, this can then be compared (on a period-by-period basis) with the progress actually achieved in relation to the differing conditions and a degree of lost productivity equated with the changed conditions by inference.

[Please refer to Figure 17.10]

17–147 In this example, the loss of productivity in period 2 is assignable to a combination of high water ingress and the predominantly "very hard" rock type that coincides with it. By extending the pitch line on the graph, moreover, it can be deduced that, if the cumulative advance against time had proceeded at the same relationship during the disrupted period as it had during the period taken as undisrupted by D's risk events, the work would have been completed 47 days earlier. In other words, lost productivity as a result of D's time and cost risk events caused 47 days' prolongation of that activity.

Judicial consideration of the measured mile approach

17–148 There have been numerous US cases in which the Boards of Contract Appeals have considered versions of a measured mile analysis. In *Centex Bateson*,[93] for instance, having eliminated the likelihood of other causes, the court accepted that the productivity analysis offered was representative of the effect of those events for which D was liable.

17–149 In *Lamb Engineering*,[94] in relation to the evidence taken in the measured mile calculation in order to ascertain that the calculations were reasonable, the Board observed:

> "This was a fixed price contract. [C] did not, and was not required to, maintain a job cost or change order accounting system. Nevertheless, because of the sequencing of work, the daily record of equipment usage, and the allocation of equipment usage to Mod. 3, which [C's sub-contractor] made in its daily reports, we conclude that equipment usage and labour could be allocated to various cost objectives with a reasonable degree of accuracy. [C's expert] 'coded' every hour of equipment use and labour during the relevant period and in so doing assigned them to one of five categories. The categories included stripping, cut and fill, Mod. 3, and two categories of unimpacted activities. [C's expert] testified that he did not use any of the categories upon which [C] based its claim as 'default' categories. Despite extensive discovery, [D] did not demonstrate he had done so.
>
> When, as here, the work was not performed as contracted, the party with the burden of proof must rely upon a construct for the 'would/should have cost' half of the equation for computing increased costs. Typically, where the work cannot be unit costed, the party resorts to experts who attempt to reconstruct the work as it would/should have been performed 'but for' the event that altered it, and attempt to cost that reconstructed work and arrive at an estimate based upon data available. Here, [C's expert] attempted to reconstruct the stripping and cut and fill phases as they would/should have been performed, had it not been for differing site conditions, by use of a so-called measured mile."

---

92 This will not necessarily be the best productivity actually achieved, as that may have occurred in conditions which were significantly better than those that could reasonably have been expected.

93 *Centex Bateson Construction Co* (1998) VABCA Nos 4,613, 5,162–5,165, LEXIS 14, 99–1 BCA (CCH) 30,153, affirmed *Centex Bateson Construction Co v Togo D. West, Jr, Secretary of Veterans Affairs* (2000) 250 F 3d 761 (Fed Cir).

94 *Lamb Engineering & Construction Company* (1997) EBCA 97–2 BCA 29,207.

17–150 The Board then went on to describe in some detail how C's expert approached this task:

> "[C's expert] developed and employed a measured mile in an attempt to show the productivity [C's sub-contractor] could have achieved if the site was as indicated and it had been able to use the scrapers as planned. His measured mile was based upon actual records kept of one scraper's productivity for the first six days after the scrapers resumed operation on August 12. The scraper operator maintained records of the number of hours of operation and the number of cycles (cuts and fills) completed by his scraper each day. The scraper took an average of 5.44 minutes to complete a cycle although the daily average cycles per hour varied from a low of 8.35 cycles to a high of 12.91 cycles.
>
> The expert then 'corrected' the cycle time after consultation with [C's sub-contractor] by reducing it by one minute because of the conditions at the site when the cycles were recorded, thus increasing the productivity by approximately 20%. Since the capacity of the scrapers in question was established at 16.6 cu yds., the expert then calculated a rate of production of 224 cu.yds. per hour using the 'corrected' cycle times. He then, in separate calculations, divided the volume of material for the stripping phases and for the cut and fill phase, as taken off the topographic and grading drawings of the solicitation, and arrived at a calculated number of hours for each phase, which he testified [C's sub-contractor] should have taken to complete each of the two phases under the conditions indicated by the solicitation. He then prepared a separate composite hourly rate for each of the operations as planned, drawing from actual cost records, and multiplied the calculated number of hours for each phase by the relevant composite rate to arrive at a 'but for' cost for each
>
> The expert appears to have been thorough in gathering and allocating the data necessary for his calculations and [D] did not successfully attack them. We conclude that the mechanics of the process he followed were essentially sound."

17–151 Another good example of how the relationship of actual performance in differing periods of productivity can be used to establish a degree of performance actually attainable (against which a loss of performance can be inferred to have been caused by the effects of inefficient working[95] and acceleration), appears from the US case of *Danac*.[96] This was a case concerning a contract to demolish 88 officers' and airmen's Wherry housing units and to renovate and upgrade 565 units into 21 different types of new housing, together with ancillary garage accommodation and related site work at Loring Air Force Base, Maine, for the US Air Force.

17–152 The contract divided the housing units into various heating zones, or "heat loops". A heat loop contained an average of 25 housing units that received heat supplied by a single boiler room through piping unique to those units, with a common mechanical system. The contract contemplated that D would initially release five heat loops to C for renovation and that, as C completed a heat loop, D would release another. Many housing units were occupied and D had to decant the occupants to other locations before C could renovate their units. C planned to employ a small demolition crew, a framing crew, a mechanical crew, an electrical crew, as well as small crews for the other activities. C contemplated that the crews would follow each other through the units. When the crews completed a heat loop, C planned that they would move on to the next heat loop released by D.

17–153 In fact, the workflow was badly disrupted as a result of finding asbestos, hidden defects that had to be put right and additional work as a result of defective design. In

---

95 It is worth noting that, in this case, C scheduled its work using a bar chart, without any CPM analysis. The Board accepted that as the foundation for the calculations of costs, presumably because it was used only for the purpose of comparing efficient periods with inefficient periods and not in an attempt to prove the knock-on effect of a delay to progress on the critical path to completion.

96 *Danac Inc* (1997) ASBCA No 33,394, 97–2 BCA 29,184, affirmed (1998) 98–1 BCA 29,454.

order to demonstrate the effect on production of the disrupted workflow caused by out-of-sequence work, C's expert used C's as-planned schedule to establish benchmarks. In addition to the as-planned schedule, he also developed an as-built schedule from weekly reports prepared by both parties during performance.

17–154 By comparing the as-planned and as-built schedules, C's expert determined when C was achieving the productivity rate planned and when it was not. Among the expert's conclusions were that C was achieving its planned productivity up to early November 1982, when it encountered differing site conditions and other problems. Thereafter, C was not able consistently to achieve its planned rate of housing unit completions until January 1984. However, from January 1984 until contract completion, C was successful in completing housing units at approximately the rate planned.

17–155 C's expert then developed a computer model to perform a loss of efficiency study. He compared C's expenditure of labour hours to the actual numbers of units completed. His premise was that, in an efficient project, the rate of actual labour hours expended, after an initial build-up, would closely parallel the rate of housing units completed. Treating those periods in which there was no such parallel as bad periods, he sought to demonstrate C's loss of efficiency by comparing the labour hours expended in the bad period with those expended in the good period.

17–156 He identified the bad period as the time from the beginning of construction to December 1983 because, over this entire period, C had a high percentage of labour hours, but a low percentage of housing units completed. He identified the good period as the time from December 1983 to the end of construction in January 1985 because the rate of labour hours expended was less than the rate of housing units completed. He used this period as the baseline for measuring loss of efficiency in the bad period. Thereupon, C's expert applied efficiency factors to the labour hours expended in the bad period to adjust the rate of actual labour hours expended so that it would "closely parallel" the rate of housing units completed.

17–157 The adjustments reflected C's expert's calculation that C experienced an average 55% loss of efficiency from the start of construction until August 1983, and a 25% loss of efficiency from August to December 1983. Considering inefficiencies attributable solely to out-of-sequence work, he determined that 500,000, or 83%, of C's 603,570 labour hours were efficient, and that C experienced a loss of efficiency of 103,570, or 17%, of its total labour hours.

17–158 C's expert also performed an analysis to support C's inefficiency claim on behalf of its plumbing sub-contractor. He extracted from the sub-contractor's invoices from the beginning of performance to November 1984 the amounts shown for the sub-contractor's actual labour expenditures. C's expert then plotted the sub-contractor's labour expenditures to November 1984, as well as C's labour hours for the same period. He superimposed the resulting curve for the sub-contractor on the resulting curve for C, and both curves were closely parallel. He concluded from this relationship that the fact that the rate of sub-contractor's labour expenditure was very similar to that of C indicated that both C and the sub-contractor experienced substantially the same loss of efficiency.

17–159 This was accepted by the Board as good evidence of the loss of efficiency suffered by C and its sub-contractor as a result of the reimbursable delays to progress.[97]

---

97 See also L Davis, L Stipanowich and W Bauer, "Does the 'Measured Mile' measure up? When it has, when it hasn't and what may happen under Daubert/Kumho" (2007) *Construction Briefings* (Thomson/West).

Expert opinion

17–160 So far as activity durations are concerned, the scope for useful expert opinion is limited. It is always possible, of course, to use an expert in the calculation of construction durations and productivity to determine applicable "baseline" rates of work for the tender activity and the impacted activity,[98] but in general courts and tribunals can be expected to require records to prove that productivity has in fact been lost as a result of a definable cause. In *Fru-Con*,[99] for example, the Board declined to accept expert evidence of the degree of productivity lost as a result of exceptionally hot weather, saying:

> "[C's] attempt to provide missing productivity information through the testimony of its expert did not compensate. [C's expert] focused his investigation on lost productivity. In [C's expert's opinion] opinion, productivity will decrease with an increase in temperature and difficulty of the task. A typical loss of productivity due to increased temperatures would be approximately 20% to 30%. Small increases in temperature can have a significant effect on productivity once the temperature reaches a certain point. In his efficiency analysis, [C's expert] focused on four factors: temperature, overtime, overcrowding, and difficulty of the work due to overbreak. Noting that the sum total effect of all four factors was greater than each individual factor and that other factors were not accounted for, but which would have had an impact, [C's expert] concluded that [C] lost a minimum of 31,024 hours. [C's expert's] analysis did not account for instances in which [C] was inefficient or made an error resulting in delay, e.g., the mitre gate skirt work and setting of the bulkheads. The court is unable to discern from [C's expert's] analysis a causal relationship between the weather and [C's] loss of productivity. [C's] loss of 31,024 man-hours appears to be the result of factors that were not included in [C's expert's] calculations. For example, [C's expert] does not account for physical or mental fatigue or errors such as breach of the lock culvert. Most significantly, [C's expert's] analysis does not delimit a specific loss attributable to weather. Coupled with the lack of contemporaneous records, the lack of a specific loss due to weather precludes a finding in [C's] favour. Having failed to establish that the delay was the fault of [D] or to prove its losses with sufficient certainty, [C] may not recover damages."

17–161 Similarly, in *Clark Construction*, the Board rejected expert testimony of what lost productivity there might have been saying:

> "The after-the-fact, conclusory assessments of the project managers or the opinion of its experts are not sufficient substitutes for PKC's underlying obligation to contemporaneously document the severe adverse impact on labour efficiency it now claims resulted from the changes and RFIs."

17–162 In the circumstance where C advances its claim by pursuing a valuation of varied works, including the disruptive effects of the variation, the comments above in respect of the factual nature of the as-planned schedule remain pertinent. However, it may be entirely appropriate in this circumstance to seek expert opinion on the changes to the schedule which should rightly flow from the variation and the disruptive effects upon the works as a whole, since this is a matter of objective opinion and not a matter of fact and, under many standard forms of contract, is the appropriate basis for valuing the varied works.

---

98 R Lane, "Cause – Effect Analysis for Delay and Disruption Claims" (1994) *Construction Briefings*, 2nd Series (Federal Publication Inc).
99 *Fru-Con Construction Corp v The United States* (1999) 44 Fed Cl 298 at 27.

CHAPTER 18

Concurrency, parallelism and pacing

Introduction

"First, different causes of delay may overlap, and this will be intellectually troublesome if one is an event justifying an extension and one not; eg information or access may not available, but due to culpable delay or an event not justifying an extension, [C] would not have been able to take advantage of them if they had been."[1]

18–003   Add at the end of footnote 5:
See also Jackson LJ, "Concurrent liability: where have things gone wrong" (2015) 27 SLC paper 191.

18–005   Insert in footnote 7 after (London 2008):
(January 2009) SCL paper 153.

18–007   Add at the end of footnote 10:
See also, M Balen, "Concurrent delay, over-determination and the problem of default rules" (2016) 32 Const LJ 269.

18–013   In the penultimate line of footnote 14, replace "clause" with:
"cause"

18–039   Add the following further Illustration to the existing Illustration (which should be numbered (1)):

(2)   *Facts*: S contracted with F for the dry docking, repair and refurbishment of S's cruise ship. The work was to be completed by 2 March 2012. However, the ship was not redelivered to S until 16 March 2012. Some of the delaying events were S's contractual responsibility and others F's contractual responsibility. S claimed LADs in respect of the delay. F argued that, in so far as the completion date had been delayed by two concurrent events, one of which was F's responsibility and the other of which was S's responsibility, no liability for LADs should arise in respect of that period. *Held*: that it was important to distinguish between a delay which, had the contractor not already been delayed, would have caused delay but, because of an existing delay, made no difference, and a delay that was actually caused by the event relied upon. There is only concurrency if both events in fact cause delay to the progress of the works and the delaying effect of the two events is felt at the same time. The act relied upon must actually prevent the contractor from carrying out the works within the contract period. Unless there is a concurrency actually affecting the scheduled completion date, the contractor cannot claim the benefit of it. Therefore, events for which F was responsible had delayed the completion date between 2 and 16 March 2012. This gave

---

1 I Duncan Wallace, QC (ed), *Hudson's Building and Engineering Contracts* 10th edn, 1st Supplement (1979) p. 639.

Saga a prima facie entitlement to LADs running between those dates. Whilst a number of events for which S was responsible had occurred within that period that might have been capable of causing delay, they did not operate to "cancel out" the delays F caused. F was not entitled to rely upon delays for which S was responsible as stopping time running under the LADs clause. S was entitled to LADs: *Saga Cruises BDF Limited v Fincantieri Spa* (2016).[2]

18–053   **In the first line of footnote 47, following "editor", insert:**
"is"

18–065   **Add at the end of footnote 59:**
See, in particular, the helpful summary of the Australian position, at 166–7 (cited at paragraph **19–071** below).

See also M Curtis QC, "Time for completion, concurrent delay and *Abu Dhabi v SD Marine Services*" (2011) 27 Const LJ 560 and the Illustration at paragraph **6–129** above.

---

2 [2016] EWHC 1875 (Comm).

CHAPTER 19

Total time, total loss and global claims

Introduction

"The expression 'total cost' is adopted only for those claims where [C] alleges a number of legal bases for financial compensation and claims as the measure of this compensation the difference between its total cost of performing the contract and payments received under the contract.[1] By analogy, a 'total time claim'[2] is the name given to a claim in which a number of legal bases for a time extension are alleged and [C] seeks as a time extension the difference between the number of days which the project took to complete less the time, including extensions allowed, provided in the contract. It will be immediately apparent that a total cost/time claim is a particular, albeit a very common, and certainly the most controversial, form of global claim. A total cost claim is one where the composite sum sought is computed by reference to the amount of money required to ensure that the total money received is not less than the total money expended, or expected to be expended on the project. By analogy, a total time claim is one where the time extension sought is calculated by reference to the time required to ensure that the total time allowed under the contract including any time extensions is not less than the total time actually spent on the project."[3]

19–061 Add the following Illustrations:

(1) *Facts*: DM Drainage and Constructions Pty Limited (C) entered into a contract with Karara Mining Limited (D) to construct a 135km water pipeline and claimed that D re-sequenced and redesigned the works causing delay, disruption and additional costs. D sought to strike out parts of the

---

1 *Boyajian v United States*, 423 F 2d 1231, 1240 (Ct Cl 1970) at 1234.
2 *WRB Corporation v United States*, 183 Ct Cl 409 (1968) at 427.
3 The Honourable D Byrne, "Total costs and global claims" [1995] ICLR 531 at p. 532.

statement of claim as failing to disclose a reasonable cause of action, on the basis that global claims were being made. *Held*, by Beech J (in the Supreme Court of Western Australia), striking out parts of the statement of claim and ordering the re-pleading of others, that: (1) C's claims were in the nature of a modified total costs claim and were global, because no attempt had been made to draw any causal link between any particular items of claim and any particular consequences; (2) in order for a total costs claim to succeed, the contractor must establish that there were no operative causes of its loss and expense that were not the responsibility of the employer; without demonstrating that alternative causes are excluded, the inference of causation cannot be drawn; (3) it is for the contractor to prove that the employer is liable for the whole of its total loss and that there are no alternative causes of the total loss; (4) it is for the contractor to prove that the additional costs incurred were incurred reasonably, because, otherwise, the inference that the costs were caused by the employer's conduct cannot be drawn; on a re-pleading, that element of reasonableness should be specifically pleaded; (5) in the circumstances of this case, it was appropriate to require C to plead that it was impossible, or impracticable, to identify that part of the loss attributable to each head of claim, or conduct, on the part of the employer; (6) C must specifically plead that the combined effect of the variations was that none of the work done thereafter in respect of the affected works was within the scope of works to which the stipulated contractual sums and rates applied, so that all such work done was varied work; that assertion would need to be supported by material facts and particulars and was a fundamental and necessary step in C's civil case: *DM Drainage and Constructions Pty Limited v Karara Mining Limited* (2014).[4]

(2) *Facts*: Lamio Masonry Services (C) sought to have an adjudication determination quashed on the basis that it has been denied natural justice; the contractor had only provided C with evidence of its labour hours by the provision of site diaries in its adjudication application and not in its payment claim. It argued that, due to the fact that the diaries were only provided in the adjudication, the respondent was not able to raise the argument that the labour hours were not the applicable rates for the relevant personnel in its payment schedule. *Held*, by the NSW Supreme Court: that the claims met the requirements of a payment claim, since they identified the job, gave a brief description of the work done, how many men did it, how long it took and the amount charged: *Lamio Masonry Services Pty Limited v TP Projects Pty Limited* (2015).[5]

(3) *Held*, by the Singapore Court of Appeal, that: an adjudication application can be challenged prior to the issue of the determination, but that the adjudication process will not be stayed. Under s 27(5) of the Building and Construction Industry Security of Payment Act (SOPA), security must be provided by the respondent before it applies to court to challenge the determination. If no such security is provided, the application will be

4 [2014] WASC 170.
5 [2015] NSWSC 127.

dismissed: *Lau Fook Hoong Adam v GTH Engineering and Construction Pte Limited* (2015).[6]

(4) *Facts*: Probuild (D) submitted a payment claim and also made an adjudication application, after which Netball (C) applied for an interlocutory application, restraining D from taking any further steps in adjudication, since it claimed that the payment claim relied upon was not valid. C argued that the injunction would prevent it from incurring further costs in preparing its adjudication response. *Held*, by Ball J, that: D would suffer more prejudice if it lost its right to recover the payments under the Building and Construction Industry Security of Payment Act 1999 (NSW); the injunction preventing D from enforcing the determination was granted, but not from taking any further steps in the adjudication and C was required to prepare a response. The judge concluded that the court does not have the power to interfere with the statutory timetable and processes set out in the statute: *Probuild v NSW Netball* (2015).[7]

(5) *Facts*: This case was the follow-up to the immediately preceding case. The matter proceeded to adjudication and Probuild (C) was awarded only a fraction of what it was actually claiming (AUD 125,000 instead of AUD 10m). *Held*, by Stevenson J, that: the payment claim was not valid, but was not constructed to mislead the opponent: *Probuild v NSW Netball* (2015).[8]

(6) *Facts*: The Building and Construction Industry (Security of Payment) Act 2002 (Vic) contains provisions that seek to limit the application of the Act (unlike in other Australia jurisdictions), particularly with regard to the quantum of variation claims, where the contract provides a method of resolving disputes (thus using the latter, instead of the one provided under the Act). *Held*, by the Victorian Supreme Court, that: the "method of resolving disputes" within the meaning of the Act means that the contract has a dispute resolution clause, which provides for a final and binding outcome, determined by a third party. By contrast, where it is optional, or allows for an appeal, it is not a "method of resolving disputes", and the Act is available with regard to disputed variations: *SC Plenty Road Pty Limited v Construction Engineering (Aust) Pty Limited* (2015).[9]

---

6 [2015] 5 SLR 516 (SGHC).
7 [2015] NSWSC 408.
8 [2015] NSWSC 1339.
9 [2015] VSC 631.

CHAPTER 20

Apportionment

Introduction

> "*Socrates thought that if all our misfortunes were laid in one common heap, whence everyone must take an equal portion, most persons would be contented to take their own and depart.*"[1]

20–046   **Add at the end of footnote 49:**
See also V Moran QC, "Causation in construction law: the demise of the 'dominant cause' test" (November 2014) 27 SLC paper 190.

20–055   **Add the following Illustration:**

---

(1)   *Facts*: Pathman Construction Co (R) was employed by the General Services Administration (GSA) for the construction of a federal office facility in Evansville, Indiana. Hi-way (A) was R's sub-contractor for all the electrical

---

1 J Bartlett, *Familiar Quotations*, 10th edn (1919). (Attributed to Plutarch (AD 46? – AD c 120), *Consolation to Apollonius*.)

work on the project. R sued A for damages due to an alleged delay in performing the works. The trial court entered judgment for R in the amount of $92,553.93, which was to be set off against a previous judgment obtained by A against R in the US District Court for the Eastern District of Michigan. A appealed and the following issues were raised: (1) whether R had failed to plead and prove the necessary elements of its case; (2) whether the trial court had erred in apportioning the damages for delay; (3) whether the trial court had erred in failing to credit A with an extension granted on the prime contract; (4) whether the trial court's findings were against the manifest weight of the evidence; (5) whether the damages were supported by substantial evidence; (6) whether the trial court had erred in refusing to admit certain testimony as judicial admissions against R; and, (7) whether the trial court had lacked authority to enter the supplemental order. *Held*, by the appellate court, that: (1) an objection which was not preserved in the trial court could not be raised for the first time on review and that such an objection can only be raised whenever a complaint with all the intendments in its favour failed to state a cause of action; (2) the defendant waives any defect by answering a complaint without objection and proceeding to trial; (3) since R chose to seek recovery, as provided in paragraph 14, the 48-hour notice provision did not apply; (4) the trial court was right in apportioning the damages to arrive at A's aliquot share; (5) the trial court was right to exclude the extension from consideration in the computation of damages for delay regarding the steelhauler's strike, as this was unrelated to A's performance; (6) there was no merit in A's contention that the trial court lacked jurisdiction to set off the judgment awarded to R and, as a consequence, the judgment of the trial court was affirmed: *Pathman Construction Co v HiWay Electric Co* (1978).[2]

20–068 Add at the end of footnote 65:

See further B McAdam, "Apportionment and the common law: has *City Inn* got it wrong?" (2009) 25 Const LJ 79.

---

2 [1978] 65 Ill App 3d 480.

CHAPTER 21

Damages

Introduction

"According to the law of nature it is only fair that no one should become richer through damages and injuries suffered by another."[1]

21–009 Add the following further Illustration after the existing Illustration (which should be numbered (1)):

(2) *Facts*: Having previously found that these were manifests errors in the council's tender evaluation in a successful challenge to the procurement procedure, the court set aside the council's original decision finding that C's tender had been the most economically advantageous. However, the court declined to issue a mandatory injunction forcing the council to award the contract to C, noting that such a remedy would only be available in exceptional circumstances and was not a remedy which C had claimed in its pleaded case. Furthermore, the court had found the whole tender process to be flawed and it would be inappropriate to award a contract arising out of a flawed process. The court decided that damages were an adequate remedy as it would be possible for C to demonstrate both its wasted costs and loss of profit arising from the flawed tender process. It was appropriate to award damages, as the council had breached the procurement regulations and, if it had not, it was likely that C would have been awarded the contract: *Woods Building Services v Milton Keynes Council (No. 2 Remedy)*.[2]

21–018 Add the following Illustration:

Facts: This case concerned a form of contract providing for interim certification by an architect (under the Architecture and Surveying Institute standard form). *Held*, by Schiemann, Sedley and Jacob LJJ, that: a party not satisfied with an amount incorrectly certified can either request correction in a subsequent certificate, or adjudicate on that very certificate, as to the correct application of the valuation rules. The same applies if the contractor has obtained an adjudicator's decision in its favour on the amount certified, on the basis that it is the amount certified; this is because such a decision decides that the amount is due, not that it is correct: *Rupert Morgan Building Services (LLC) Limited v Jervis (2003)*.[3]

1 Cicero, Marcus Tullius, *Pomponius* (106–43 bc).
2 [2015] EWHC 2172 (TCC).
3 [2003] EWCA Civ 1563; [2004] 1 WLR 1867; [2004] 1 All ER 529.

21–136 Add the following Illustration after the existing Illustration (which should be numbered (1)):

(2) *Facts*: C engaged D as a sub-contractor to supply and install mechanical and electrical services at a site in London. However, during the work, Carmel entered administration and C therefore terminated the sub-contract. Several years later, after the works had been completed, D applied for payment of the value of work executed but not paid for, together with interest. The dispute went to arbitration. The arbitrator held that D was entitled to payment for work properly carried out. D sought interest in accordance with the *Late Payment Act*. C argued the JCT *Sub-contract Conditions* included a "substantial remedy" for the late payment and, therefore, the *Late Payment Act* had no application. C relied specifically upon the following generally worded provision contained in cl. 4.10.5 of the JCT conditions, which stated that "If the Contractor fails properly to pay the amount, or any part of it, due to the Sub-Contractor under these Conditions by the final date for its payment, the Contractor shall pay to the Sub-Contractor in addition to the amount not properly paid simple interest thereon at the Interest Rate for the period until such payment is made." *Held*: that cl. 4.10.5 was not applicable and awarded interest under the *Late Payment Act* in D's favour (although for different reasons). Although worded generally to refer to payments due "under these Conditions", cl. 4.10.5 was situated within cl. 4.10, which deals exclusively with interim payments. Clause 4.10 also refers to the payment of interest not being a waiver of D's right to suspend work for non-payment, which is a right only applicable to interim payments. A similar interest provision was contained in a subsequent clause dealing with the final payment, suggesting that cl. 4.10.5 was not to be of general application: *John Sisk and Son Limited v Carmel Building Services Limited* (2016).[4]

21–140 Add the following Illustration:

Facts: Sabic UK Petrochemicals Limited (C) was a Saudi company based in the Netherlands. Simon Carves Limited (SCL) was part of Punj Lloyd Limited group and a subsidiary of Punj Lloyd Limited, which was based in India (D) and provided a parental company guarantee. C employed SCL to develop a plant at Wilton. By the end of 2006, delays occurred and both parties agreed to extend the completion date and increased the contract price by under £5.3m. Further delays arose, leading to a second agreement and variation of the main contract, dated 2 July 2008 (SSA2), containing the following key provisions: (1) SCL would carry out certain works previously claimed outside its scope; (2) that the ethylene in date (EID) should be on 5 December 2008 and that LADs should be paid by reference to the

4 [2016] EWHC 806 (TCC).

EID; (3) to procure services from specific key sub-contractors; (4) that C would pay the whole balance of the existing contract price of £14,338,609 made in early July 2008; (5) SCL would provide an advance payment guarantee for £15m, made on 24 June 2008; (6) C agreed to pay the additional £15m in advance of completion of the works, which it did on 2 September 2008; (7) any claims either party had up to 2 July 2008, were compromised and subject to immaterial exceptions. C made the above payments, in the belief that this would enable SCL to complete the works, since it was going into administration. On 3 October 2008, C sent a warning letter relying on the original contract's terms regarding breach of contract and financial difficulties that would enable D to fulfil its obligation. On 6 October 2008, D replied denying breach of contract and asserting that any delay was attributable to C's own breach of contract. On 3 November 2008, C terminated the contract and called in the advance payment guarantee of £15m and the performance guarantee of £13m. D, as the guarantor disputed this on procedural and substantive grounds, also disputing D's entitlement to call upon the proceeds of the performance bond, or the advance payment guarantee. There were claims and counterclaims. C claimed £27.5m for the additional costs of completing the project works and the losses caused by the delays in the production of ethylene. D counterclaimed for the return of the performance bond and advance payment guarantee money. The following issues were established: (1) whether C was justified in sending the warning letter dated 8 October 2008 and whether that letter was sufficient written warning for the purposes of cl. 27.2.10 of the EPC contract; (2) whether D failed to proceed with the works with due diligence, despite the warning to entitle C to terminate the employment; (3) whether D's financial position had so deteriorated to the extent that it could not fulfil its obligations under the contract and entitled C to terminate it; (4) whether D was in repudiatory breach of the contract and, if so, whether C accepted that repudiatory breach; (5) whether D was entitled to its counterclaim on the basis that C's termination was wrongful; (6) whether C's costs were reasonably incurred; (7) whether the contract limited, or excludes, the claims made by C; (8) how the payments of the advanced payment guarantee and the performance bond were to be brought into account; and (9) the balance due to either party. *Held*, by Stuart-Smith J, that: the warning letter was effective as a warning under cl. 27.2.10; that, during the warning period, insufficient progress was made and that D failed to exercise due diligence, which entitled C to terminate its employment under cl. 27.2.10 of the contract; that D's financial position had deteriorated to the point that it jeopardised the fulfilling of its obligations; that by letter of 10 November 2008, C accepted D's repudiatory breach of contract; that the counterclaim failed because there was a substantial balance due to C, after taking into account the £28.5m it received as bond monies; that C had not behaved unreasonably regarding costs to complete the unfinished work left by D; that whereas cl. 35.2 applied to liabilities resulting from breaches of contractual, or tortious, obligations, cl. 35.1 did exclude D's liabilities for loss of production, or profit, but not interest on increased capital expenditure; that the bond money should be considered when computing the total cost to C, as a consequence D should pay C £11,797,514: *Sabic UK Petrochemicals Limited v Punj Lloyd Limited* (2013).[5]

---

5 [2013] EWHC 2916 (TCC).

21–192 Add the following further Illustration after the existing Illustration (which should be numbered (1)):

---

(2) *Facts*: Aspects Contracts Limited (R) was engaged by Higgins Construction plc (A) to carry out an asbestos survey and to report upon certain blocks of maisonettes in Hounslow. A subsequently discovered asbestos, which had not been identified in the report and, after failed negotiation and mediation, brought its claim to adjudication for £822,482 for breach of contractual and/or coterminous tortious duties to exercise reasonable skill and care. The adjudicator's decision dated 28 July 2009 found that R was in breach of such duties, ordering it to pay £490,627, plus interest amounting to £166,421.05. On 6 August 2009, R paid A £658,017, inclusive of the interest accumulated from the date of that decision. R did not initiate any proceedings for the balance of £331,855 plus interest. The limitation period for any claim for breach of the construction contract expired on 27 August 2010 and (by early 2011) for any action in tort. None of the parties agreed to treat the adjudicator's decision as final. After the limitation period, R brought an action to recover the sum it had paid to A on the basis that no existence of asbestos had been identified besides those mentioned in the report. A sought to counterclaim for the £331,855 balance of its claim and interest, but was met by R with a plea of limitation and an alternative claim in restitution. *Held*, at first instance, by Akenhead J, that: (1) there was no such implied term; (2) R could have sought a declaration of non-liability at any time within six years after performance of the contract and that, based upon that, the court would have had ancillary and consequential power to order repayment; (3) the above claim was then time-barred and therefore no claim in restitution existed. On appeal, R did not pursue its restitutionary claim. *Held*, by the Court of Appeal, that: any overpayment could be recovered. The case was brought to the Supreme Court by R in restitution (as an alternative to its primary claim based upon an implied term). *Held*: that the Court of Appeal decision should be affirmed and therefore that the appeal was dismissed: *Aspects Contracts Asbestos (Limited) v Higgins Construction plc* (2015).[6]

21–212 Add the following Illustration:

---

(1) *Facts*: Portsmouth City Council (C) and Ensign Highways Limited (D) entered into a PFI contract, under which D was to undertake works to the highways infrastructure and maintain it for twenty years. D was to receive a monthly fee, less deductions made for breaches of the contract. These deductions were calculated by reference to "service points" listed in the contract. C treated the service points as a discretionary range, with a minimum and maximum level, reflecting the seriousness of the breach and deducted these monthly.

---

6 [2015] UKSC 38. See also, I Hitching, *Aspect Contracts (Asbestos) Ltd v Higgins Construction Plc* [2015] UKSC 38 – first Supreme Court decision on construction adjudication (2015) 31 Const LJ 338.

Following budget cuts, C began awarding maximum service points for every breach and saved up notifications so as to notify them together and trigger termination thresholds under the contract. A dispute arose as to whether an express obligation of good faith in one part of the contract applied to the whole, or whether there was implied duty of good faith on C. *Held*, by Edwards-Stuart J: that the express good faith provision did not apply to the whole contract, because there were a number of other express provisions to act in good faith throughout the contract. The parties had therefore agreed express terms of good faith, which applied merely to specific parts of the contract. Furthermore, an obligation of good faith could only be implied, where the contract provided for one party to exercise discretion, which involved a balancing exercise, the implied term was intrinsic and the contract would not make sense without it. The service points list was found to represent a range that C could award in the event of a breach and, in doing so, required C effectively to undertake a balancing exercise, since the number selected from the range could vary depending upon the severity of the breach: *Portsmouth City Council v Ensign Highways Limited* (2015).[7]

21–213   Add the following Illustration:

Facts: Biffa Waste Services (D) entered into an EPC contract with MW High Tech Projects (C) for the design and construction of a waste treatment plant. C was obliged under the contract to procure a retention bond, under which a condition precedent required that the employer must first make a call on the parent company guarantee (PCG). After the termination of the contract, D called the PCG and, when no payment was forthcoming, it called the retention bond. C rejected the call, claiming that it was not valid. *Held*: by Stuart-Smith J, that, in the absence of fraud, there was no justification for implying a term that the call on the PCG should be valid; there were therefore no grounds upon which the call on the bond could be restrained: *MW High Tech Projects UK Limited v Biffa Waste Services Limited* (2015).[8]

21–224   Add the following further Illustration:

(3)   *Facts*: Mr Makdessi (R) was an influential Lebanese businessman and owner of a group of companies across the Middle East (Team Y&R). In 2008, R sold shares to Team Y&R, which later were transferred to Cavendish Square Holdings BV (A). The contract contemplated some "restricted activities" and "prohibited areas", with which R had to comply, until two years after he ceased to hold any shares in Team Y&R, or the date of the final instalment of any payment. Failure to comply with this, would imply losing the entitlement to an interim payment

7 [2015] EWHC 1969 (TCC).
8 [2015] EWHC 949 (TCC).

and/or the final payment according to cl. 5.1 of the contract. R breached this by getting involved with one of Team Y&R's companies and A sought a declaration that R was a defaulting shareholder and was not entitled to the interim payment or the final payment. *Held*, by Lord Mance, that: cl. 5.1 was not a penalty and that there was a perfectly respectable commercial case for saying that C should not be required to pay the value of goodwill in view of D's actions and consequently A's appeal was allowed: *Cavendish Square Holdings BV v Talal El Makdessi* (2015).[9]

21-227 Replace the penultimate word on the first line with:
"time"

21-232 Add the following Illustration:

Facts: At 2:29 pm on 15 April 2013, Mr Beavis (A) parked his car at a car park in Chelmsford administered by Parking Eye (R). R had displayed about 20 large and prominent signs at the entrance of the car park and at frequent intervals throughout it stating a two-hour maximum stay. The signs also warned that failure to comply with the above will result in a parking charge of £85. A overstayed the limit and R sent him a "First Parking Charge Notice" for £85 payable within 28 days and, if paid within 14 days, it would be reduced to £50 and informing him of an appeal procedure. A ignored this and all the reminders. R commenced proceedings in the county court to recover the alleged £85. R argued that the charge was unenforceable at common law, because it was a penalty and/or it was unfair and therefore unenforceable by virtue of the 1999 Regulations. The judge rejected his arguments and the Court of Appeal upheld the judge' decision. A then appealed to the Supreme Court. *Held*, by Lord Mance, dismissing the appeal, that: (1) there was a contract between A and R, which stated that A could not stay for more than two hours and that on breach he would have to pay £85; (2) the £85 was not a charge for the right to park, nor for the right to overstay the two-hour limit, but as there was no fixed period of time for which the motorist was permitted to stay after the two-hour period, this sum could be regarded as consideration; (3) the £85 can only be regarded as a charge for contravening the terms of the contractual licence and not a penalty and, consequently, it was not unfair for the purpose of the 1999 Regulations: *ParkingEye Limited v Beavis* (2015).[10]

21-242 Add at the end of footnote 278:
See further M S Mohd Danuri; M E Che Munaaim and L C Yen, "Liquidated damages in the Malaysian standard forms of construction contract: the law and the practice" (2009) 25 Const LJ 103 and D H Lal, "Liquidated damages" (2005) 25 Const LJ 569.

21-261 Add at the end of footnote 310:
See also, R Fenwick Elliott, "Penalties: a brief guide to three recent revolutions" (2016) 32 Const LJ 644.

---

9 [2015] UKSC 67.
10 [2015] UKSC 67.

CHAPTER 22

Settlements and dispute resolution

Introduction

> *"The partisan, when he is engaged in a dispute, cares nothing about the rights of the question, but is anxious only to convince his hearers of his own assertions."*[1]

---

1 Plato (427 BC–347 BC) *Dialogues, Phaedo.*

22–004 **Add at the end of footnote 2:**
See also E Geisinger, "Dispute avoidance in internation construction projects: the use of outside counsel as contract manager" (2009) 25 Const LJ 11 and M S Mohd Danuri, S M N A Shaik Mohd Hussain, N E Mustaffa and M S Jaafar, "Growth of dispute avoidance procedures in the construction industry: a revisit and new perspectives" (2010) 26 Const LJ 349.

22–019 **Add the following Illustrations:**

(1) *Facts:* Essar Oilfields Services Limited (C) brought a claim against Norscot Rig Management Pvt Limited (D) under section 68 of the Arbitration Act 1996 (the Act) to set aside the fifth partial award of the sole arbitrator dated 17 December 2015 (the award). The award found C liable to pay d US$12m for damages for repudiatory breach of an operations management agreement and the cost of litigation funding which D had obtained in order to fund the arbitration, as part of "other costs" under section 59(1) of the Act. Arbitration funding was provided by Woodsford Litigation Funding, in exchange for a fee of 300 per cent of the funding, or 35 per cent of any recovery in the event of success. The arbitrator was very critical of C's conduct towards D, which justified an indemnity costs order. By article 28(6) of the ICC *Rules* (under which the arbitration proceeded), the parties excluded any right to appeal under section 69 of the Act. D argued that, in interpreting section 59(1)(c), "other costs" did not include costs of litigation funding and, as a consequence, the arbitrator had committed a serious irregularity under section 68(2)(b) of the Act, exceeding his powers, which would cause substantial injustice to C. D argued that C's claim was out of time and that no extension of time had been granted. Furthermore, D argued that no irregularity had been committed by the arbitrator, but an error of law at best and that, even if there was an irregularity, no substantial injustice had been caused to C and, finally, that C had lost its right to any claim under section 68(2)(b) by statutory waiver, its pre- and post-award conduct.

Held, by HH Judge Waksman, that: (1) if the arbitrator's interpretation of section 59(1)(c) of the Arbitration Act 1996 was mistaken, this only amounted to an error of law and did not represent an excess of power under section 68(2)(b) of the Act; (2) in fact, the arbitrator's interpretation was correct, since "other costs" could include the costs of securing litigation funding; (3) pursuant to section 73, C had in any case, waived its right to challenge the award, by not addressing such irregularity to the arbitrator pre- or post-award; hence dismissing the claim: *Essar Oilfields Services Limited v Norscot Rig Management Pvt Limited* (2016).[2]

(2) *Facts:* Elkamet Kunststofftechnik GmbH (C) (a German company) brought patent proceedings before the English High Court against Saint Gobain Glass France SA (D), in which it was awarded 90% of its costs of the invalidity issues and 100% of the costs of infringement, assessed (upon the indemnity basis) in the sum of £458,000. C sought a compensating order for the losses suffered, in view of the drop-in value of Sterling since it had paid the costs, since it had to exchange Euros into Pounds in order to pay its solicitors' bills. The exchange rate had fallen from €1.39 to €1.41 Euros to the Pound

---

2 [2016] EWHC 2361 (Comm).

between the first and the last invoice paid. D argued that, since the order for costs was made to compensate a party for the costs incurred in litigating in England and Wales, any such order needed to be expressed in Sterling, without taking notice of the origin of the funds used to pay the costs.

Held, by Arnold LJ, that: where a foreign company had to exchange its local currency to Sterling in order to pay costs, it should be compensated for any additional costs resulting from the losses in exchange rate, similar to the right to be compensated by the payment of interest for being kept out of its money; he therefore awarded an additional £20,000 so as to compensate it for the exchange rate loss on payments to its solicitors, taking account of the significant fall in the value of Sterling against the Euro since the UK referendum to leave the EU: *Elkamet Kunststofftechnik GmbH v Saint-Gobain Glass France SA.*[3]

22–027   Add at the end of footnote 16:
See also L Robinson, "Claims for compensation events – How should a contractor prove its claim for time?" (2012) 28 Const LJ 507.

22–030   Add at the end of footnote 26:
See also J Smalley and J Charlson, "A critical review of the effective use of expert witnesses on construction disputes" (2014) 30 Const LJ 268; J Charlson and J Smalley, "Expert witnesses update for 2014" (2015) 31 Const LJ 210; and G McLean, "Expert evidence in adjudication" (2016) 32 Const LJ 498.

22–043   Add the following Illustration:

(2)   *Facts*: An independent expert witness took the witness evidence of Van Oord UK Limited (C) at face value and did not undertake any factual investigation himself, thereby relying solely upon C's witness statements to prepare his report. *Held*, by Coulson J: that the evidence of the expert witness should be rejected in its entirety: *Van Oord UK Limited v Allseas UK Limited* (2015).[4]

22–054   Add at the end of footnote 79:
See also S Nyambo, "The abolition of expert witness immunity: implications of *Jones v Kaney*" (2012) 28 Const LJ 539.

22–059   Add at the end of footnote 83:
See also M Wheater, "Reasonable settlement revisited" (2011) 27 Const LJ 259.

22–068   The case reference in footnote 99 should read:
"[2000] BLR 530 at 545 [131]".

Add, following that citation:

See also *Carillion Construction Limited v Felix (UK) Limited* [2001] BLR 1 at 6 [24], per Dyson J; *Capital Structures plc v Time & Tide Construction Limited* [2006] BLR 226 at

---

3 [2016] EWHC 3421 (Pat).
4 [2015] EWHC 3074 (TCC).

230 [16]–[18], per HH Judge Wilcox; *Ansalem v Raivid* [2008] EWHC 3028 (TCC) at [78], per Akenhead J; *Holcim (Singapore) Pte Limited v Kwan Yong Construction Pte Limited* [2009] 2 SLR 193 at 210 [65] – 213 [72], per Lai Siu Chiu J.; *Farm Assist Limited (in liq) v Secretary of State for Environment, Food & Rural Affairs*[2009] BLR 80 at 82 [8], per Ramsey J; *Siemens Industry Software Pte Limited v Lion Global Offshore Pte Limited* [2014] SGHC 251 at [25]–[27], per Chan Seng Onn J. See further *B&S Contracts and Design Limited v Green* [1984] ICR 419; Bigwood, "Economic Duress by (Threatened) Breach of Contract" (2001) 117 LQR 376; Tan, "Constructing a Doctrine of Economic Duress" (2002) 18 Const LJ 87; Lal, "Commercial Exploitation in construction Contracts: the Rôle of Economic Duress and Unjust Enrichment" (2005) 21 Const LJ 590, [2005] ICLR 466. In an Australian case, White J observed that "[c]haracterising conduct as constituting duress in a commercial setting is fraught with difficulty": *Isicob Pte Limited v Baulderstone Hornibrook (Qld) Pty Limited (in liq)* [2001] QSC 066 at [5].

22–068   The final number in footnote 100 should be:
"1".

22–091   Add at the end of footnote 143:
See also S Mau, "Arbitration to mediation to arbitration with the same parties in the same international commercial dispute before the same neutral: innovative evolution, or recipe for disaster?" (2015) 31 Const LJ 429 and M Goodrich, "Arb-Med: ideal solution or dangerous heresy?" (2016) 32 Const LJ 370.

22–100   Add at the end of footnote 132:
See also C Freedman, "Non-statutory adjudication: is it expert determination, or something different?" (2011) 27 Const LJ 3 and C O'Neil and Dr M Hammes, "60-day expert determination – structured to meet the commercial expectations of business management" (2012) 28 Const LJ 181.

22–106   Add at the end of footnote 148:
See further T Kennedy-Grant, "A review of the cases on the New Zealand Construction Contracts Act 2002" (2013) 29 Const LJ 371, S Magintharan, "Construction adjudication in Singapore – *Lee Wee Lick Terence v Chua Say Eng*" (2014) 30 Const LJ 73, J M E Lyden, "Construction Contracts Act Ireland 2013:some problems in practice" (2016) 32 Const LJ 484 and A Burr and Magintharan, "Malaysia: construction industry *Payment and Adjudication Act 2012*" (2016) 32 Const LJ 699.

Add the following further Illustration:

> (3)   *Facts*: A construction contract did not make any express provision for the timing of progress payments. *Held*, by the NSW Supreme Court, that: in such instances, a claimant will be able to rely upon the times for making progress payments under s 8(2)(b) of the *Building and Construction Industry Security of Payment Act 1999 (NSW)*, which allows for progress claims every month during the course of the project and for 12 months from the date upon which any construction work was last carried out. As a result, the claimant can continue to make payment claims every month, even where no new work has been carried out, or

when the contract has been terminated: *Broadview Windows Pty Limited v Architectural Project Specialists Pty Limited* (2015).[5]

(4) *Facts*: Allied P & L Limited (C) was engaged by Paradigm Housing Group Limited (D) to construct certain dwellings and further works in Hertfordshire. Payments were made monthly after a notice of payment on an interim basis. On 1 May 2009, D issued a notice of withholding payment for a gross sum of £2,418,727, alleging that C has failed to complete the contract by the completion date, which was caused by its unjustified suspension of the design and construction of the works, amongst other breaches to the contract. On 8 May 2009, C replied that, unless payment was made within five working days, it would be at liberty to terminate the contract. On 19 May 2009, D served the first notice, stating the same claims above against C. C denied the claims. On 14 June 2009, D served C a second notice, insisting upon its default and ejected C from that date. On 6 July 2009, C served upon D a notice of adjudication, seeking relief that D had wrongfully terminated the contract and thus that C is entitled to the sum of £248,016.80 plus £8,567.15 of expectation interest. D disputed the adjudicator's jurisdiction. On 3 September 2009, the adjudicator issued his decision, which stated that D's first and second notices were invalid, and therefore that C's eviction form the site had amounted to D's repudiation of the contract, accepted by C leaving the site, awarding C the sum of £274,279.35, plus £13,800.35 for its fees. On 9 September 2009, D wrote to C, alleging that the decision was invalid. C issued proceedings on 9 October 2009 to enforce the decision and to pursue a summary judgment application. D argued that no dispute had arisen because it had not received a letter of claim before referring the matter to adjudication. C replied that there were disputes about D's claims in the first notice. *Held*, by Akenhead J, that: D did not make any effective reservation regarding the adjudicator's jurisdiction and, as a result, his jurisdiction was unchallengeable and the decision should be enforced, ordering C's 100% costs and £20,500 in costs: *Allied P&L Limited v Paradigm Housing Group Limited* (2009).[6]

(5) *Facts*: Camporeale Holdings Pty Limited (C) emailed Mortimer Construction Pty Limited (D), attaching four invoices, which stated that they were made under the *Building and Construction Industry Payments Act 2004 (Qld)*, whilst the email itself did not expressly state that it was a payment claim under the *Act*. *Held*, by Henry J, that: the email and its attachments were a single payment claim under the Act; he rejected the argument that C had either not submitted, or had submitted, more than one payment claim with regard to a single reference date: *Camporeale Holdings Pty Limited v Mortimer Construction Pty Limited* (2015).[7]

(6) *Held*, by Christopher Clarke J, that: the adjudicator had no jurisdiction to act under the modified notice. He concluded that it was a strict obligation that any request for nomination must be made at the same time, or following service of a notice of adjudication. The judge had misgivings about this conclusion, in that the amendment made was of limited importance to the dispute as a whole, but felt that this was overwhelmed by the possibility that an amendment introduced in this way could, in other instances, be much more

---

5 [2015] NSWSC 955.
6 [2009] EWHC 2890 (TCC).
7 [2015] QSC 211.

significant. The judge thought it preferable that this question of jurisdiction should not be decided on the particular significance of the amendment: *Vision Homes v Lancsville* (2009).[8]

22-107 Add the following Illustrations:

(1) *Facts*: Bovis Lend Lease Limited (C) engaged Cofely Engineering Services (D) to carry out and complete the mechanical and public health works, at a cost of £9,651,946.70. A dispute arose for C's withholding of around £198,000 and D referred the matter to adjudication. This first adjudication decided on 21 November 2007 that C had wrongfully deducted the money. A second dispute arose concerning D's entitlement to an EoT and referred to the same adjudicator as before. C objected his jurisdiction and reserved its rights. On 23 June 2007, the decision was made granting D a partial EoT. A third dispute arose concerning design-related claims and was referred to the same adjudicator as before, with D no objecting him. On 6 November 2007, the decision was made favourable to D. A fourth dispute arose regarding D's entitlement to a further EoT and again referred to the same adjudicator as above, with C not objecting to him. The adjudicator's decision of 16 October 2007 found that D was entitled to such EoT. A fifth dispute arose with D serving a notice of adjudication at 7.40am on 1 April 2009, regarding D's claim for a further EoT. At 7.50am on the same day, D applied to RICS to nominate an adjudicator, who was nominated on the morning of 2 April 2009. At 5.30pm on 1 April 2009, C issued a sixth adjudication on the same matter than fifth, applying to appoint a certain adjudicator, who nominated another DLE partner in his place. C applied to the court to determine which adjudicator has the jurisdiction to decide the dispute, under Pt 8. *Held*, by Coulson J, that: the appendix to the sub-contract was the most important document for the purposes of this application, which stated that in the event of a dispute there would be an adjudication and that both parties clearly agreed that the nominating body would be the RICS. As a consequence, the adjudicator had the necessary jurisdiction and C's claim under Pt 8 was dismissed: *Bovis Lend Lease Limited v Cofely Engineering Services* (2009).[9]

(2) *Facts*: In adjudication enforcement proceedings, the issue was whether there was an absence of a crystallised dispute at the time of the notice of adjudication. There was a novel alternative argument to the effect that the adjudicator acted in breach of natural justice in seeking to obtain (and obtaining) further information from the claiming party, which had not been provided before. *Held*: that (1) the adjudicator rejected the "no dispute" point, noting that there had been a five-month gap as between the application for payment on 31 March 2015, and the notice of adjudication on 2 September 2015. Coulson J agreed with the adjudicator, noting that he had observed before that "this argument is frequently advanced and almost as frequently rejected by the courts"; it was "wrong in principle" to suggest that a dispute had not arisen until every last particular of

---

8 [2009] BLR 525.
9 [2009] EWHC 1120 (TCC).

every last element of the claim had been provided; (2) the learned judge rejected the submission that it was somehow unfair if the adjudicator was given information during the adjudication, which had not previously been available (whether, or not, it had been previously requested); it would be contrary to the *Scheme for Construction Contracts* and the basic principles of adjudication not to allow the adjudicator a wide leeway to seek information that they believed to be important: *AMD Environmental Limited v Cumberland Construction Company Limited* (2016).[10]

(3) *Facts*: In a first adjudication, the contractor succeeded on the basis of the sum applied for as interim payment and the absence of notices from the employer; in a second adjudication, the employer sought a review of the sum properly payable. *Held*, by HH Judge Hicks QC, that: the adjudication proceeded on the basis that the second adjudicator could review and revise the application and determine the proper sum that ought to have been applied for. The issue of jurisdiction was not raised in this case: *VHE Construction Plc v RBSTB Trust Co Limited* (2000).[11]

(4) *Facts*: In the appeal in *Paice v MJ Harding (t/a MJ Harding Contractors)* (2015),[12] the Court of Appeal (Jackson, Rafferty and Gloster LHH) *held*: that *ISG Construction Limited v Seevic College* (2014)[13] and *Galliford Try Building Limited v Estura Limited* (2015)[14] did not apply to final accounts and, therefore, that failure to serve a valid pay less notice did not mean that the employer was deemed to have agreed to the value of the contractor's termination account and it was entitled to adjudicate in order to determine the correct value of the termination account: *Harding (t/a MJ Harding Contractors) v Paice* (2015).[15]

(5) *Facts*: RMP Construction Services Limited (C) sought enforcement of an adjudicator's decision regarding an interim application for payment it had made. The adjudicator decided that Chalcroft Limited (D) had failed to serve a pay less notice in time and so the amount applied for by C was to be paid by D. No formal contract had been entered into. The parties agreed that C had carried out its works pursuant to a construction contract, but disagreed the manner in which the contract had been formed. The parties agreed that the Scheme for Construction Contracts (England and Wales) Regulations 1998 (the Scheme) applied, but the dates for serving payment, or pay less, notices differed depending upon which documents formed part of the contract. *Held*, by Stuart-Smith J, that: it was not clear precisely how the contract had been formed and it was not possible as part of the enforcement proceedings to conduct a mini-trial to determine this issue. However, the manner in which the contract had been formed did not affect the enforceability of the adjudicator's decision. The *Scheme* applied to all of the possible formations of the contract and the adjudicator had been correctly appointed in accordance with the *Scheme*. The adjudicator therefore had jurisdiction to determine the dispute: *RMP Construction Services Limited v Chalcroft Limited* (2015).[16]

---

10 [2016] EWHC 285 (TCC).
11 [2000] BLR 187; (2000) 2 TCLR 278; 70 Con LR 51.
12 [2015] EWHC 661 (TCC).
13 [2014] EWHC 4007 (TCC).
14 [2015] EWHC 412 (TCC).
15 [2015] EWCA Civ 1231.
16 [2015] EWHC 3737 (TCC).

(6) *Facts*: Seevic College (D) failed to pay ISG Construction Limited (C) and issue a payment, or pay less, notice; C therefore started (the first) adjudication proceedings and succeeded. D then issued a second adjudication notice, before the decision in the first adjudication was given, in which D sought to determine that the value of C's works was less than that given in the application. The second adjudicator confirmed this, ordering C to repay the difference. An application by C to enforce the decision in the first adjudication was contested by D on the basis of the decision in the second adjudication; subsequently, C applied to the court to decide whether the second adjudication was invalid, due to lack of jurisdiction. *Held*, by Edwards-Stuart J, that: in cases where the employer fails to serve any valid notices, they must be taken as agreeing the value stated in the application served upon them and the contractor becomes entitled to the amount stated in the interim application (irrespective of the true value of the work). The employer cannot start a second adjudication on the same interim payment application: *ISG Construction Limited v Seevic College* (2014).[17]

(7) *Facts*: St Austell Printing Company Limited (C) engaged Dawnus Construction Holdings Limited (D) to design and construct certain industrial units in Cornwall. D applied for an interim payment, but no payment was received. D commenced adjudication proceedings, limited to the measured value of 115 specific changes and variations. The adjudicator decided that D was owed £417,000. C applied for a declaration that the adjudicator lacked jurisdiction to award D any payment, because the dispute had not crystallised and because D had chosen to refer only part of the items included in the application for interim payment to adjudication. *Held*, by Coulson J, that: C's application was dismissed. The crystallisation argument "is almost never successful" because "crystallisation may require no more than the service of a claim by the claiming party and subsequent inactivity for a further short period by the responding party". On the alternative jurisdictional challenge, it was *held* that a claimant is entitled "to prune his original claim for the purposes of his reference to adjudication" and that, in its response to such a claim, the responding party was entitled to rely upon all matters open to it to place reliance upon, by way of defence. The responding party was not limited to those matters which the referring party had chosen to refer to adjudication: *St Austell Printing Company Limited v Dawnus Construction Holdings Limited* (2015).[18]

(8) *Facts*: The Trustees of the Marc Gilbard 2009 Settlement Trust (C) employed OD Developments and Projects Limited (D) to carry out works in Mayfair, London. The contract provided that the final certificate was conclusive, save for matters raised in proceedings commenced within 28 days of the date of issue of the certificate. A final certificate was issued showing a sum due from D to C. Within 28 days, D issued proceedings disputing that certificate. After 28 days had lapsed, D sought to commence adjudication to challenge the final certificate. C argued that the certificate was conclusive and could not be challenged in any adjudication commenced after 28 days. *Held*, by Coulson J, that: D could not commence an adjudication challenging the final certificate outside of 28 days. On a proper construction, the contract allowed D to first commence adjudication and later to commence court, or arbitration, proceedings

---

17 [2014] EWHC 4007 (TCC).
18 [2015] EWHC 96 (TCC).

within the 28-day period, but not otherwise; it was business commonsense that, following the issue of the final certificate, the contract envisaged only one set of proceedings to challenge the final certificate within the 28-day period. This did not fetter D's right to adjudicate at any time, since D could still adjudicate, but would find that C could rely upon the final certificate as conclusive evidence on the matters it covered: *Trustees of the Marc Gilbard 2009 Settlement Trust v OD Developments and Projects Limited* (2015).[19]

(9) *Facts*: Topevent Limited (D) engaged Wycombe Demolition Limited (C) to carry out demolition works. C commenced adjudication proceedings, claiming payment of outstanding invoices and damages for wrongful termination. D counterclaimed and challenged C's valuation and sums which it alleged were due. D requested that the adjudicator visit the site in order to complete the re-valuation, but the adjudicator refused to do so. The adjudicator found that the parties had ended the contract by mutual consent and awarded C £114,000 plus costs and dismissed D's counterclaim. D did not pay and C sought to enforce the decision. D argued that the adjudicator lacked jurisdiction, since he had determined multiple disputes, had acted in breach of natural justice by refusing to visit the site and by deciding the valuation upon a basis that had not been argued by either party. *Held*, by Coulson J, that: the notice of adjudication made it clear that the dispute concerned the outstanding payment due to C, following works having been stopped. Both parts of the payment alleged to be due were part of the same dispute; they were simply different parts. The *TeCSA Rules* also stated that an adjudicator could deal with "any further matters" that the parties agreed should come within the scope of the adjudication. D's agreement and failure to object to the adjudicator dealing with both disputes gave the adjudicator jurisdiction if there were two disputes. Furthermore, it was for the adjudicator to decide what he needed to do to reach a decision; the adjudicator had explained why a site visit was not proportionate, or cost-effective. Finally, the adjudicator had not gone beyond the boundaries of natural justice by improving upon the deficiencies in the claim by reaching a conclusion that was not advanced by either party: *Wycombe Demolition Limited v Topevent Limited* (2015).[20]

(10) *Facts*: Vinci Construction UK Limited (D) entered into a contract with Ecovision Systems (C) for the design and installation of a ground source heating and cooling system. The contract contained three sets of terms, under which the parties could make a referral to adjudication, each with different procedures. A dispute arose between the parties and D commenced adjudication proceedings. During the course of the adjudication, C disputed the jurisdiction of the adjudicator and requested D to confirm which rules had been applied, but D did not so confirm. The adjudicator gave directions that he was proceeding under one set of rules under the contract. D was successful in the adjudication and C was ordered to pay the adjudicator's fees. C sought a declaration that it was not bound by the decision. *Held*, by HH Judge Havelock-Allan QC, that: an adjudicator lacks jurisdiction to determine whether he has jurisdiction, including choosing between two, or more, sets of adjudication rules, if the choice makes a material difference as to the manner in which the adjudicator should be

---

19 [2015] EWHC 70 (TCC).
20 [2015] EWHC 2692 (TCC).

appointed. Because there was uncertainty (due to D not stating which rules it was relying upon in its notice) and the rules had real differences in procedure, since each put forward different methods of appointing the adjudicator, the adjudicator should have asked D to explain which rules it was following. The court found that a different set of rules applied than those used by the adjudicator; accordingly, the adjudicator had not been properly appointed and lacked jurisdiction: *Ecovision Systems v Vinci Construction UK Limited* (2015).[21]

(11) *Held*, by Edwards-Stuart J (clarifying his decision in *ISG Construction Limited v Seevic College* (2014),[22]) that: an employer, which fails to submit a payment, or pay less, notice will only be held to have agreed to the sum in the application on the valuation date relevant to the particular payment certificate and not on any other date. The employer cannot therefore bring a second adjudication to determine the value of the work, but it can challenge the value of the work upon a further application. In this case, the court granted a partial stay of the adjudicator's decision, since it would otherwise cause "manifest injustice": *Galliford Try Building Limited v Estura Limited* (2015).[23]

(12) *Held*, by HH Judge LLoyd QC, that: in a first adjudication, the contractor was entitled to the sum for the interim payment applied for, in the absence of a notice from the employer; the adjudicator in a subsequent adjudication on the correct valuation of the interim payment, was held not to have jurisdiction (under the JCT *Design and Build* payment terms). The judge was, however, apparently of the view that there was a separate dispute between the parties as to the correct valuation: *Watkin Jones & Son Limited v Lidl UK GmbH (No 2)* (2001).[24]

(13) *Held*, by Lord Wheatley, that: the adjudicator had not reached her decision within the time limits provided for either by the *Act*, or by the standard contract. Whilst the statute is silent on the question of communication of the decision, there is a contemporaneous duty to communicate the decision to the interested parties, once it has been reached. Otherwise, the purpose of the legislation would be meaningless. Rendering a decision "forthwith" means immediately via facsimile, or similar, and not by first class post, which might be regarded as "archaic". Furthermore, the adjudicator was not entitled to delay communication of the decision until her fees had been paid, because nothing in the Scheme, or the contract, provided for that possibility. However, whilst the failure to comply with the timing was a serious matter, it did not render the decision a nullity: *St Andrews Bay Development Limited v HBG Management Limited* (2003).[25]

(14) *Held*, by the Scottish Lord Justice Clerk, that: the proper interpretation of paragraph 19 of the *Scheme* was that jurisdiction ceased upon the expiry of the 28-day time limit, unless it had already been extended in accordance with the *Scheme*. The court had to choose between two alternatives, first, that jurisdiction expired at the end of the 28th day, or, secondly, that it continued after that date and remained in existence until one of the parties served an adjudication notice under paragraph 19(2) of the *Scheme*. The Lord Justice Clerk felt that this interpretation reflected the natural meaning of paragraph

---

21 [2015] EWHC 587 (TCC).
22 [2014] EWHC 4007 (TCC).
23 [2015] EWHC 412 (TCC).
24 [2001] EWHC 453 (TCC), [2002] CIIL 1847.
25 [2003] ScotCS 103.

19(1)(a). It was a simple and straightforward approach. Paragraph 19(1) states that an adjudicator shall reach his decision not later than 28 days after the date of the referral notice (unless extended): *Ritchie v Philp* (2005).[26]

22-108 Add the following Illustrations:

(1) *Facts*: Geoffrey Osborne Limited (D) engaged PP Construction Limited (C) to act as its sub-contractor and to carry out works on the concrete frame at Chichester Festival Theatre, the contract making provision for the correction of errors in an award within 14 days of notification of the decision. Any such correction was to be notified within seven days from when such initiative was taken, or such request was made. The adjudicator issued an award on 26 November, directing D to pay C. On 5 December, the adjudicator corrected his decision, but the requests to correct the error previously made had been unclear. C applied for summary judgment, relying upon the correction made by the adjudicator, whilst D resisted on the basis that the correction was made out of time and was of no effect. *Held*, by Stuart-Smith J, that: for a request to be operative and to engage the time periods in the contract, the error had to be identified with sufficient clarity, so that a reasonable adjudicator would understand that they had made an error, what the error was, why it was an error and what alteration was necessary: *PP Construction Limited v Geoffrey Osborne Limited* (2015).[27]

(2) *Facts*: The Science and Technology Facilities Council (C) issued two adjudication applications. MW High Tech Projects UK Limited (D) sent C a letter, including a clear reservation of rights regarding challenging the jurisdiction of the adjudicator. D sent a further letter, agreeing to the identity of the adjudicator, but again reserving the right to challenge the appointment. The adjudicator issued a decision and apportioned his fees as between both parties, which D duly paid. C sought enforcement of the two decisions, but D argued that the adjudicator lacked jurisdiction to determine the dispute. C argued that the decisions were enforceable, because D had entered into an ad hoc agreement to have the dispute decided by adjudication and that, by paying the adjudicator's fees, D had treated the decisions as binding, thereby waiving any right to challenge jurisdiction. Held, by Fraser J, that: the agreement on the identity of the adjudicator did not prevent D from raising jurisdictional challenges at the enforcement stage. Furthermore, payment of the adjudicator's fees did not mean that a party lost its right to challenge jurisdiction upon enforcement: *Science and Technology Facilities Council v MW High Tech Projects UK Limited* (2015).[28]

22-108 Add at the end of footnote 154:

See also, R Klein "Securities provided under statute: Part 2 Housing Grants Construction and Regeneration Act 1996 (as amended)" (2015) 31 Const LJ 266 and J Bowling, "Adjudication enforcement and insolvent companies – the unsatisfactory sate of the law" (2016) 32 Const LJ.

---

26 [2005] BLR 384.
27 [2015] EWHC 325 (TCC).
28 [2015] EWHC 2889 (TCC).

22-109 Add the following Illustration:

(1) *Held*, by HH Judge LLoyd QC, that: where an adjudicator fails to issue his decision within the timescale agreed between the parties (although the adjudicator sent a draft of his decision to both parties' solicitors by email on 20 May, it was not until 22 May, when the final decision was signed and dispatched using the Document Exchange (DX), arriving with the parties one day later on 23 May), it will not, of itself, mean that the decision is not binding upon them. The court will consider each case on its facts and, if the decision is only a day, or so, late, decide whether such delay is excusable as being within the tolerance and commercial practice that one has to afford to the legislation and to the contract: *Barnes & Elliot Limited v TaylorWoodrow Holdings Limited* (2003).[29]

22-110 Add the following Illustration:

(1) *Facts*: C sought to enforce two decisions made by an adjudicator. In accordance with paragraph 8(1) of Pt I of the *Scheme for Construction Contracts (England and Wales) Regulations 1998*[30] (the *Scheme for Construction Contracts 1998*), an adjudicator cannot adjudicate on more than one dispute at the same time without the parties' consent. *Held*, by Coulson J that: one adjudication decision should be enforced, but not the other. Section 108(1) of the *Housing Grants, Construction and Regeneration Act 1996* granted permission for a party to give more than one notice of adjudication (each referring to a separate dispute), and for each adjudication to be referred to the same adjudicator. Further support was provided by the fact that a party may refer a dispute "at any time" when giving effect to s 108(2)(a) of the *Construction Act 1996*. Separate dispute referrals to the same adjudicator at the same time would have to cease unless the parties agreed to do otherwise, where the *Scheme for Construction Contracts 1998* applied. Nonetheless, if parties wish the same adjudicator to decide a dispute, they may do so by waiting for adjudicator's decision on one referral before proceeding with their subsequent referral: *Deluxe Art & Theme Limited v Beck Interiors Limited* (2016).[31]

(2) *Facts*: Eurocom (C) was employed by Siemens (D) under a sub-contract to install communications systems at Charing Cross and Embankment underground stations (the sub-contract), as part of a main contract of D with London Underground Limited. A dispute arose between both parties due to delay and disruption of the work, which ended with C serving a notice of adjudication on D, on 20 July 2012. On 1 August 2012, D sought to terminate C's employment under the sub-contract. As C's first notice of adjudication lapsed, C gave a second notice of adjudication on 8 August 2012, leading to Matthew Molloy's appointment as adjudicator for the first adjudication. On 7 September 2012 he made a decision, determining that C owed D a net amount of £35,283.98, which led to no payment at that stage. On 21 October 2013, C issued a claim document

29 [2003] EWHC 3100 (TCC).
30 SI 1998/649.
31 [2016] EWHC 238 (TCC).

against D requiring it to satisfy the claim within 28 days, otherwise C would issue proceedings. On 18 November 2013, C responded requesting documents. On 21 November 2013 C served notice of adjudication on D, stating that they would applied to RICS for appointment of an adjudicator. When filling the RICS form, C replied to the question of who would have a conflict of interest in the case, by putting the name of Matthew Molloy, among others. On 22 November 2013 the RICS nominated Anthony Bingham as adjudicator for this second adjudication. He made his decision on 28 January 2014, deciding that C was entitled to £1,521,313.75, together with £93,029.38 interest, totalling £1,614,343.13. On 27 May 2014, C threatened enforcement proceedings against D if it did not pay the sums awarded by the adjudicator. D replied that if enforcement proceedings were brought, it would resist, particularly regarding the nomination process for the appointment of this second adjudicator. On 25 July 2014, C commenced proceedings against D, issuing an application for summary judgment. The following issues were raised against the enforcement of the second adjudication by summary judgment: (1) whether the appointment of the adjudicator in the second adjudication was invalid, since C appeared to have misled the RICS in declaring that Matthew Molloy had a conflict of interest and by the RICS failing to raise this with D in accordance with the procedure in their explanatory notes; (2) whether the second adjudication adjudicated on the same matters already decided in the first adjudication; (3) whether the adjudicator in the second adjudication had adopted a procedure contrary to the rules of natural justice; and (4) whether should have been a stay of enforcement of any sums awarded by way of summary judgment. *Held*, by Ramsey J, that: there was a very strong *prima facie* case that C had either deliberately, or recklessly, falsely answered the question regarding conflict of interest, therefore making a fraudulent representation to the RICS; as a consequence the exercise of the RICS' discretion as an independent body was invalidated and is as if no application had been made; as a result, the appointment was null and the adjudicator did not have jurisdiction and C's application for summary judgment was unsuccessful, on the basis that D had established real prospects of successfully defending the claim: *Eurocom Limited v Siemens plc* (2014).[32]

(3) *Facts*: Kier Construction Limited (D) made an "open offer" to Dorchester Group Limited (C), stating that "for the purposes of the proceedings only, and without making any admissions of liability save as set out below", D accepted that C was entitled to certain declarations. C argued that the letter contained an admission and that it was therefore entitled to judgment. *Held*, by Coulson J, that: there was no admission pursuant to CPR 14.1. The letter made no reference to CPR 14.1, did not admit the truth of C's case generally, but only for the purposes of the offer, and it made no reference to an important part of D's defence. The admission was not "clear and unequivocal", as required by CPR 14.1. The offer was a whole "package" of terms, which were to be wholly accepted, or wholly rejected. It would be contrary to the point of the offer as a package of terms, if C could accept parts of the offer, whilst rejecting other parts of it: *Dorchester Group Limited (t/a the Dorchester Collection) v Kier Construction Limited* (2015).[33]

---

32 [2014] EWHC 3710 (TCC).
33 [2015] EWHC 3051 (TCC).

(4) *Facts*: Paice (C) lost two adjudications, involving the same adjudicator (the first adjudicator). C then telephoned the first adjudicator's office to discuss the adjudications. MJ Harding (D) initiated a third adjudication, decided by a different adjudicator, which C also lost. C then initiated a fourth adjudication, in which the first adjudicator was again appointed. D requested telephone records from the first adjudicator and C; the request was ignored and a subsequent injunction to prevent adjudication proceedings was not granted. The adjudication concluded with a decision that D should repay C the majority of its final account payments. Evidence of telephone contact between the first adjudicator and C emerged after the decision and enforcement was challenged on the grounds of bias. *Held*, by Coulson J, that: the application should be refused, since the following gave rise to a real possibility of bias: failure by the adjudicator to disclose the conversations, the "ill-judged" criticisms of D's case and a statement made in support of C's application for summary judgment: *Paice v MJ Harding (t/a MJ Harding Contractors)* (2015).[34]

(5) *Held*, by HH Judge Coulson QC (as he then was), that: cl. 41A.4.1 of the JCT contract expressly recognised that an adjudicator should not be appointed until after the seven-day period has expired and he considered that the words of this clause were mandatory. The effective date of the notice was held to be 20 September 2006. However, the referral notice was not a nullity, since cl. 41A had to be operated in a sensible and commercial way. A sensible interpretation of cl. 41A was that, if the appointment of the adjudicator happens late, on day 7, the referral notice must be served as soon as possible thereafter and, if that means that it is served on day 8, then service on day 8 would be in accordance with cl. 41A. Judge Coulson stated that it would be contrary to business common sense to rule that the provision of the referral notice in this case was out of time. Although cl. 41A sets out a mandatory timetable, it was a timetable which needed to be operated in a sensible and businesslike way. Therefore, the referral notice was validly provided in accordance with the contract and the adjudicator had the necessary jurisdiction: *Cubitt v Fleetglade* (2006).[35]

(6) *Held*, by HH Judge Seymour QC: that, having considered the circumstances in which the first and the final decisions were issued, on the facts, the first decision was not a decision. Therefore, the adjudicator only made his decision when the final decision was published. The question was, therefore, whether the late delivery of the decision meant that it was not binding upon the parties. The judge considered the terms of the adjudication agreement and, in particular, cll. 5.1 and 5.2 thereof, which reflect paragraph 19 of the *Scheme*. Clauses 5.1 and 5.2 provided that the parties might jointly terminate the adjudication agreement at any time upon written notice and, if the termination was due to the adjudicator's failure to give their decision within the relevant period, then the adjudicator was not entitled to their fees and expenses. Where an adjudicator fails to issue their decision within the appropriate time, then this will not, of itself, mean that the decision is not binding upon the parties. Time may be of the essence for issuing the decision, but the parties have the ability to terminate the adjudicator's appointment, if the time for issue of the decision expires without it being given and, if they do

---

34 [2015] EWHC 661 (TCC).
35 [2006] EWHC 3413 (TCC).

not, then they are likely to be bound by the adjudicator's late decision. Since the parties had taken no such steps (under either course of action) before the decision was published, the decision was binding: *Simons Construction Limited v Aardvark Developments Limited* (2003).[36]

22–111   Add the following Illustration:

Facts: Khurana and Khurana (C) engaged Webster Construction Limited (D) to undertake building works to a property. A dispute arose and the parties entered into an adjudication agreement, using the *Scheme for Construction Contracts 1998*, under which, an adjudicator's decision was only temporarily binding. D suggested in correspondence that the decision of the adjudicator "shall be binding on all the parties". C agreed. C then commenced court proceedings to have matters dealt with in the adjudication determined. D argued that the matters already dealt with by the adjudicator were "finally binding". *Held*, by HH Judge Davies, that: the parties had agreed that the adjudicator's decision would be finally binding; the adjudication agreement used the term "shall be binding", without which the proposal to use the Scheme would have evidenced an agreement between the parties that the decision would only be temporarily binding. Both parties were taken to have been aware that the proposal for adjudication using the Scheme carried with it an implicit, but obvious, proposal that, unless expressly stated to the contrary, the decision would be only temporarily binding: *Khurana and Khurana v Webster Construction Limited* (2015).[37]

22–112   Add at the end of footnote 164:
See further C Winser, "Adjudicators' entitlement to their fees" (2012) 28 Const LJ 369 and N Morris and Professor I Ndekugri, "The timetable of challenges of adjudication under the Housing Grants, Construction and Regeneration Act 1996" (2013) 29 Const LJ 343.

Add the following Illustrations:

(1)   *Facts*: Company A (a ship bunker supply company) concluded a bunker oil sales agreement with company B (a shipowner). There was a choice of court clause in the sales agreement that all disputes should be referred to the exclusive jurisdiction of the English High Court. Because B failed to pay the sales price of the bunker oil, A sued B before Ningbo Maritime Court. B then objected to the jurisdiction, because there was a valid choice of court clause. A countered that this choice of court clause was invalid because London had no connection with the dispute. *Held*, by the Ningbo Maritime Court, that: B's objection to jurisdiction should be dismissed. B appealed to Zheijang High People's Court, which maintained the decision of the Ningbo Maritime Court, because: (1) although there was a choice of the English High Court clause in the sales agreement, London was not the place of conclusion of the agreement, the place of performance of the agreement, the

36 [2003] EWHC 2474 (TCC).
37 [2015] EWHC 758 (TCC).

place of the subject-matter, or the place of business of the parties; (2) hence, London had no connection with the disputes and this choice of court clause was therefore invalid; (3) upon seeing A's application, Ningbo Maritime Court attached B's bank account in a bank in Zheijang Province and, as the court was seated in the place where such assets were attached, Ningbo Maritime Court should therefore have jurisdiction: *ZXZZ No 98* (2013).[38]

(2) *Facts*: Forge (C) was hired by Hammersley (D) to design and construct two fuel hubs. Prior to completion of the works, C went into voluntary administration and receivers and managers were appointed by its principal secured creditor. C secured an adjudication determination against D for AUS$14,335,778.07, plus GST. D did not pay the determined amount and C brought an application before the Supreme Court, seeking leave to enforce the determined amount. D presented evidence that it had counterclaims consisting of costs which either had been, or would have been, incurred by it as a direct result of C's insolvency. D asked for such costs to be offset against C's determined amount by operation of s 553C of the *Corporations Act 2001 (Cth)*. *Held*, by Beech J, that: (1) the party resisting enforcement should demonstrate why leave should not be given; (2) there was a serious question to be tried as to whether D's counterclaim exceeded C's determined amount; (3) D's counterclaim constituted a "mutual dealing" for the purpose of s 553C and that s 553C operated as at the date C appointed voluntary administrators and that, from that time onwards, only the net balance remained as between C and D; (4) the application for leave would be suspended pending resolution of D's counterclaim: *Hammersley Iron Pty Limited v James* (2015).[39]

(3) *Facts*: Gazprom (D), a company in the gas sector, acquired shares in Lietuvos Dujos AB (D), which conveys and distributes gas in Lithuania, also managing the gas pipelines and transporting gas to the Region of Kaliningrad of the Russian Federation. An agreement under Lithuanian law was signed between both companies to supply natural gas to consumers in the Republic of Lithuania (C) for ten years, based upon fair prices. Section 7.14 of the agreement contemplated that any claim, dispute, or contravention, should be finally settled by arbitration according to the *Rules of Arbitration of the Institute of Stockholm Chamber of Commerce* and with Stockholm, Sweden, as the seat of arbitration. On 8 February 2011, C wrote to one of D's general manager and two other board members, alleging that they had not acted in the interest of the company when calculating the formula of the gas price. On 25 March 2011, C brought an action against the above three in order to investigate D's activities, claiming that the interests of the country as shareholder of D, had been damaged and that the other D's interests on the contrary, had been unduly favoured by the amendments to the long-term gas contract, with an unfair price. C also asked the three board members to be removed from their posts and to require one of the Ds to renegotiate with the other D a fair and correct price for the purchase of gas. D thus filed a request for arbitration before the Stockholm Chamber of Commerce, on 29 August 2011, requesting to order C to withdraw the action before the Lithuanian courts. D initiated further international arbitration before the Permanent Court of Arbitration in The Hague, disputing

---

38 [2013] Zheijang High People's Court, PRC.
39 [2015] WASC 10[1].

C's decision, which effectively removed one of the Ds as a shareholder, as well as claiming that C had breached its obligations under the Treaty of 29 June 1999 between the Russian Federation and Lithuania on encouragement and mutual protection of investments. On 31 July 2012, the arbitral tribunal made a final award, granting D's request in part. That award referred to the proceedings brought by the Ministry of Energy before the Viliniaus Apygardos Teismas as a breach of the arbitration agreement. As a consequence, it ordered the Ministry of Energy to withdraw some of the requests submitted to the Vilniaus Apygardos Teismas, specifically the request to negotiate with D a fair and correct price for the gas purchase. On 3 September 2012, the Viliniaus Apygardos Teismas upheld the action brought by the Ministry of Energy, finding that the action fell within its jurisdiction and could not be subject to arbitration under Lithuanian law, hence appointing experts to conduct an investigation. One of the Ds and the board members appealed the decision before the Lithuanian Court of Appeal, whilst the other D brought a court action to recognise and enforce the arbitral award under the *New York Convention 1958*. In October 2012, C commenced arbitration against the latter before the Arbitration Institute of the Stockholm Chamber of Commerce on the grounds that the amendments to the long-term gas contract between 2004 and 2012 were against the terms of the agreement for the sale and sought damages amounting to £1.9 bn. On 17 December 2012, the Lietuvos Apeliacinis Teismas refused D's application. On 21 February 2013, the Lietuvos Apeliacinis Teismas dismissed the appeal brought by the other D and the board members against the decision to initiate an investigation of D's activities. Both of the above orders were brought in cassation, which, on 21 November 2013, decided to stay examination of the appeal against the investigation of D's activities until it had decided the appeal regarding the recognition and enforcement of the arbitral award. D claimed that the order of 17 December 2012 should be quashed and a new order made, upholding its request for recognition and enforcement of the arbitral award. The Lietuvos Auksclausiasis Teismas then stayed proceedings and referred to the European Court for a preliminary ruling. *Held*, by Wathelet Advocate-General, that: the recognition and enforcement of the arbitration award in the main proceedings was exclusively within the scope of the *New York Convention 1958* and that the *Brussels I Regulation* could not be seen as a public policy provision; of 22 December 2000 regarding jurisdiction and enforcement of judgments in civil and commercial matters must be interpreted as not requiring the court of a member state to refuse to recognise and enforce an anti-suit injunction issued by an arbitral tribunal and, as a consequence, whenever an arbitral award contained an anti-suit injunction, it would not automatically imply refusing to recognise and enforce on the basis of art. V(2)(b) of the *New York Convention 1958*: *Gazprom OAO* (2014).[40]

(4) *Facts*: ICS (P) was an electrical contractor, which hired Opron (D) as a sub-contractor for the "non-process buildings" at the Canaport LNG facility at a fixed price of $552,000. Over 20 change orders adjusting the works were carried out by P to a final price over $2m. Disagreements arose and

---

40 [2014] Case C-536/13.

a mechanics' lien proceeding was commenced. Both parties were involved in a motion, with P claiming alternative relief. Further proceedings were brought before another judge. P then invoked art. 8.2.5 of the general condition of the contract, to proceed to arbitration on the issue of delay and impact against D. *Held*, by McLellan J, that: the filling of a claim for a lien and any subsequent enforcement of an arbitration award through the enforcement of a claim for lien should all work together; that the delay and impact issues could not be separated from the other parts of P's claim; that the arbitrators would have jurisdiction to consider the interaction of that arbitration with the arbitration involving the other Ds and also jurisdiction to consider whether the application of any part of that s 36 dispute resolution provision applied to the dispute between P and D and, consequently, the motion was allowed and the action would stay subject to dealing with costs on the motion: *ICS State v Irving Oil Limited* (2012).[41]

(5) *Facts*: Thameside Construction Company Limited (C) was employed by Mr and Mrs Stevens (D) to carry out building works at their home for originally £600,000, although some variations took place later, raising the amount to over £1m. The completion date was 14 March 2011. There were delays and an EoT was granted until 8 August 2011. C took possession of the property in three stages: October 2011, December 2011 and March 2012. On 23 March 2012, a certificate of non-completion was issued against D. On 21 June 2012, C submitted its interim application in the sum of £1,310, 998.39. D replied with a new valuation of £1,185,533.01 less £58,105.44 for contra-charges. On 1 March 2013, C served a notice of adjudication for failure to pay amounts due and seeing a peremptory decision from the adjudicator and, by this time, D had already paid over £1.1m. On 24 April 2013, the adjudicator made his decision that D should pay C within 14 days, £88,606.22 plus VAT, or else interest would accrued thereafter according to cl. 4.8 of the contract and that his fees and expenses should be paid 50/50 by each party. On 30 April, C issued an interim payment certificate for a net sum due for payment of £88,606.22 plus VAT. On the same day, D issued a withholding notice for £40,000 for LADs and paid the balance. On 20 June 2013, C issued proceedings for the balance of £40,000 resulting from the adjudicator's decision. D argued that they were entitled to set off their LADs claim against the decision. *Held*, by Akenhead J, that: C was entitled to the sum of £40,000, plus interest in the sum of £328.76 and costs: *Thameside Construction Company Limited v Stevens* (2013).[42]

(6) *Facts*: The Russian Federation (C) signed the *Energy Charter Treaty* (the *ECT*) in December 1994 regarding exploitation of oil in the region. In 1996, C presented a legislative proposal to Parliament to ratify the *ECT*. This was never done and, on 20 August 2009, C notified Portugal (depository under art. 49 ECT) that it would not become a signatory. Veteran Petroleum Limited, Yukos Universal Limited and Hulley Enterprises Limited (D), were all companies of Yukos, operating in the oil field in Russia. By 2003, C seized and sold D's assets, following a claim of systemic and large tax evasion. D claimed that this action amounted to an unlawful expropriation of their investment and requested arbitration under art. 26, paragraph 4 sub-paragraph b *ECT* and the *Arbitration*

41 2012 NBQB 191.
42 [2013] EWHC 2071 (TCC).

Rules of the United Nations Commission on International Trade Law. Arbitration started in October 2005 in The Hague as the arbitral seat. In 2009, the tribunal gave an interim award that: (1) each signing party had agree to apply the *ECT* provisionally, pending its entry into force for such signatory in accordance with art. 44 and, as long as that provisional application would not be clashing with the constitution, or domestic laws, and contained an "all-or-nothing" approach; (2) conversely, in the interpretation of the Limitation Clause in art. 45(2)(c), the phrase "such provisional application", had a different meaning, which referred to the *ECT* as a whole; (3) if the signatory parties were to agree to modulate, or eliminate the *ECT*'s provisional application whenever inconsistent with the domestic law, that agreement must have been clearly and unambiguously expressed, which was not the case with art. 45(1); (4) as a result, the principle of provisional application was consistent with C's constitution and domestic laws and, consequently, the whole *ECT* applied provisionally in C's territory, until such provisional application was terminated; (5) that art. 26 of the *ECT* was not inconsistent with C's domestic laws and, as a result, the ECT applied provisionally in its entirety until October 2009, dismissing objections to jurisdiction. The final award of 18 July 2014, C was ordered to pay compensation of $8,203,032.751, plus $1.846.000.687 and $ 39.971.834.360 in damages to each one of the companies comprising D. C brought proceedings before The Hague District Court seeking to quash the interim and final awards and that the court order D to pay the costs of those proceedings, plus interest at the statutory rate from the 14th day following judgment. *Held,* by The Hague District Court, that: (1) the tribunal's interpretation of the limitation clause was wrong, since relying upon a conflict between a treaty provision and domestic law is not contrary to the *pacta sunt servanda* principle, nor to the principle of art. 27 VCLT; (2) C was not obliged to submit a prior declaration for successfully relying on the limitation clause of art. 45(1); (3) that disputes between investors and a state such as the nature of these proceedings, can be arbitrated under C's law; (4) the arbitration clause of art. 26 ECT was incompatible with C's law; (5) that this was not a matter for an "all or nothing" approach; (6) C never made an unconditional offer for arbitration and, as a result, D's notice of arbitration was not a valid arbitration agreement; (7) therefore, the tribunal lacked jurisdiction to decide the claims and issuing awards; as a consequence, the interim and final awards were quashed and D was ordered to pay C the costs of the proceedings: *Russian Federation v Veteran Petroleum Limited, Yukos Universal Limited and Hulley Enterprises Limited.*[43]

22-114 **Add a new footnote 170A at the end of the final sentence:**
See also M Raeside QC, "Techniques for handling the cross-cultural tribunal" (2009) 25 Const LJ 30 and A Burr, "Publication of International Adjudication Decisions and Arbitral Awards: Confidentiality v Transparency", *IBA Construction Law International,* Lawyer Issue, April 2017.

---

43 The Hague District Court, C/09/477160/HA ZA 15–1; C/09/477162/HA ZA 15–2./ C/09/481619/ HA ZA 15–112.

Add the following Illustrations:

(1) *Facts*: Alessandro Benedetti and Bertrand des Pallierès (D) applied to the court to stay the proceedings against them by Christian Kruppa (C), pursuant to s 9 of the *Arbitration Act 1996* (the Act). D claimed that "governing law and jurisdiction" in the agreements signed between both parties constituted an "arbitration agreement" under s 6(1) of the Act and, consequently, the dispute should be submitted to arbitration. The relevant clause in the agreement contemplated two ways to resolve a dispute, first through Swiss arbitration, followed by litigation in the English courts. *Held*, by Cooke J, that: the clause did not require the parties to refer any dispute to arbitration (as stated by the Act), but rather attempted to refer the matter to arbitration by agreement between them, failing which, the parties could reach for the English courts. In consequence, D's application was dismissed with costs: *C Kruppa v A Benedetti* (2014).[44]

(2) *Facts*: In September 2007, Sentosa UK Limited (C) engaged JPA Design and Build Limited (D) to carry out design and construction of a new medical centre in Brentford. The contract was under the JCT *Design and Build* form and contained adjudication provisions. By November 2008, the relationship between the parties deteriorated. By April 2009 the relationship between the parties had broken down completely and the contract came to an end, with each side blaming the other. Three separate disputes were referred to adjudication: (1) a claim for the advance payment of £300,000; (2) the dispute about interim valuation 12 and the subject of the arbitrator's decision dated 23 June 2009; and (3) the dispute as to EoTs, LADs and the like and the subject of the decision dated 3 August 2009. D sought to enforce the adjudicator's decision in their favour in the sum of £300,000 plus interest. In a separate claim, C sought a declaration that another adjudicator's decision in their favour in the sum of £180,000 should be declared to be an enforceable decision, entitling it to set off against the £300,000 claimed by D. In addition to that, C claimed that, whether the sum due to D was £300,000 or £120,000, enforcement of any such a sum should be stayed pursuant to RSC Ord. 47. *Held*, by Coulson J, that: (1) D's entitlement to the £300,000 could be set off in the sum of £180,000. Accordingly, C should pay D the remaining sum of £169,784.48, including interest; (2) given D's poor financial position and C's contractual right to repayment, it was fair to stay the execution of the judgment sum: *JPA Design and Build Limited v Sentosa Limited* (2009).[45]

22-115 **Add the following Illustrations after the existing Illustration (which should be numbered (1)):**

(2) *Facts*: A (D) contracted with B (C) for the joint development and sale of security solutions for various goods, with C paying the fees for the development of such products. C complained about the poor performance of the products and looked to recover the moneys paid to D for the development

---

44 [2014] EWHC 1887 (Comm).
45 [2009] EWHC 2312 (TCC).

and purchase thereof. D denied C's allegations and counterclaimed for payment of the outstanding balance of the development fees and purchase price for the products. The dispute was referred for arbitration to HKIAC, with the tribunal upholding C's claims and dismissing D's counterclaim. However, the tribunal failed to address whether C's claims fell within the limitation defence, since they were contractually time-barred. D then applied to the court to set aside the award, on the basis that failure to consider the limitation defence was contrary to public policy. *Held*, by Chang J, that: (1) there was no need for the tribunal to provide detailed reasons in the award, because this was private and confidential and intended to be read only by the parties and, as long as the parties could understand the manner in which the tribunal had reached its conclusions upon any given issue, the reasons for the award need not be elaborate, or lengthy; (2) the reasons in this particular award with regard to the rejection of the limitation defence, were insufficient; (3) when applying the concepts of fairness, due process and justice, material issues ought properly to be considered and dealt with fairly; (4) the limitation defence raised by D was a material issue and, as a consequence, the tribunal's failure to provide any explanation about the manner in which this was dealt with was unfair to D, causing a real risk of injustice; (5) the setting-aside proceedings would be suspended for 90 days: *A v B* (2014).[46]

(3) *Facts*: Cofely (C) was employed by Stratford City Development Limited and the Olympic Delivery Authority for construction works at the Olympic Park and Westfield Shopping Centre in Stratford, London. When disputes arose, C appointed Knowles (D1) to provide advice on these issues and to prepare the time claim and money claim on C's behalf. Further disputes arose with D1 about the increasing costs and delay, which led to an agreement. Soon after, D1 started adjudication against the employers on behalf of C. C however became concerned about D1's handling of the adjudication and the advice and directly negotiated with the employers the agreed settlement of the time claim, money claim and other issues. D1 subsequently argued that C had breached their agreement and claimed around £3.5m. D1 notified C of arbitration and applied to the CIArb for the appointment of an arbitrator. Mr Bingham was appointed (D2). D2 made a partial award, directing C to pay D £1m, with which C complied. C then made its own application for partial awards under s 46 of the 1996 Act, seeking a decision as to whether the moneys owed to C were the actual value of D1's money claim. Later, C raised concerns about D2's appointment, as the judgment in *Eurocom Limited v Siemens plc* had stated that the adjudicator (D2) had no jurisdiction, because of a fraudulent misrepresentation made by D1, which resulted in D2's appointment. D2 concluded that the tribunal was properly constituted and that he had no conflict of interest. C asked D2 to recuse himself, but D2 did not respond. C then sought an order to remove D2 as arbitrator, on the grounds of apparent bias. *Held*, by Hamblen J, that: C had established grounds for D2's removal as arbitrator and an order for removal would be issued if D2 did not resign: *Cofely Limited v Anthony Bingham* (2016).[47]

---

46 [2014] HCCT 40/2014.
47 [2016] EWHC 240 (Comm).

(4) *Facts*: Monaco Yachting and Technologies (D) commenced arbitration against Swallowfalls Limited (C) for breach of a construction agreement. C then began proceedings to enforce a loan agreement and guarantee against Monaco Yachting and Technologies (D). D raised (by way of counterclaim) claims for set-off, the arbitration claims. Proceedings were stayed in the court, pending the resolution of the arbitration. D failed to comply with the tribunal's orders during the arbitration, requiring security for costs to be provided to C, leading to the tribunal issuing a final and peremptory order against D. C then applied to dismiss the claim under s 41(6) of the *Arbitration Act 1996*, which the tribunal granted, issuing a partial final award and a second award on costs. Based upon this, C looked to lift the stay of the court proceedings. D contended that the dismissal of the arbitration proceedings did not constitute a determination on the merits of its claim and, as a consequence, should be allowed to use the same grounds in the court proceedings. *Held*: that D's submissions should be rejected on the basis that D's dismissal of the arbitral claim, even on the narrow ground of non-compliance, had the ordinary consequences of finality and that allowing D to raise the same arguments in the court proceedings would therefore amount to an abuse of process: *Swallowfalls Limited v Monaco Yachting and Technologies SAM* (2015).[48]

(5) *Held*, by Clarke J, that: where the defendant did not admit the claim and there remained a dispute falling within the ambit of the arbitration agreement, the defendant was entitled to a stay of proceedings as of right, even if the defendant did not have had an arguable defence to all, or part, of the claim; the appeal of the case was dismissed: *Halki Shipping Corp. v Sopex Oils Limited* (1998).[49]

22–116 Add at the end of footnote 172:
See also HH Judge Toulmin CMG QC, "Arbitrators taking procedural control – a good or a bad idea?" (2009) 25 Const LJ 3 and A Burr and P A Karrer, "'Chess clock' arbitration and time management techniques in international commercial arbitration: from the perspective of the arbitrator and counsel" (2010) 26 Const LJ 53.

Add the following Illustration:

(1) *Facts*: B (D) claimed to have made two contracts with A (C) for the purchase of cotton, under which A defaulted. B further argued that the contracts provided for the *International Cotton Association Limited (ICA) Rules* and arbitration. On 8 February 2012, B brought a reference under the *Bylaws* of the ICA and claimed over $7m. A denied making the contracts and having agreed to ICA (or any) arbitration and disputed the jurisdiction of the tribunal. On 26 February 2013, the tribunal made an award, concluding that it had jurisdiction to decide the reference and upheld the claim. Under the ICA Rules, parties have a right to appeal and, on 22 March 2013, C sent the ICA a notice of appeal. However, C did not pay the ICA's fees, a deposit and outstanding costs and, after being required to do so on several occasions, ICA sent C a notice that the appeal had been dismissed. On 3 May 2013, C sent the ICA the requested payments and

48 [2015] EWHC 2013 (Comm).
49 [1998] 1 WLR 726; [1998] 2 All ER 23; [1998] CLC 583.

sought an EoT to pay, which was refused. No tribunal was ever appointed to deal with the appeal. On 22 May 2013, C brought proceedings before the court, seeking an order to set aside the award "and/or declare it to be of no effect on the grounds of lack of jurisdiction and/or serious irregularity, which has or will cause substantial injustice to" it. A preliminary issue was heard to determine whether C's challenge to the first tier award dated 26 February 2013 was precluded by the terms of s 70(2) and/or s 73(2) of the *Arbitration Act 1996* (the *1996 Act*). To address this, two questions were identified: (1) whether there was an available arbitral process of appeal, or review, and, if so, (2) whether C had exhausted it. *Held*, by Smith J, that: whenever a party takes part in arbitral proceedings, whilst challenging the jurisdiction, they thus confer powers upon the arbitral, or other institution, or person that would have had powers in relation to the matter if they had entered into an applicable arbitration agreement. As a consequence, there was an arbitral process of appeal, or review, available to C, even when it was not a party to any relevant arbitration agreement and C had first exhausted that arbitral appeal before bringing the proceedings. The answer to the preliminary issue was therefore that C's challenge to the first tier award dated 26 February 2013 was not precluded by the terms of ss 70(2) or 73(2), of the *1996 Act*: *A Limited v B Limited* (2014).[50]

22–117 Add at the end of footnote 173:

See also C Ennis, "Arbitration of disputes in UK construction projects: what is left after adjudication?" (2012) 28 Const LJ 585.

Add the following Illustration:

Facts: Mr and Mrs Shaw (C) engaged MFP to perform works of extension, repair and conservation to their lodge in Cheshire, for a sum of £168,253. Works were delayed and, on 28 February 2007, C terminated the contract, due to D's refusal to replace some defective stone windows. The dispute was brought to arbitration. Award no 1 decided that D's refusal to replace the defective stone windows amounted to repudiatory breach. C also claimed that D did not carry out work in a competent manner, causing delay, as well as claiming for the cost of completing the work which was incomplete, or defective. Award no 2 decided that a balance of £47,509.97 was due to D, inclusive of interest, and that D should complete the work by Christmas 2007, being entitled to an EoT with loss and expense. C sought permission to appeal Award no 2 and to challenge it under s 68 of the *Arbitration Act 1996*, and sought an EoT to lodge the claim form. C later claimed that it was their intention that C's mother would move into the lodge and pay some rent, which caused a loss of rent. *Held*, by Edwards-Stuart J, that: the arbitrator had addressed the issues raised before him at the time and, since this ground was not mentioned then, there was no irregularity by the arbitrator; the challenge under s 68 of the *Act* failed and permission to appeal was refused under s 69 there of *Act*: as a result, there was no entitlement to an EoT and the claim was dismissed with costs: *Shaw v MFP Foundation and Pilings Limited* (2010).[51]

---

50 [2014] EWHC 1870 (Comm).
51 [2010] EWHC 1839 (TCC).

22–118 Add the following Illustration after the existing Illustration (which should be numbered (1)):

(2) *Facts*: One issue in an adjudication between the parties was whether, or not, D had achieved the first milestone. C asserted that the adjudicator had failed to take into account the evidence on this issue presented by them. This evidence was that, during a site visit, photographs of the work had been taken and that, although during the site visit C had concluded that the first milestone had been achieved, subsequent analysis of the photographs taken during the site visit showed that the milestone had not in fact been achieved. The adjudicator did not refer to the photographs in giving reasons for his decision that the milestone had been achieved. On enforcement, C asserted that an adjudicator's decision was "flawed and invalid" because the adjudicator did not take its evidence into account. That was a breach of natural justice. *Held*: that, since there was no other evidence in support of the submission that the first milestone had not been achieved, the adjudicator must have taken it into account because, if he had simply overlooked that evidence, he would not have thought that there was anything to decide. The adjudicator listed all the written submissions that had been made to him, which he said he had considered fully when making his decision. Given that the evidence of fact before the adjudicator was largely confined to the issue about the achievement of the milestone, it was hard to see how the adjudicator could have overlooked that evidence when considering the question of the state of the work: *Manor Asset Limited v Demolition Services Limited* (2016).[52]

22–119 Add the following further Illustrations after the existing Illustration (which should be numbered (1)):

(2) *Facts*: C employed SH to build houses under a contract signed under hand. SH was acquired by D. Clause 2.5.5 provided that: "The Employer will register the site with NHBC under the Employer's registration and the contractor warrants to accept responsibility for any defect and any expense incurred due to defective work for the period of 10 years for the NHBC warranty." C sold the houses in 2002, with the benefit of NHBC cover that expired in 2012. As a result of defects in the foundations of three houses, successful claims under the NHBC cover were made. The NHBC notified C it was seeking reimbursement for those claims in spring 2011. C notified D of the defects on 24 May 2011 and followed this up on 22 November 2011. D replied on 3 September 2013, stating any claim against it was time-barred. C commenced court proceedings on 14 April 2014. The issue was whether the claim was time-barred founded on the wording of cl. 2.5.5. *Held*: that the claim was not time barred. Clause 2.5.5 rendered D responsible for defects under the NHBC cover; the reference in cl. 2.5.5 to a ten-year period was to identify the period for which NHBC cover applied and during which a home owner could make a claim under it for defects. It was not a limitation period. The clause expressly referred to defects and expenses incurred during the ten-year period of NHBC

---

52 [2016] EWHC 222 (TCC).

cover and did not limit responsibility to claims notified during that period. For a contract signed under hand, the limitation period for claims in contract is six years from the date of breach and in tort (for negligence) the limitation period is six years from when the alleged negligent act or omission caused loss. On the facts of this case, C's cause of action under cl. 2.5.5 arose when the contractor refused or failed to accept responsibility for the defects and therefore court proceedings had been commenced within the limitation period: *Larkfleet Limited v Allison Homes Eastern Limited* (2016).[53]

(3) *Facts*: Forest Heath District Council (C) engaged ISG Jackson Limited (D) for the construction of a community sports centre and two pools at a school. The contract was in the JCT standard form of building contract, with 19 June 2007 as the date for completion. Asbestos and contamination were discovered on the site, which caused a delay. D then proceeded to paint the steelwork in situ, and claimed EoT for 29 weeks for delays associated with the scaffold and relying on cl. 25.4.5 compliance with architect's instructors. On 29 April 2009 D referred the matter to adjudication and on 22 July 2009 the adjudicator produced a decision determining that the net delay was 24 weeks and three days. C sought a declaration under CPR Pt 8 against D regarding the determination by the adjudicator, which C claims form a large part of the remaining issues between the parties who were then seeking to conclude final account negotiation. C sought a determination of why D made the decision to change from a pre-finished to a site applied paint system, as this could have been something different from what the adjudicator found. *Held*, by Ramsey J, that: no declaration could be made in relation to these Pt 8 proceedings as the scope of the factual issue was likely to widen on further investigation and that a declaration would not amount to a final determination of the dispute: *Forest Heath District Council v ISG Jackson Limited* (2010).[54]

(4) *Facts*: The parties entered into a contract for the development of accommodation, cl. 8.5.3 thereof stating that, as from the date the contractor became insolvent, whether, or not, the employer had given notice of termination, cl. 8.7.3 would apply, as if such notice had been given. Clause 8.7.3 stated that the employer need not pay any sum that had already become due if the contractor, after the last date upon which a payless notice could have been given, had become insolvent. Harbour View Developments (D) suspended work on the grounds it had not been paid sums in interim certificates. D later notified Wilson and Sharp Investments Limited (C) that it was going to present a winding-up petition against C, which then applied for an injunction to restrain D from doing so, claiming that the sums were disputed on substantial grounds and that C had cross-claims exceeding those sums. D later passed a special resolution that it be wound up voluntarily, since it was insolvent. C argued that, in accordance with TCC practice not to enforce interim payment obligations in favour of insolvent contractors, D should not be permitted to enforce an interim payment obligation by way of a winding-up petition, given that it was insolvent. *Held*, by the Court of Appeal, that: on a proper construction, cll. 8.5.3 and 8.7.3 could apply after termination of the contract.

---

53   [2016] EWHC 195 (TCC).
54   [2010] EWHC 322 (TCC).

Payment of the sums due under the interim certificates was therefore disputed upon substantial grounds. Furthermore, there was no absolute rule that summary judgment would be refused because an employer was able to show that a contractor was insolvent and each case would be reviewed on its merits: *Wilson and Sharp Investments Limited v Harbour View Developments* (2015).[55]

22–120 **Add the following further Illustrations:**

(19) *Facts*: GSK Project Management Limited in liquidation (C) was employed by QPR Holdings Limited (D) to carry out works at Queen's Range Park Rangers' Loftus Road soccer ground. C claimed payment of £806,675 plus £ 824,038 in costs, whilst D counterclaimed that the works were defective, opposing C's costs as excessive. The issues to be identified were: (1) work carried out by C; (2) C's entitlement to payment under the contract, or upon a quantum meruit basis; (3) were there grounds to set off and counterclaim for defective works? The parties agreed at the CMC that four days would be enough and agreed directions on that basis. At this stage, the court had to decide on the proportionality of C's costs budget. *Held*, by Stuart-Smith J, that: C's incurred costs/ approved costs budget would total £425,000 and that C's original costs requests offended against the obligation to keep costs to a reasonable minimum, represented a waste of the court's and the parties' time and, consequently, C should pay to D £1,000 for costs incurred in defending this costs claim: *GSK Project Management Limited v QPR Holdings Limited* (2015).[56]

(20) *Facts*: This claim arose in relation to the construction of a roof that was damaged during heavy winds. The roof was unusual in that it was a sealed structure, which meant that C could only rectify the damage by replacing the entire roof at a cost of over £5m. There was also no chance of any reduction for contributory negligence and so the contractor would either be found liable for the full amount or would not be found liable at all. C's Pt 36 offer that D pay "95% of our client's claim for damages" was therefore not an outcome that could ever have been reached during trial. D did not respond to the offer, but later conceded liability during a pre-trial review. The issue was whether a claimant was entitled to the benefits of a Pt 36 offer where that offer did not reflect a possible outcome of the case. *Held*: that there was nothing in the authorities to prevent a Pt 36 offer being valid on the basis that it was a purely commercial offer, rather than one that was available to a prospective judge during a trial. So long as it was a genuine attempt to settle, there was no reason to hold that it was not a valid Pt 36 offer, even in circumstances where the offer was only for a very modest discount. C was therefore granted indemnity costs from the date at which D could reasonably have put itself in a position to make an informed assessment of the strength of the claim on liability, ie later than the expiry of the relevant period: *Jockey Club Racecourse Limited v Willmott Dixon Construction Limited* (2016).[57]

---

55 [2015] EWCA Civ 1030.
56 [2015] EWHC 2274 (TCC).
57 [2016] EWHC 167 (TCC).

22–121   Add the following Illustrations:

(1) *Facts*: An employer (E) engaged a contractor (C) to build eight town-houses in Sydney, Australia. There were various delays and variation claims, with C suspending work on three occasions. Both parties argued that the other had repudiated the contract. C claimed that it was entitled to EoTs for the variations that it had carried out and E claimed LADs for delay. Under the contract, C was entitled to an EoT for delays beyond its sole control, being required to give written notice to E, within ten working days of becoming aware of the "cause and extent of the delay". E claimed that C had failed to provide the requisite notice and therefore the claims were time-barred. EoTs should be calculated by reference to the critical path and that, since the project had been abandoned, this was no longer possible. *Held*, by the Supreme Court of New South Wales, that: C had complied with the notice requirements, since it had given notice once it knew of the cause of the delay; since the question of whether delay occurred was a factual one, it was not necessary to have a programme in order to make an assessment of the EoT to which C was properly entitled: *Champion Homes Sales Pty Limited v DCT Projects Pty Limited* (2015).[58]

(2) *Facts*: Sykes & Son Limited (the respondent) was to carry out extension and refurbishment works at a property in Surrey for which Teamforce Labour Limited (the petitioner) was the sub-contractor. On 6 December 2011, the petitioner submitted to the court to wind up the company on the grounds that the latter was heavily indebted to the petitioner due to a final account and unpaid labour and, despite numerous requests for payment, the outstanding debt had not been paid. The company applied for an injunction restraining the petitioner from advertising, or otherwise proceeding with, the winding-up petition and to strike out that petition. It contends that the petitioner has been paid all monies due to it and that any money for unpaid labour would be set off because of a larger cross-claim. *Held*, by Richard Snowden QC (sitting as a High Court Judge), that: (1) consistent with the general practice of the Companies Court not to attempt to resolve factual disputes that would involve the rejection of credible evidence without cross-examination, as the petition was founded upon the sums claimed in respect of the sub-contract works, it should not be permitted to continue and must be dismissed; (2) as the amount claimed under unpaid labour was paid shortly after the petition was presented, this claim could proceed; (3) that the company was solvent and, consequently, the petition should be dismissed and removed from the court file: *Sykes & Son Limited v Teamforce Labour Limited* (2012).[59]

22–122   Add the following Illustration:

(1) *Facts*: Malmaison Hotel Limited (R) employed Henry Boot Limited (A). A dispute concerning the proper construction of cl. 25 of the contract, whether the architect should have granted a further EoT, was referred to arbitration. An interim award was made and A challenged it in the Mercantile Court of

---

58 [2015] NSWSC 616.
59 [2012] EWHC 883 (Ch).

Manchester, under s 69(1) of the *Arbitration Act 1996*. The matter was transferred to the TCC at the Royal Courts of Justice and Dyson J upheld the arbitrator's interim award. A sought leave to appeal under s 69(8) of the *1996 Act*, which was refused. A then sought leave from the judge to appeal his refusal of leave. A first decision by Waller LJ held that the refusal of leave by the High Court, or the county court, was not a decision within s 16 of the *Supreme Court Act 1981* and thus could not be reviewed in the Court of Appeal. However, an addendum judgment had to be made by virtue of s 55 of the *Access to Justice Act 1999*, which came into force on 27 September 1999, before Dyson J's decision. A further argued, at this stage, that the wording of s 55 referring to an appeal from an arbitrator to the High Court, or the county court, was in relation to "any matter" and, as a result, s 55 covered the afore-mentioned judge's decision. Furthermore, A argued that, in applying s 55 to the facts, it had actually repealed s 69(8) and that Dyson J lacked jurisdiction to deal with the permission to appeal, leaving the Court of Appeal as the only court that had jurisdiction. *Held*, by Waller LJ, that: (1) s 55 had no effect over s 69(8) and consequently had not repealed it; (2) a decision of the High Court, or the county court, could not be challenged in the Court of Appeal under s 69 without leave of the High Court, or county court, and the refusal of the High Court, or the county court, could not be challenged in the Court of Appeal; (3) in the event that the High Court judge granted permission to appeal under the *1996 Act*, s 69(8), A must still obtain permission from the Court of Appeal under s 55 of the *1999 Act* and, as a consequence, the previous judgment should stand: *Henry Boot Construction Limited v Malmaison Hotel Limited* (2000).[60]

22–136   Add the following Illustration:

Facts: Multiplex Constructions Limited (C) engaged Cleveland Bridge UK Limited (D) as sub-contractor. On 24 August 2004 the contract was repudiated, with each party alleging that it was each other who repudiated the contract. Both parties claim damages for repudiation. C's offers to settle were not accepted by R, with the judge holding on 5 June 2006 that R was the party in repudiatory breach. R appealed. In August 2006, A served on the amended Scott Schedule, highly increasing its claim for damages for repudiation, the majority of which was for temporary works for the roof. R challenged the legal basis of the Scott schedule, claiming that it had no continuing responsibility for the design, or fabrication, works for the roof, which was favourable resolved in preliminary issue 11. A appealed and by consent R's application for costs was stood over for a later date. *Held*, by Jackson J, that: (1) A's claim for roof temporary works under the Scott schedule was a new claim, linked to what became preliminary issue 11; (2) as R won preliminary issue 11, then A's claim under the Scott Schedules fell away; (3) consequently, A's should pay the costs for that new claim; (4) that A should pay 85% of R's costs of responding to the Scott Schedule and R's costs occasioned by preliminary issue 11, therefore payment on the account of the costs: *Multiplex Constructions (UK) Limited v Cleveland Bridge UK Limited* (2007).[61]

---

60 [2001] QB 388.
61 [2007] EWHC 659 (TCC).

CHAPTER 23

Adjudication in the United Kingdom

Introduction

"The [Housing Grants, Construction and Regeneration] Act provides that a party to a construction contract is to have the right to refer a dispute arising under the contract for adjudication under a procedure, complying with its requirement,[1] which are that the contract must:

(a)   *enable a party to give notice at any time of their intention to refer a dispute to adjudication;*

(b)   *provide a timetable with the object of securing the appointment of the Adjudicator and referral of the dispute to the Adjudicator within seven days of such notice;*

(c)   *require the Adjudicator to reach a decision within 28 days of referral, or such longer period as is agreed by the parties after the dispute has been referred;*

(d)   *allow the Adjudicator to extend the period of 28 days by up to 14 days, with the consent of the party by whom the dispute was referred;*

(e)   *impose a duty on the Adjudicator to act impartially; and*

(f)   *enable the Adjudicator to take the initiative in ascertaining the facts and the law.[2]*

The contract must also provide that the decision of the Adjudicator is binding until the dispute is finally determined by legal proceedings, by arbitration (if the contract provides for arbitration, or the parties otherwise agree to arbitration), or by agreement, although the parties may agree to accept the decision of the Adjudicator as finally determining the dispute."[3]

---

1 *Housing Grants, Construction and Regeneration Act 1996* s 108(2).

2 *Housing Grants, Construction and Regeneration Act 1996* s 108(3).

3 *Hudson's Building and Engineering Contracts* Twelfth Edition, by Atkin Chambers (Sweet & Maxwell, 2010), paragraph 11–021.

23–004 **In the first line, the first name of the statute should be capitalised, as:**
"Local"

23–006 **Add the following Illustrations:**

---

(1) *Facts*: Loppingdale Plant Limited (D) and Stansted Airport entered into a framework agreement, pursuant to which works were instructed via task orders. Imtech Inviron (C) was subsequently engaged as sub-contractor via a purchase order. C's order contained a classic "awareness" clause, relating to the terms of the framework agreement and, under the latter, disputes were to be referred to adjudication using the NEC *Adjudicator's Contract*. When D failed to pay C, the latter initiated adjudication proceedings; however, D claimed that the adjudicator lacked jurisdiction, whilst C, on the other hand, took the view that the adjudication provisions of the framework agreement could not have been incorporated into the sub-contract. *Held*, by Edwards-Stuart J, that: a provision making adjudication a condition precedent to litigation (as in the framework agreement) is an onerous provision, which requires extremely clear wording and that this intention was not clear in this particular case; the adjudicator's decision should therefore be enforced: *Imtech Inviron Limited v Loppingdale Plant Limited* (2014).[4]

(2) *Held*, by Jackson J (as he then was), that: "where the parties to a construction contract engage in successive adjudications, each focused upon the parties' current rights and remedies, in my view the correct approach is as follows. At the end of each adjudication, absent special circumstances, the losing party must comply with the adjudicator's decision. He cannot withhold payment on the ground of his anticipated recovery in a future adjudication, based upon different issues. I reach this conclusion both from the express terms of the *Act* and also from the line of authority referred to earlier in this judgment. . .": *Interserve Industrial Services Limited v Cleveland Bridge UK Limited* (2006).[5]

23–014 **Add at the end of footnote 12:**
See also R Gwilliam, "Open season for ambush? How 'disputes' have changed from *Nuttall v Carter* to *Catillon v Urvasco*" (2010) 26 Const LJ 456.

23–035 **Following the fourth line, the quotation should be inserted in a smaller font.**

23–038 **Add the following Illustration:**

Facts: Husband and Brown Limited (C) were engaged by way of an oral agreement to negotiate the purchase of a site for a care home for Mitch Developments Limited (D), a property developer. During negotiations, the vendor went into liquidation and the liquidator agreed a reduced price for the site. A dispute arose over the incentive

---

4 [2014] EWHC 4006 (TCC).
5 [2006] EWHC 741 (TCC); [2006] All ER (D) 49 at [43].

fee payable to C; C began an adjudication to obtain the fee. In the TCC, C claimed the fee and the adjudicator's costs, one issue being whether the adjudication costs were recoverable. *Held*, by HH Judge Moulder, that: for a contract to be covered by the adjudication provisions of the *Housing Grants Construction and Regeneration Act 1996*, it had to be an agreement to carry out construction operations, or to arrange for the carrying out of construction operations. The oral contract in question involved negotiating a price for land and did not involve building, or works, upon the land. The adjudicator who had issued a decision on the dispute did not therefore have jurisdiction to make it and C could not recover such costs as part of the court proceedings: *Husband and Brown Limited v Mitch Developments Limited* (2015).[6]

23–039   Add the following Illustration:

(1)   *Facts*: A consultancy agreement was entered into by the parties, which contained an ICC arbitration clause; a settlement agreement was subsequently entered into, providing that when a dispute arose, the English courts were provided with exclusive jurisdiction. When a dispute arose under the latter, Monde Petroleum SA (C) issued both court and arbitration proceedings. Westernzagros Limited (D) counterclaimed in arbitration proceedings, but the tribunal decided that it did not have the jurisdiction and dismissed D's claim. *Held*, by Popplewell J, that: the jurisdiction clause in the settlement agreement superseded the arbitration clause, relying in the ruling upon the case of *Fiona Trust and Holding Corp v Privalov* (2007)[7]: *Monde Petroleum SA v Westernzagros Limited* (2015).[8]

23–041   Add at the end of footnote 23:
See Illustration (4) under paragraph 23–063 below.

23–063   Add the following further Illustrations:

(6)   *Facts*: C and D had a dispute over the construction of two properties, which D threatened to refer to adjudication. C contended out that adjudication was out from the contract and that it was instead a residential occupier and thus outside the statutory provisions relating to adjudication. On 16 April 2015, C issued a claim form in the TCC under CPR Pt 8, seeking a declaration that there was no right to adjudicate, and D withdrew its threat. D proposed, instead, that the issue of who terminated the contract should be resolved by litigation, and a possible mediation to deal with quantum. The court directed that there should a CMC and, whenever possible, the parties were to agree directions to resolve disputed matters, including the termination issue. *Held*, by Edwards-Stuart J, that: C's costs of issuing the proceedings

---

6 [2015] EWHC 2900 (TCC).
7 [2007] UKHL 40, [2007] All ER (D) 233.
8 [2015] EWHC 67 (Comm).

should be paid by D; D's costs of the action between 17 April and 21 May 2015 should be paid by C upon an indemnity basis; 50% of D's costs of attendance at the CMC should be paid by C and that parties and their solicitors must litigate taking proper account of proportionality of the costs being incurred at the forefront at all times: *Gotch v Enelco Limited* (2015).[9]

(7) *Facts*: C applied for summary judgment against D in relation to a contractual claim for payment of an outstanding balance of an adjudicator's award. The dispute had been referred by D, as the paying party, in order to determine the value of C's claim under a sub-contract. D agreed to pay a portion of the sums due under the adjudicator's award, although disputed that it was due to pay the outstanding balance of "debt recovery costs" claimed under the *Late Payment of Commercial Debts Act 1998*. D claimed that the adjudicator had no jurisdiction, as the claim in respect of debt recovery costs was not specifically referred to in the initial notice of adjudication. being mentioned for the first time in the rejoinder. *Held*: that the "debt recovery costs" were held to be connected with and ancillary to the referred dispute, and were considered to be a part of it. It did not matter that the costs were not referred to in the notice of adjudication, but were included for the first time in a rejoinder. This was because the adjudication had been initially referred by D the paying party: *Lulu Construction Limited v Mulalley & Co Limited* (2016).[10]

---

9 [2015] EWHC 1802 (TCC).
10 [2016] EWHC 1852 (TCC).

CHAPTER 24

Dispute boards

Introduction

"[. . .] *but with fairness to all involved. Above all, it needs teamwork. Management jargon calls 'seeking win-win solutions'. I prefer the immortal words of the Dodo in Alice's Adventures in Wonderland, 'Everybody has won and all must have prizes'. The prize is enhanced performance in a healthier atmosphere. It will involve deeper satisfaction for clients it will lead to a brighter image and better rewards for a great industry.*"[1]

24–009 **Add at the end of footnote 6:**
See also J Papworth, "Avoidance of disputes through the use of FIDIC DABs and DRAs" (2016) 32 Const LJ 362.

24–012 **Add at the end of footnote 10:**
See also M Armes, "'Putting your money where your mouth is' or 'practising what you preach': the funding (or not) of dispute boards by the international funding banks" (2013) 29 Const LJ 111.

---

1 Taken from the Foreword to the Latham Report, *Constructing the Team* (HMSO, 1984), in which Sir Michael Latham quotes from Lewis Carroll's *Alice in Wonderland*. See also the article by Murray Armes at (2011) 27 Const LJ 552.

24–014 **Add at the end of footnote 13:**
See also P Gerber and B Ong, "Look before you leap: avoiding the traps and maximising the benefits of you DRB" (2012) 28 Const LJ 310.

24–044 **Add at the end of footnote 55:**
See also Dr S Kratzsch, "ICC dispute resolution rules: ICC dispute boards and ICC pre-arbitral referees" (2010) 26 Const LJ 87.

24–057 **In the penultimate line, remove the second:**
"has".

24–068 **Add at the end of footnote 85:**
See also G Butera, "The Persero Saga" (2016) 32 Const LJ 383.

24–070 **Add at the end of footnote 90:**
See also P Genton and P Gélinas, "Compliance with and enforceability of a dispute board decision: recommendations by the international Beau-Rivage Palace forum working group" (2012) 28 Const LJ 3 and, generally, A Burr, *International Contractual and Statutory Adjudication* (informa law by Routledge, 2017).

CHAPTER 25

Mandatory law in international construction contracts

Introduction

> *"Speak in French when you can't think of the English for a thing. . .He's an Anglo-Saxon Messenger – and those are Anglo-Saxon attitudes."*[1]

25–005   Add the following Illustration:

Facts: Construction of an extension to Toronto's subway system was being undertaken, extending a line to York University, with part of the works involving the construction of a new station beneath an existing university building. Concerns regarding potential damage to the buildings during construction and tunnelling operations led to the conception and implementation of a monitoring scheme, involving ground stabilisation, which was carried out by Advanced Construction Techniques Limited (ACT) (C), working under a sub-contract with OHL Construction Canada (D), the general contractor responsible for the subway extension on behalf of the Toronto Transit Commission (TTC). Ontario provincial law provided statutory protection for building contractors through the Construction Lien Act (the CLA).

A dispute arose, leading to D removing C from site, which resulted in C registering a lien against the York University land title. D promptly bonded off the lien. The court was asked to decide whether to grant the lien, whilst D sought to vacate the lien and release the university land title. D's defence centred upon two main arguments, namely that the CLA was unenforceable on public policy grounds, or that the works were considered a "Railway right of way" and therefore exempt under the CLA.

---

1 Lewis Carroll, *Through the Looking Glass* (1877), chapters 2 and 7.

Held, by Master Short, that: since the lien was promptly bonded off, realistically there was no threat to the unfinished subway being sold off under the CLA, therefore offering no support for the argument to override the CLA on public policy grounds. Discussing the possibility of having to set aside the Act on policy grounds, he stated:

> "...*a party having done work to improve lands, could have absolutely no potentially enforceable lien rights*",

suggesting that this goes against the very intention of the CLA and is therefore untenable.

The second argument by D was based upon the works falling within a "railway right of way" provision and therefore exempt from being subject to the CLA. After reviewing case law, it was found that the works did not fall within the railway right of way, due to express terms agreed between TTC and York University receiving the "benefit of the works" and therefore being the owner under the CLA.

The lien made by ACT was therefore found to be valid under the CLA, requiring release of the bond values: *Advanced Construction Techniques Limited v OHL Construction Canada* (2013).[2]

25–010 Add the following Illustrations:

> (1) *Facts*: A contract based upon the FIDIC *Red Book* (1999) related to the construction of a hospital in Trinidad and Tobago. Disagreements arose between the parties and the contractor (NHIC) suspended work and later purported to terminate. A number of issues were refereed to arbitration, leading to five arbitration awards, two of which were appealed on points of law. Under cl. 2.4 of the FIDIC *Red Book*, the contractor is entitled to request evidence from the employer (NIPD). Unsatisfied with the letters sent in response, it initially suspended works and then issued a notice of termination, NHIC disputed that the contract had validly been terminated. The arbitrator held that it had been and, in doing so, concluded that the evidence required under cl. 2.4 must go beyond merely showing that the employer is able to pay. After this decision was reversed by the Court of Appeal, the Privy Council upheld the arbitrator's finding that NHIC was entitled to terminate. The second appeal related to cl. 2.5, which gives the employer a right of set off. The Court of Appeal, agreeing with the arbitrator, found that the clause prohibits the employer from exercising its right of set off in another way. The Privy Council disagreed, noting that cl. 2.5 makes it clear that any claim by the employer must be notified promptly and particularised and that failure to comply with the notice requirement would invalidate the claim: *NH International (Caribbean) Limited v National Insurance Property Development Company Limited (Trinidad and Tobago)* (2015).[3]
>
> (2) *Facts*: A dispute arose out of a £30m contract for design and construction work to Gibraltar Airport, including the construction of a new dual carriageway and a tunnel under the eastern end of the airport runway. This contract incorporated the *FIDIC Conditions of Contract for Plant and Design Build for Electrical and Mechanical Plant, and for Building and Engineering Works, designed by the*

---

2 [2013] ONSC 7505.
3 [2015] UKPC 37.

Contractor, First Edition 1999 (commonly known as the *Yellow Book*). The contract works were due to be completed in two years, but, after over 30 months and with only 25% of the work completed, the contract was terminated by the employer (the Government of Gibraltar). The Spanish contractor (Obrascon Huarte Lain) (C) commenced proceedings for an EoT (EoT) and associated loss and expense (L and E). C argued (amongst other things) that it had encountered more rock and contaminated material than would have been reasonably foreseeable by an experienced contractor at the time of tender. It also argued that a report that it had commissioned (which concluded that airborne contamination posed a health and safety risk) meant that it was necessary to suspend the excavation works and redesign the tunnel. Akendead J disagreed with C's arguments and found that it had failed to proceed with the design and execution of the works with due expedition and without delay. Of the EoT of 660 days originally claimed (reduced to 474 days in the amended particulars of claim submitted during the trial), it was awarded only a single day of EoT for a small amount of unforeseen rock. No weight whatsoever was given to the expert's report commissioned by C, which was found to be neither "independent nor competent".[4] Instead, it was decided that D was fully entitled to and did effectively terminate the contract. Quantum was left to be decided at a later date. *Held*: that (1) D had lawfully terminated the contract by notice of termination dated 28 July 2011 (delivered to C's site office), alternatively by notice dated 4 August, 2011 (redelivered to C's head office in Madrid); (2) D was entitled to serve a notice of termination pursuant to cl. 15.2(a) of the contract, by reason of C's failure to remedy defects notified in the notices to correct issued by the engineer under the contract; (3) D was entitled to serve a notice of termination pursuant to cl. 15.2(a), because C had clearly abandoned, or otherwise plainly demonstrated the intention no longer to continue, performance of its obligations under the contract pursuant to cl. 15.2(b); (4) since C was entitled to only a single day of EoT, such limited entitlement did not mean that D was no longer entitled to serve a notice of termination pursuant to cl. 15.2(b); (5) D was entitled to serve a notice of termination pursuant to cl. 15.2(a), because C had failed, without reasonable excuse, to proceed with the works in accordance with cl. 8, pursuant to cl. 15.2(c)(i); (6) D's notice of termination was a valid and effective notice pursuant to cl.15.2, even though it was not served at C's head office in Madrid, which was the address for service stated in the appendix to the tender; The contract was lawfully terminated by D on 20 August 2011 (when it wrote to inform C that it was terminating the contract and, shortly thereafter, took possession of the site) pursuant to cl. 15.2 of the contract; (7) the service of the notice of termination dated 28 July 2011 at the site office (rather than at the head office in Madrid, as specified in the appendix to the tender) did not amount to a repudiation of the contract and C was not therefore entitled to elect to accept it as a repudiation on 3 August 2011, as it had purported to do. C's letter dated 3 August 2011 therefore itself constituted a repudiatory breach, albeit that it was never expressly accepted as such by D; (8) the service

---

4 At [332].

of the notice of termination dated 28 July 2011 in the terms in which it was written did not amount to a repudiation of the contract (or an anticipated repudiation) by D, which C either accepted, or was entitled to accept, on 3 August 2011; (9) C's conduct when it left the site evinced the intention no longer to be bound by the terms of the contract and therefore amounted to a repudiatory breach, albeit that D did not expressly accept this; (10) D was entitled to the relief provided for by cll. 15.3 and 15.4 of the contract, together with interest as allowed for under the contract, or to the extent that the court had a discretion pursuant thereto: *Obrascon Huarte Lain SA v Her Majesty's Attorney-General for Gibraltar* (2014).[5]

(3) *Facts*: The contractor (C) referred to arbitration a dispute regarding the refurbishment of a hotel in Tripoli, when the engineer informed C that, having ceased his rôle under the contract, he would not determine the dispute. The employer (E) did not appoint a replacement engineer. Clause 67.1 of the *Red Book* required C to refer any dispute to the engineer, who should issue a decision within 84 days, only allowing C to refer the dispute to arbitration once the engineer had issued his decision after the 84 days had expired. C referred the dispute to arbitration before the 84 days expired. E challenged the jurisdiction of the arbitrator on the ground that C was required to wait for the 84 days to expire before appointing an arbitrator. The court was asked to interpret the effect of cl. 67.1. *Held*, by HH Judge Raeside QC, that: in accordance with *Belize*,[6] there are implied terms that: (1) the parties will co-operate in the performance of the contract; (2) each party will do what is necessary to enable the other to perform their duties; (3) no party should benefit from the non-fulfilment of a condition, the performance of which has been hindered by himself; and (4) that, by not appointing an engineer, E had breached the first two of these implied terms; as a consequence, E could not take advantage of its own failure to deny C its right to refer the dispute to arbitration and, therefore, C was entitled to bring the dispute to arbitration, without waiting for the 84 days to expire: *Al Wadden Hotel Limited v Man. Enterprise Sal* (2014).[7]

25–013 Add at the end of footnote 37:

See also C Ennis and W Breyer, "Comparison of treatment of claims for extension of time and compensation under the FIDIC *Red Book Form* according to civil law and common law jurisdictions" (2014) 30 Const LJ 3.

25–017 In footnote 41, correct the book title to:

"*Keating*".

25–023 Add at the end of footnote 49:

See also C Misu, "Termination for employer's convenience under the FIDIC Yellow Book 1999" (2013) 29 Const LJ 138; this topic will be further developed in the *Second Supplement* hereto, or the *Sixth Edition* hereof.

---

5 [2014] EWHC 1028 (TCC).
6 *Attorney General of Belize v Belize Telecom* [2009] UKPC 10.
7 [2014] EWHC 4796 (TCC).

25–027   Add the following paragraphs after paragraph 25–026:

Use of UK standard forms of contract overseas

25–028 Important considerations which must be addressed with care, when using UK standard forms of construction contract overseas, are the local legal system and the cultural differences determining the precise manner in which such provisions are interpreted, Sir Vivian Ramsey (previously Senior Judge at the London TCC) told delegates attending the JCT Povey Lecture at Local Government House, London on 12 November 2015:[8]

> "English language standard forms have become the norm overseas, which makes UK standard forms of contract an appropriate choice.
>
> However, the way in which the contract provisions are used and interpreted will differ depending upon the cultural or legal systems in which the contract is being operated and care needs to be taken to ensure these aspects are taken into account.
>
> Unless that is done the provisions will not properly deal with important aspects and may even render the contract or parts of it unenforceable."

In addition, Sir Vivian explained that the principles and practices of common law systems versus regions primarily operating under a civil law jurisdiction provides another area of potential conflict, when considering the use of UK contracts abroad:

> "(. . .) in English law there are commonly implied terms relied upon by construction lawyers. These terms relate to co-operation and non-hindrance by the employer [and] carrying out work in a good and womanlike manner, with good and proper materials by the contractor.
>
> In civil law jurisdictions, there is also an obligation of "good faith" in the performance of the contract [but] all relevant evidence is generally admissible [so] there is an ability to rely on conduct which has taken place after the formation of the contract and generally, up to the point where there is a dispute.
>
> This can alter the approach to the interpretation of the terms of any agreement and can impose wider obligations in terms of the requirement to act fairly than would apply in common law jurisdictions."

25–029 Sir Vivian Ramsey addressed various important areas of the contractual process in order to highlight various differences in practice and approach, including the position of the architect/engineer, contractual interpretation, notices, unforeseen conditions, interest, liquidated damages, termination, limitation of liability, mediation, adjudication and arbitration. To this list must also be added the widespread absence of use in civil law jurisdiction of either quantity surveyors, or bills of quantities.

---

8 See the article in the February 2016 issue of *JCT News* entitled "Use UK standard forms of contract overseas but take care of cultural and local aspects, says Sir Vivian Ramsey".

CHAPTER 26

Construction delay insurance

This is an entirely new chapter.

The need for insurance

"Words are innocent, neutral, precise, standing for this, describing that, meaning the other, so if you look after them you can build bridges across incomprehension and chaos. But when they get their corners knocked off, they're no good any more.

I don't think writers are sacred, but words are. They deserve respect. If you get the right ones in the right order, you can nudge the world a little, or make a poem which children will speak for you when you're dead."[1]

26–001 Most construction projects are undertaken in expectation of generating a profit after completion. The profit arises from sales or other income that can be earned by the project once it is in operation.

26–002 Delays usually mean a loss of money, for both contractor and client.

26–003 In the contractor's case this loss is predominantly in the form of continuing site establishment costs, and possibly unproductive time for labour. The contractor may also be exposed to the risk of liquidated damages under the terms of the contract, if the delay is his fault.

26–004 For the client, delay means that the project will not commence on the date planned. The client would therefore be losing the proceeds of the commercial activity that should have occurred during the period of delay, but may still incur the costs of

---

1 Tom Stoppard, *The Real Thing.*

servicing debt incurred to finance the project, and any other fixed costs of the business that would be in place by that time.

Illustration

> *Facts*: C owned and operated the Moyle Interconnector, which provided an undersea cable link between the electricity systems of Northern Ireland and Scotland. By a contract of insurance, D agreed to provide insurance against the risk of failure of the Moyle Interconnector. There were two separate cable failures that led to a loss of power flow. Loss adjusters assessed the value as £41,022,504. D did not agree to pay and so C commenced a claim against them for £17,630,067. D alleged deliberate non-disclosure by C due to their knowledge of previous cable failures. The issue was whether the reference in the insurance policy to "deliberate . . . non-disclosure" meant that the contract could be avoided in circumstances where C had honestly, but mistakenly, decided not to disclose a particular document or fact; or whether the words meant that avoidance was only available if there had been a deliberate decision not to disclose a particular document or fact which C knew was material, such that the non-disclosure involved an element of dishonesty. *Held*: that "deliberate" non-disclosure meant that C must have known that what it was doing was wrong; as with "fraudulent" non-disclosure, an element of dishonesty was required. Commercial business sense dictated that the insured should be punished if it had behaved dishonestly, but not if it had made an honest (but deliberate) mistake. C had not behaved dishonestly so there had been no deliberate non-disclosure: *Mutual Energy Limited v Starr Underwriting Agents Limited* (2016).[2]

26–005 Insurance policies have therefore been devised to indemnify the consequences of delay.

The material damage policy and its limitations

26–006 Insurance for projects under construction are typically "all-risks" material damage policies. They insure against accidental damage to the works, temporary works, and, in some cases, temporary site installations and construction equipment. Specified perils (such as defect) are excluded.

26–007 The project policy might be purchased by the owner or the contractor, but typically both owner and contractor will be named as insured parties in the policy. Other parties may be listed as insureds, usually in respect of their particular interests, such as financiers, suppliers, consultants, sub-contractors and the like.[3]

Illustration

> *Facts*: SSE Generation Limited (C) engaged Hochtief Solutions AG (D) to design and build a new hydro-electric scheme at Glendoe, Fort Augustus. After completion, in August 2009, a major tunnel collapsed, ceasing to generate electricity. The parties

---

2 [2016] EWHC 590 (TCC)

3 P Mead, "Contract works insurance: loss scenarios and the impact of policy exclusions" (2011) 27 Const LJ 345.

did not agree upon the remedial works and C hired another contractor (BAM) to deal with this from 2010 to 2012. Proceedings were brought by C seeking to recover over £130m in loss and damage as a result of the tunnel collapse. In the alternative, C claimed £102m to recover the difference between the amount that it had paid to BAM and the total amount it would have paid to D to carry out the remedial works. D counterclaimed for nearly £10m from the loss of profit if it had carried out the remedial works itself, along with the costs of investigating the tunnel collapse, which it attributed to C's event. The contract was based upon the NEC second edition and, in accordance therewith, D took out a policy in joint names of itself and C, with regard to contractor's risk events. Thus, D submitted that C was barred from the court proceedings, since it should have made a claim on the joint names policy. *Held*, by Woolman LJ, that: the provision for joint names insurance did not displace the parties' liability under the NEC contract; as a result, C was not barred from initiating court proceedings: *SSE Generation Limited v Hochtief Solutions AG* (2015).[4]

26–008 These policies are almost always material damage policies; in other words they will only be triggered by physical loss or damage to insured property. The traditional material damage policy excludes "consequential loss" that is to say pure financial loss stemming from the accident, and this would normally exclude the financial consequences of delay.

Illustration

Facts: A contractor was engaged to design and build a hospital wing; during construction, it was discovered that the slab floors were cracking and over defecting. The contractor subsequently sought indemnity from its insurers with respect to a Course of Construction (Builder's Risk) policy. *Held*, by the British Columbia Court of Appeal, that: LED 2/96 (it was the first time that the wording of this exclusion was interpreted) excludes "only those costs of repair that would have remedied the defect immediately prior to the occurrence of the damage" and "the exclusion does not exclude the costs of rectifying or replacing the damaged property itself". *Further held*, that the design of the slabs was not defective, but the result of faulty shoring procedures: *Acciona Infrastructure Canada Inc v Allianz Global Risks US Insurance Company* (2015).[5]

26–009 Extensions to the standard policy may create some cover for the "consequential loss" that might stem from physical damage. For instance, expediting costs may be covered. These are generally limited to expediting the execution of the repair of physical damage itself. Sometimes these costs are specified, such as overtime, or express and air freight. Sometimes the coverage may be more broadly expressed.

26–010 The intention is to reduce the possible impact on the project schedule that might be caused by the need to carry out the repairs.

26–011 Other extensions may go further, and cover the increased cost of the unbuilt works that may arise as a result of the delay (usually the increase in cost due to inflation). A more broadly worded clause might allow consideration of increase in cost due to alterations in access conditions.

---

4 [2015] CSOH 92.
5 [2015] BCCA 347 [CanLII].

26–012 Changes in statutory requirements affecting the reconstruction of the damaged part of the works (and hence increasing cost) may be covered by a specific extension.

26–013 There are clauses available that will reimburse the contractor for the additional cost of continuing the rest of the project. This is intended to cover the contractor's extra expense incurred to maintain the project schedule as far as possible, to overcome the disruption caused by the need to execute the repairs.

26–014 Almost all material damage policies will exclude contractual penalties (ie liquidated damages or their equivalent) and any other financial loss.

Delay policies

26–015 Liquidated damages insurance has been written by the insurance market. This was for the benefit of the contractor and simply indemnified liquidated damages incurred by any cause not specifically excluded. These covers were not found to be economic for insurers, and the terrible loss experience mean that they are rarely offered today.

26–016 Thus, while within the conventional material damage policies, extensions may be provided to assist (primarily) the contractor to mitigate the delays caused by the need to repair physical loss or damage, there is usually nothing to indemnify liquidated damages, or continuing establishment costs.

26–017 Similarly, should the promoter suffer financial loss that is not offset by liquidated damages, there is nothing in the material damage policy to alleviate that loss.

26–018 The lack of indemnity for the promoters' financial loss was perceived to be a problem for financiers, and has led to the development of Delay in Start-Up (DSU) insurance, also sometimes known as "Advance Loss of Profit" (ALOP) insurance (even though profit is not always part of the indemnity offered).

26–019 These policies are of great interest to the project financiers who are concerned about the ability of the project to service the debt incurred by the project's financing arrangements.

Delay in start-up insurance

26–020 Insurance of the promoters' loss resulting from delay can be in the form of a separate insurance contract, but is more usually added as a separate section of the project all-risks policy. This means that where a project policy contains a DSU section, the whole insurance package will have been arranged and purchased by the promoter rather than the contractor.

26–021 It is this type of insurance that we will examine here.

26–022 The insurance concerns itself with the loss that will be suffered by the promoter if the start of commercial activity (let us call it "the business") is delayed.

26–023 The insurance therefore restricts its attention to the possible impact on the business. This may be a loss of revenue that would otherwise have been accruing and which would have been used to cover operating costs, create profit and/or service debt.

26–024 The fact that the insurance only considers the promoters' business is yet one more obvious reason why it cannot render any benefit to the contractor. The contractor will not (usually) be part of the operating business.

26–025 These insurances were developed out of conventional business interruption insurances. They therefore look to establish the delay that arises solely out of indemnifiable material damage. Just as in conventional business interruption insurance principles, the material damage might be insured under a separate policy, but as we have remarked above it is more common to find this as part of a project insurance "package" policy.

26–026 The package policy may also include a marine cover, and delays arising out of damage/delay covered by that section may also be indemnifiable. Alternatively a separate marine cargo and marine DSU policy may have been purchased.

26–027 The marine policy may cover all property in transit to the site or alternatively may be restricted to "critical items" that have been identified when the policy is placed. These might be the turbines and transformers in the case of a power station, or large reactor vessels in the case of a process plant.

The policy period and the indemnity period

26–028 The DSU cover is triggered by delay resulting from insured material damage.

The material damage policy covers any accidental loss or damage occurring during the period of construction, ie before handover. Handover may not necessarily have been established contractually. If a client has taken beneficial occupation of the works, even without issuing any formal written acknowledgment to the contractor, insurers may consider that the works have effectively been handed over. However, insurers may also accept other specified dates (see below).

26–029 The DSU coverage therefore addresses any delay to the date of handover, or alternatively the intended date of commencement of commercial business.

26–030 In some cases, such as specialist process plants, the works may be handed over to the client after mechanical completion, and the client then commissions the plant using their own staff. It is the intended date of the start of the business that the policy should really address. In this example, that would be after the client's staff have successfully commissioned the plant.

26–031 Thus the policy period runs from the start of the works, until the *intended* date of commencement of the business.

26–032 There may be several phases involved. Consider for instance a power plant consisting of several separate units capable of independent operation: Individual units may be completed on a staggered schedule to maximise the contractor's use of resources and manpower. As each unit is completed, it may enter service and start earning revenue. A delay policy covering such a project would have to recognise several different dates of commencement of business, and the distinct revenue streams attaching to each unit.

26–033 The insurance buyer should therefore satisfy themselves that they have purchased a sufficiently long indemnity period. In considering what that might be, they must assess what are the worst delays that could affect the project. That may be related to the construction timespan, and possible the number of winters, rainy seasons or other environmental conditions that might impinge on the project.

26–034 Furthermore the effects of delay in start-up might affect the business for quite some time after commercial operation has actually been achieved (**Figure 26.1**). Some

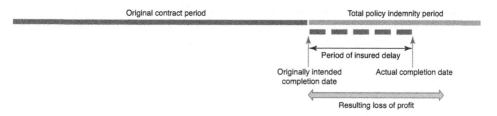

Figure 26.1 The available indemnity period, the delay, and the effect of delay

plants take time to ramp up production. There may have been a loss of market if a competitor is entering the market at the same time.

26–035 European policies normally state the maximum indemnity period (such as 12, or 36, months). The indemnifiable loss of profits may persist beyond the end of the project delay itself, and will only be limited by the maximum policy indemnity period. North American policies often restrict the indemnity to the physical delay itself, and limit it to the time to that in which, with reasonable diligence, the damage could have been repaired, or the affected article replaced.

The deductible

26–036 Policies almost always carry a self-insured deductible, ie a certain level of loss that must be borne by the insured before the policy begins to contribute.

26–037 It can be expressed simply as a sum of money, but is more commonly expressed as a number of days (a time deductible).

26–038 The time deductible may take the form of pure time expressed as "The first X days", or as an average value. The average value deductible demands that the total commercial loss from all insured delay is evaluated, and then a daily average loss is calculated. The deductible can then be turned into a sum of money by multiplying the X days by the average daily value of the loss.

26–039 Some policies decline to consider delays of less than a minimum period. However, more commonly, DSU policies aggregate all the delays occurring due to insured incidents, even if the material damage value is below the separate material damage deductible under the material damage part of the policy.

26–040 The time deductible is likewise the aggregate of all those delays up to X days.

Extending the policy

26–041 As we have observed elsewhere, delays in large projects are commonplace, and therefore insurers are regularly approached to extend the period of cover afforded by the construction project policy.

26–042 When contemplating a pure material damage policy, this is usually a simple enough matter and the additional premium usually reflects the original rate.

26–043 Where delay is also insured, the matter of extending cover is more complicated.

26–044 If no insured delay has occurred, but the project will be late for other, uninsured reasons (**Figure 26.2**), the whole project period for both material damage and delay can usually be extended without too much trouble.

If the project has been delayed on account of an insured loss, and this is the reason why an extension is sought, it will be argued that the original delay policy has been triggered. The additional cover being sought is for any future event that might occur during what is the indemnity period of the original policy (**Figure 26.3**).

26–045 The material damage cover can be extended in the normal way, but the original delay insurance cannot. The original delay insurance was a promise to pay for any delay

Extension to project
period

Figure 26.2 Extension due to uninsured events

Figure 26.3 Extension made necessary by insured delay

resulting in an overrun of the original contract period, due to an insured event in that original contract period. There is no cover for any insured event happening after the end of the original contract period.

26–046 In the eyes of purists, this means that a fresh insurance contract is required for the new extension period.

26–047 In reality, this would be difficult to achieve if new underwriters had to be found. Insurers not engaged in the risk from its inception will be reluctant to underwrite it at a late stage. When a project is nearing completion, any delay is more likely to be impact the critical path, and so the exposure for the delay insurer is much higher. They would be likely to demand very high rates of premium if they accepted the risk at all.

26–048 In practice, the most common solution is for the original insurers to issue an endorsement to the existing policy granting cover for this additional period, but attaching a separate deductible to the new period.

26–049 It is possible then to have a project policy with a series of endorsements for a sequence of periods (as the delays continue and compound) each with its separate deductible.

Establishing an indemnity

26–050 Establishing an indemnity comes in two parts: First one must establish the delay that arises out of the insured material damage that has occurred.

26–051 Once the delay is known, the financial loss attaching to that delay can be calculated.

26–052 In practice, work on these two aspects is usually pursued in tandem.

Establishing delay

26–053 The delay that is to be considered for the purposes of a DSU insurance is fundamentally different from those considerations that arise when considering delay entitlements under the construction contract. All the contractual provisions can effectively be disregarded since insurance asks a much simpler question.

26–054 The question can be paraphrased as follows:

> *"How much earlier would this contract have been completed* **but for** *the need to repair or replace the insured property that has been lost or damaged?"*

26–055 In other words, these policies are based upon the principle of indemnity. They seek to put the insured back in the position they would have enjoyed had the indemnifiable event not happened.

26–056 To assess this question, one must (usually) wait until the final completion of the contract. That is because, in the course of a construction project, all sorts of unexpected events may occur that cause delay or disruption to the project schedule, and none of these may be incidents of material damage. Consider the following:

1. Suppliers being late in delivery
2. Labour outputs being lower than anticipated
3. Strikes
4. Changes in design
5. Unforeseen problems in execution
6. Defective workmanship that must be rectified.

26–057 None of these is (normally) an insured peril. All may cause delay. If any of these delays were to occur in parallel with an insured delay, they would erode or even eclipse that delay. That is because if the insured delay had not occurred, the uninsured delay would still have been taking place and delaying the project to the same extent.

26–058 Therefore, the occurrence of the insured delay might not cause the project to complete any later than it otherwise would have done. Where the insured delay persists beyond that of the uninsured delay, it is this extra period that is indemnifiable (**Figure 26.4**).

26–059 Analysis of these delays is conventionally in the form of a collapsed as-built analysis. However, it must be recognised that when an insured delay occurs, the insured may take advantage of this to implement changes, or re-schedule other works to make better use of resources during the repair period. Equally, there may be signs of concurrent delay or consequential delay impacts not immediately apparent from activity relationships alone. For this reason, it may prove necessary to perform a windows analysis as a second step.

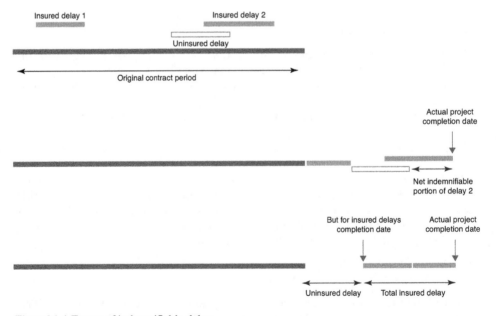

Figure 26.4 Extent of indemnifiable delay

26–060 Whilst the collapsed as-built analysis will model the critical impact of the insured delay, the complementary windows analysis will enable the analyst to understand the driving mechanisms of delay from a contemporaneous basis, to more accurately model the project's likely path of progression had the insured delay not occurred.

26–061 This, in turn, will form the basis of the analyst's interpretation of the "but for" as-built logic and durations. Insurers will need to be satisfied that any alterations or re-scheduling would not have been contemplated in the absence of the insured event.

26–062 Things sometimes go wrong with the new design changes or the redeployment of labour, leading to yet further delays. Insurers need to be very clear-eyed in assessing what delays are reasonably attributable solely to damage, as opposed to other opportunistic actions by client or contractor.

26–063 The existence of an insured delay is always dependent on the policy conditions and exclusions. Almost every policy will contain exclusions for defects. In the first case we should say that insurers make a clear distinction between defect and damage. Something may have been created in a defective condition. That may need to be remedied, but no physical damage may have taken place. In such a situation, no claim arises.

26–064 If, however, the defect gives rise to damage, there may be an indemnifiable claim, depending upon the exact nature of the defect exclusion that exists in the policy. Some exclusions are a blanket exclusion of all costs arising in connection with a defect. Some limit the exclusion to any improvement that may arise when a repair is executed, and other exclusions provide coverage that falls somewhere in between these extremes.

26–065 Insurers have considered that the exclusion will similarly limit the attaching delay incurred by the necessity to repair, although this is not universally accepted.

Establishing financial loss

26–066 The DSU section of the policy may be written on several different bases: Traditional business insurance policies consider the loss of "gross profit". This is measured as fixed costs and net profit. If a business is not in operation, there is a presumption that variable costs are not being incurred. This version of "gross profit" is not one recognised by accountants practising in the commercial sphere, and is peculiar to the insurance industry.

26–067 Some clients may prefer to reduce the value being insured by neglecting net profit, and only insuring fixed costs. The fixed costs are often specified in the policy. In many cases only selected fixed costs are insured, such as debt service costs (of primary interest to the project financiers).

26–068 For some projects with few or no variable costs, it may be more appropriate to simply insure on the basis of anticipated revenue (for instance toll roads or bridges).

26–069 The task confronting the insurers is to establish what revenue or profit the project might have enjoyed, had the project completed on the earlier date implied by the delay analysis.

26–070 This may require a lot of specialist consulting input. Economists may be required to create suitable models to predict what the market would have been in the relevant period. Had the project been operational, and its products been sold into an existing market, there may be a reasonable presumption that the additional supply could have depressed the market price.

26–071 For insurers being invited to insure fixed costs or debt service only, a philosophical problem may arise: Suppose for some reason, even had the project never been delayed, market conditions obtaining in the relevant period mean that the project would never have been profitable and it could never have covered its fixed costs. Payment by insurers of the fixed costs in their entirety might then be more than strict indemnity. That is because in reality, in such situations, debt service costs might not have been paid in full to the original schedule, and some relief might have been sought from the lenders.

26–072 For this reason, insurers may draft the indemnity to be a proportion of the fixed costs in a ratio reflecting the size of the would-have-been revenue rather than the originally projected revenue.

26–073 The insured may have the opportunity to recoup some of the loss by increasing production above the original plan, once production has actually started, or by substituting output from other existing plants. In such situations it may be difficult to prove that these measures would not have been taken anyway if the market conditions are favourable, and so the insured may argue that there has been no mitigation.

26–074 Where a delay arises from accidental material damage for which, under the contract, the contractor is culpable, the client may be entitled to receive liquidated damages from the contractor. In principle, such liquidated damages are intended to make good the reasonably estimated economic loss that the client would suffer in consequence of such delay. Of course, it is exactly that economic loss that the DSU policy insures. Therefore the underwriters will consider that the insured loss is partly (or even completely) made good by such payments, and any such payments are usually deducted when evaluating the indemnifiable loss under the policy

26–075 If it is found that would-have-been revenues or profits during the indemnity period are greater than those original foreseen, the sum insured in the policy may be too low. Most policies will apply "average" to reduce any indemnity pro-rata to the shortfall between the sum insured and the actual loss that could have occurred in the entire indemnity period.

Acceleration and increased cost of working (ICOW)

26–076 When a project is faced with a delay, the usual reaction of all the contractual parties is to look to see how this can be minimised. Where the delay is the fault of the contractor, the contractor may devise remedies that can minimise the delay or reduce it to nothing. These would be implemented at the contractor's cost. The client will have sought details from the contractor of their revised schedule and want to be satisfied that the contractor is doing or has done everything possible to restore the project schedule.

26–077 The extent of mitigating measures that the contractor is willing to contemplate may be limited economically by the value of the LADs and other continuing establishment costs being avoided.

26–078 In the situation where the contractor has already incurred the full extent of LADs under the contract, the economic limit may be reduced to merely the continuing establishment costs, and that might preclude doing very much to restore the project schedule.

26–079 Where the client is faced with a contractor who is not prepared to take effective measures at his own cost, the client may be compelled to contemplate issuing instructions to the contractor to undertake certain actions to accelerate. The implication is that these additional measures would be at the client's cost.

26–080 A similar result may arise where there is a misalignment between the LADs stipulated under the contract, and the actual economic loss that the client may suffer due to any delay.

26–081 Where the delay is due to a cause for which the client bears responsibility under the contract, any acceleration measure must, obviously, also be paid for by the client.

26–082 Where the client is bearing the cost of an accelerating measure to avert or reduce delay, this may reduce or avert what would otherwise be a commercial loss that would be claimed from insurers. Clearly, in equity, insurers have an interest in any measure that may reduce loss under the policy, and should accept the costs incurred in executing such measures. Most DSU policies expressly cover such ICOW in the operative clause of the policy wording.

26–083 Almost all policy wordings insist that such measures should be economic – that is to say the cost of the mitigation measures should not exceed the amount of commercial loss avoided.

26–084 It is possible to buy additional cover that removes the requirement for the "economic" test ("additional increased cost of working") but this will be subject to a monetary cap.

26–085 In reality, the suggestion that acceleration measures be implemented poses a number of problems:

1. The efficacy of any particular measure proposed can never be guaranteed. Contracting history is littered with examples of acceleration schemes that have simply not worked for various reasons.
2. Insurers will want to have a detailed understanding of the project schedule to be sure that the scheme only mitigates a delay that has arisen due to an insured loss, and not any other difficulty that the contractor (or the project) may be experiencing.
3. The delay mitigation scheme may work as expected, but some other unanticipated development may subsequently delay the project to the same or even greater extent, rendering the mitigation measures useless.
4. The future commercial loss being avoided may still be several years into the future. Pricing this would-have-been delay is very difficult and uncertain, so applying the economic test becomes a very academic exercise.

26–086 Because no one can be sure in advance of the effectiveness of a mitigation scheme, it is strongly recommended that insurers and insured formally agree the extent of costs that may be accepted under the policy, before such costs are incurred, and regardless of the actual outcome. There must always be a temptation to be wise with hindsight, and it would be unfair for insurers only to decide how much they will pay when they have been able to see the effect.

26–087 The existence of a deductible under the DSU section of the policy means that the mitigation measure may be averting a loss that would otherwise partly fall to insurers, and partly on the insured themselves. It is only fair that the parties should bear the costs pro rata to the losses that it is hoped will be avoided.

26–088 Consider a policy which has a deductible of 60 days. The first significant insured event occurs, and this threatens to result in a 140-day delay. An acceleration measure is proposed that promises to reduce the resulting delay to zero. This would save the insured their deductible of 60 days, but it would also save insurers a net insured delay of 80 days. Insurers will normally insist that the cost of the proposed measure should be shared in a 60:80 ratio.

26–089 Implementing an ICOW measure does not reduce the time deductible. It may or may not be successful. The actual delay experienced at the end of the project remains to be seen, and the deductible remains undiminished.

26–090 It is sometimes possible to mitigate the effects of any delay in start-up by making alternative business arrangements. Again, these would be "increased cost of working" measures.

26–091 For instance, once start-up has actually been achieved, the plant might be capable of producing at a higher level than that originally envisaged, which would allow some of the lost production to be made up. Alternatively it may be possible to sub-contract the manufacture of components of an intended product to others, both before and after the eventual start-up. If any such measure reduces the resulting loss during the delay indemnity period, it will be reflected in the adjustment of the net resulting claim.

CHAPTER 27

An introduction to Nordic construction law

This is an entirely new chapter.

Introduction

> *"Good Hamlet, cast thy nightly colour off,*
> *And let thine eye look like a friend on Denmark.*
> *Do not for ever with thy vailèd lids*
> *Seek for thy noble father in the dust.*
> *Thou know'st 'tis common – all that lives must die,*
> *Passing through nature to eternity."*[1]

27–001 This chapter comprises a brief introduction to Nordic construction law, first in general terms and then through a comparative analysis of three key issues: namely, delay damages, limitation of liability and defects liability.

Defining features of Nordic construction law

27–002 The Nordic countries include Denmark (including the partially autonomous territories of Greenland and the Faroe Islands), Finland, Iceland, Norway and Sweden, whereas the cultural and linguistic region (usually called Scandinavia) is limited to Denmark, Norway and Sweden.

27–003 The Nordic countries share a closely intertwined history; for instance (as recorded by Shakespeare in Act I, Scene 1. lines 79-107 inclusive, of *Hamlet*), Denmark, Norway and Sweden were for a long period united as a state under the Danish monarch.

---

1 William Shakespeare, *The Tragedy of Hamlet, Prince of Denmark, per Queen Gertrude*, Act 1, Scene 2, lines 68–73.

This common past, as well as the Nordic countries' relatively isolated geographical position explain the pronounced ties uniting them on many levels, which results in the same type of societal organisation, characterised by strong welfare states and a high level of taxes.

27–004 Similarities between the Nordic countries can be observed from a legal point of view as well. In the 13th and 14th centuries, Nordic laws were codified on a provincial basis. In 1683, a general code of law, the *Danish Code 1683 (Danske Lov)* was adopted by the Danish monarch. Since Norway was a part of Denmark at that time, the *Danish Code* was also put into force in Norway as the *Norwegian Code (Norske Lov)*.[2] Although it is called a code, *Danske Lov* differs from a proper code in the ordinary civil law sense in several aspects. First of all, it does not systematically regulate the main areas of law, but is a compilation of rules on scattered subjects such as civil and criminal procedure, religion and clergy and maritime matters. Secondly, its rules are of casuistic nature, providing examples of the application of rules, rather than exposing them in a general and abstract manner. In Sweden, a code compiling the medieval rules was enacted in 1734. Like the *Danish* and *Norwegian Codes*, it contains rules of both private and public law nature; it extended to Finland and is still valid in both countries as the latest global restatement of the law. A few rules of the original Nordic codes are still in force, but most of them have been overtaken by more recent and specialised legislation, or became obsolete.

27–005 A Nordic legislative co-operation started with the Convention of Nordic Lawyers held every third year since 1872 and created in the context of a political movement called "Scandinavism",[3] which was based upon the idea of a Nordic federation.[4] Within the framework of the Convention, Nordic lawyers and academics (inspired by the movement leading to the adoption of the German BGB), attempted to codify various part of private law. The most significant achievement of this collaboration is the adoption of the *Sale of Goods Acts* and the *Contracts Act*, which have almost identical content in all the Nordic countries.

27–006 The *Contracts Act* and the *Sale of Goods Acts* are the most important legislative sources of Nordic private law, which is generally divided into two distinct disciplines. The first, called *contract law*, covers the formation, invalidity and interpretation of contracts as well as agency; it is governed by the different *Contract Acts* adopted in the Nordic countries between 1915 and 1929. The second is the *law of obligations* and covers matters of performance, breach of contract and corresponding remedies, termination and so forth. This part is not codified in legislation, but based upon general principles, either judge-made and/or founded in legal doctrine. Due to this absence of specific legislation corresponding to the *Codes of Obligations* of many countries of continental Europe, some of the provisions of the *Sales Acts* are applied by analogy to contracts other than sales contracts.[5]

27–007 Since the Nordic countries do not apply the doctrine of *stare decisis* doctrine and since Nordic legal concepts are (to a very large extent) inspired by laws of continental Europe (in particular, German law), Nordic law is generally speaking assimilated to the civil law family. However, Nordic law also presents features resembling common law, such as the absence of codified rules in certain areas where case law and scholarly literature then function as main sources of law. As a consequence, Nordic law is often considered to be a "legal family" on its own.

---

2 Mads Bryde Andersen and Eric Runesson, *An Overview of Nordic Contract Law* in *The Nordic Contracts Act – Essays in Celebration of its One Hundredth Anniversary,* Copenhagen, 2015, p. 15.
3 Bryde Andersen and Runesson, *op. cit.,* p. 17.
4 Ruth Nielsen, *Contract Law in Denmark* (Aalphen aan den Rijn, 2011), p. 23.
5 Ruth Nielsen, *op. cit.,* p. 25.

27–008 The absence of legislative provisions concerning commercial[6] construction contracts has led to the adoption of *standard contracts* in this area. Each Nordic country has its own set(s) of national standard construction contracts.[7] In Norway (and due to the importance of the offshore oil and gas sector which accounts for a significant part of the country's BNP), a distinct set of standards apply for offshore construction. All the Nordic standards have the character of *agreed documents* and are the results of detailed negotiations between organisations representing the interests of all parties involved in the construction industry.[8] In order to be applicable, standards have to be formally incorporated into individual contracts; however, some of the rules contained in the standards are considered as a codification of general principles of construction law and, as a consequence, apply even if the parties did not specifically incorporate the standard into their contract.[9] Both the *Danish* and the *Swedish* standards are currently undergoing a process of revision; the new Danish standards are expected for the Spring of 2018.

27–009 The standard contracts represent the main source of Nordic construction law, together with the related case law and academic doctrine. The nature and availability of construction case law depends upon the country in question. In Denmark, a large majority of construction disputes are settled through a system which is a hybrid between arbitration and state proceedings; the most important decisions rendered under this system are published in one of two specialised law journals,[10] which means that a significant body of case law is available, by comparison with countries where most disputes are settled by ADR not leading to published decisions.

27–010 In the other Nordic countries, various dispute resolution models exist and the availability of published decisions depends upon several factors, such as the model chosen by the parties – bearing in mind that mediation is growing in importance in the Nordics countries, as much as in the rest of the world – and whether the standard adopted by the parties proposes court proceedings as standard dispute resolution process, like it is, for instance, the case in Norway for cases where the amount in dispute is below a certain limit.

Key issues

Delay damages

27–011 Parties to a construction contract almost always agree that the works have to be completed within a certain period of time. If delay occurs, two situations must

---

6 Several Nordic countries have legislative provisions concerning construction services provided to *consumers*. For instance, Norway has legislation about consumer construction in form of a statute governing the construction of residential dwellings and a statute on services provided by craftsmen to consumers, and Denmark has a specific standard contract for construction services provided to consumers. The focus of the present chapter is on commercial construction contracts and these statutes will therefore not be dealt with here.

7 Denmark: *AB 92* (build only), *ABT 93* (design and build), *ABR 89* (consultants). Sweden: *AB 04* (build-only), *ABT 06* (design and build) and *ABK 09* (consultants). Norway: the NS (*Norske Standarder*) family of contracts comprises contracts meant to be used for land construction whereas the *NF/NTK* contracts apply to offshore construction and operations. Finland: *YSE 1998* (meant for building contracts but can be modified and used for design and build contracts as well) and *KSE 2013* (consultants). Iceland: *IST 30* (build-only and design and build).

8 Erik Hørlyck, *Entreprise* (Copenhagen, 2014), p. 19.

9 Hørlyck, *op. cit.*, p. 19.

10 *Kendelser for fast ejendom (KfE)* = decisions on real estate law and *Tidsskrift for Bolig- og Byggeret (T:BB)* = Journal of Tenancy and Construction Law.

be distinguished. If the delay was caused by circumstances contractually defined as excusable, the contractor (and, in some situations, also the employer) can be entitled to an extension of time (EoT) and, in some cases, also to economic compensation. If there is no ground for an extension of time, the party in delay will in the majority of cases owe delay damages (most often standardised (or liquidated damages) to the other party.

27–012 Rules concerning the circumstances giving rise to EoTs for the contractor can be found in all Nordic standard contracts, and can be classified in two main categories: *circumstances related to the employer* (such as, for instance, variation orders, or late delivery of design documents in the build-only model, or delay caused by another contractor engaged by the employer[11]) on the one hand and, on the other hand, events generally termed *neutral events* because they are not related to, or caused by, any of the parties to the construction agreement and are beyond the control of either. This second category encompasses *force majeure* types of circumstances, such as war, natural catastrophes, fire, or exceptionally inclement weather conditions, as well as several types of labour disputes, such as strikes, or lockouts, or authorities interventions, such as public bans and orders,[12] as long as they are not caused by the contractor. Danish contracts explicitly mention that the contractor is liable for delay caused by circumstances that do not entitle it to an EoT, but this conclusion is implicit in the other Nordic contracts.

27–013 All Scandinavian standard contracts provide for liquidated damages (LADs) in case of contractor delay. The possibility is only mentioned in the Danish contract, which states that unless LADs are agreed upon, delay damages are calculated according to general principles of Danish law.[13] In Sweden, LADs are presented as the usual remedy in case of contractor delay, but the parties must agree upon a rate, or method of calculation, in order for the LADs clause under the standard clause to apply.[14] The Norwegian and Finnish standards function differently, since they provides for a default rate of LADs per day of delay, which means that the parties do not need to make express provisions in order to apply LADs, but, on the contrary, explicitly opt out if they intend delay damages to be calculated according to general rules concerning the assessment of damages.[15] If the parties do not agree upon LADs in the case of contractor delay, the employer can claim the damages he actually suffers as a consequence of a delay, calculated according to the general rules on damage assessment.[16]

27–014 LADs on the one hand and general damages on the other are generally considered as *alternatives*: when LAD are agreed upon, the main rule is that the employer is barred from claiming additional damages on account of contractor delay.[17] The *Norwegian Standard* states that this rule does not apply if the delay is caused by the contractor's gross negligence, or wilful misconduct.[18] No corresponding rule exists in Denmark and Danish case law contains one example where an employer was unsuccessful in trying to obtain higher damages than the LADs, based upon the argument that the contractor

---

11 Denmark: *AB 92* § 24, s. 1, ss 1 and 2. Norway: *NS 8405* art. 24.1. Sweden: *AB 04* Chapter 4, § 3 s. 1.

12 Denmark: *AB 92* § 24, s. 1, ss. 3, 4 and 5. Norway: *NS 8405* art. 24.3. Sweden: *AB 04* Chapter 4, § 3 ss. 2 and 3.

13 *AB 92* § 25, s. 1.

14 *AB 04* Chap. 5, § 3.

15 Norway: *NS 8405* art. 34.3. Finland: *YSE 1998* § 18.

16 See for instance the Danish *AB 92* § 25, s. 3.

17 See for instance the Danish *AB 92* § 25, s. 2.

18 See *NS 8405* art. 34.1, third part.

intentionally caused the delay;[19] a renowned scholar has suggested that a rule similar to the Norwegian rule should be inserted in the *Danish Standard*.[20] The Swedish Standard does not contain an exception to the main rule for situations in which the delay represents gross negligence, or wilful misconduct by the contractor, but it is suggested in jurisprudence that, in certain situations of qualified default, such as, for instance, if the contractor deliberately dedicates resources to another (more profitable) project, it may be reasonable to allow the employer to claim general damages in addition to LADs.[21] Such a solution could be inferred from the "general clause" contained in art. 36 of the *Nordic Contract Act*, allowing for the setting-aside of unfair and/or unreasonable contract clauses and, in some situations, interpreted to the effect of making exclusions of liability for wilful misconduct and gross negligence invalid.

27–015 The Norwegian Standards expressly limit the contractor's liability for delay to 10% of the contract sum.[22] This limitation does not exist in other Scandinavian contracts, but corresponds nonetheless to a market standard and is therefore frequently inserted by parties in their contracts. Even in situations where the contract does not contain an express maximum limit for LADs, Danish construction arbitrators are known to reduce (quite frequently and often heavily) the amount of LADs due to employers based upon general considerations of reasonableness.

27–016 In situations of excusable delay, the contractor may be entitled to an extra economic compensation (corresponding to "loss and expense") in addition to an extension of time. The *Danish Standards* provide for two different types of additional economic compensation, depending upon the circumstances causing the delay. In fact, the contractor can either claim full compensation of their delay-related costs (prolongation costs) plus his loss of profits ("*erstatning for det lidte tab*", meaning compensation of the loss suffered), or solely an indemnity covering their delay-related costs, but not their loss of profits ("*godtgørelse*", literally meaning "making good again"). In short, the main criterion distinguishing the two types of grounds is *fault*; if the employer, or contractor, for whose actions or omissions the employer is contractually responsible, has acted at fault or negligently, the delayed contractor is entitled to a full indemnity (including his loss of profits), but they can only claim a simple indemnity if neither the employer, nor one of the co-contractors is at fault.

27–017 Finally, if the delay is caused by a neutral event, the contractor is entitled to an EoT, but no additional economic compensation,[23] meaning that the parties share the overall risk of such an event.

27–018 In Norwegian law, the standard contracts list a series of grounds based upon which the contractor may claim an adjustment of its remuneration, among others delay or other default by the employer.[24] The contracts contain detailed provisions regarding the manner in which the adjustment may be calculated,[25] and the leading principle is that the contractor must be fully compensated for the consequences of the delay.[26]

---

19 Decision published at *T:BB 2000.518 (2) VBA*.

20 Torsten Iversen, *Nogle bemærkninger om dagbod* in *Festskrift til Det Danske Selskab for Byggeret* (Copenhagen, 2009), p. 124.

21 Robert Deli, *Kommersiell byggjuridik i praktiken* (Stockholm, 2012), p. 102.

22 *NS 8405* art. 34.3, s. 1.

23 Sylvie Cavaleri, *Concurrent Delay in Construction Disputes* (Copenhagen, 2015), pp. 142–147. See also, S Cavalieri, "Construction disputes in Denmark: the case of concurrent delay" (2015) 31 Const LJ 57.

24 *NS 8405* art. 25.2.

25 *NS 8405* art. 25.7 to 25.9

26 Viggo Hagström and Herman Bruserud, *Entrepriserett* (Oslo, 2014), p. 269.

27–019 In Swedish law, the contractor is, as a matter of principle, entitled to economic compensation to cover the costs caused by employer-related circumstances, among other employer-related delay.[27] However, if the employer can prove that he could not reasonably have expected, prevented and overcome the hindrance, the related costs must be shared equally between the parties.[28]

Limitations of liability

27–020 All Nordic standard contracts provide for the limitation of liability and parties often agree to additional limitations, such limitations are either of a quantitative, or a qualitative, nature.

27–021 As far as *quantitative* limitations are concerned, several contracts state that liability is limited to a certain percentage of the contract sum.[29] *Qualitative* limitations (on the other hand) generally consist in excluding liability for certain types of damages. For instance, the *Danish Standards* exclude the contractor's liability for certain types of consequential damages by stating that the contractor cannot be held liable for operational losses, loss of profit, or other indirect losses.[30] Furthermore, the provisions, present in most Nordic standards, according to which agreed LADs shall be the only damages that the employer may claim on account of delay,[31] also represent a limitation of liability in the cases where the employer's losses are higher than the LADs.

Defects liability

27–022 In all Nordic countries, the definition of a defect depends primarily upon the contract, since all standard contracts state that a defect is present if the works, or parts thereof, are not in conformity with the contract, or, as far as Swedish standards are concerned, not carried out at all.[32]

27–023 Norwegian law adds a second step to the analysis of whether a defect is present, by adding that the non-conformity with the contract must be due to circumstances in respect of which the contractor bears the *risk*. Identifying such circumstances depends upon the allocation of responsibilities as between the parties to the contract. In fact, liability follows responsibility:[33] if the employer is, for instance, in charge of providing the design, they are (as a starting point) liable if such design is defective, or not provided at the correct time.

27–024 Although this is not expressed in the provisions of the standard contract, the contractor can (under Danish law and similarly to Norwegian law) avoid being held liable for defects if he proves that the defect is caused by circumstances for which the employer is responsible (for instance, defective design), or that the works were carried out correctly in accordance with the state of the art rules and guidelines applicable at the

---

27 *AB 04* Chapter 5, § 4, referring to Chapter 4 § 3 s. 1 concerning employer-related circumstances.
28 *AB 04* Chapter 5, § 4, second sentence.
29 Sweden: *AB 04* Chap. 5, § 11, limiting the contractor's liability to 15% of the contract sum; the provision only applies to a limited type of damages. Norway: *NS 8405* § 34.3, s. 3, limiting the contractor's global liability for liquidated damages to 10% of the contract sum.
30 *AB 92* § 35, s. 2.
31 See for instance *NS 8405* § 34.1, s. 3.
32 *AB 92* § 30, s. 1. *NS 8405* art. 36.1. Sweden: *AB 04*, definition chapter.
33 Henning Nordtvedt, Dag Arne Ruud, Olav Bergsaker, Arve Martin Bjørnvik and Johnny Johansen, *NS 8407 – Kommentarutgave*, p. 622.

time of the operations.[34] In addition, Danish law has specific and more detailed provisions with respect to defects linked to the *materials* used. In fact, the materials are deemed to be defective if they are not as agreed, or of customary good quality, unless the contractor proves that materials conforming with the contract do not exist or could not be procured because of force majeure-type of circumstances, such as war, or import bans, or unless the materials prescribed by the employer cannot be provided due to circumstances that the contractor ought not to have foreseen at the time of concluding the contract.[35]

27–025 In Swedish law as well, the contractor is liable for defects unless he can prove that the defect is caused by circumstances for which the employer is responsible.[36]

27–026 The standard Nordic defect liability period is five years from taking-over, with the following modifications.

27–027 In Denmark, the standard rule only applies to building works and engineering works connected to (meaning carried out at the same time as) building works, whereas independent engineering works are subject to a different régime, according to which the contractor's right and duty to remedy the defects only exists for one year, but the employer can claim damages for defects according to general rules of Danish law concerning time-bars,[37] ie ten years. The explanation for this difference is that, in the negotiations leading up to the adoption of the Danish standard contracts, organisations defending the interests of employers did not accept the shorter period of five-year liability for long and complex engineering works.

27–028 Furthermore, the employer's five-year deadline to invoke defects does not apply if the contractor has contractually agreed to extend his liability period, if it is established at taking-over that agreed quality assurance measures have failed materially, or if the contractor is guilty of gross negligence.[38] In Sweden, the contractor is fully liable for five years if the defect is due to the contractor's workmanship, but only two years (or a longer liability period granted by the supplier to the contractor) for materials and goods.[39] When these periods have expired, the contractor's liability can only be invoked in case of material defects and if the defect is caused by the contractor's negligence.[40] The Finnish standard provides for a similar gradation of the contractor's defect liability, with full liability during a two-year guarantee period and a liability limited to defects caused by the contractor's gross negligence for up to ten years from taking-over.[41]

27–029 *Defect notification rules* apply in all Nordic jurisdictions. In Denmark, the employer must give written notice of a defect that was not taken note of at taking-over within a reasonable time after the defect was or ought to have been discovered, but this rule does not apply if the defect is due to the contractor's gross negligence. In Norway, the employer must give notice of defect without undue delay and (in any case) within five years from taking-over, but these notices do not apply if the defect was caused by the contractor's gross negligence, or wilful misconduct.[42]

27–030 In all Nordic countries, the primary remedy for defects is *specific performance*: the contractor has both a right and a duty to carry out remedial works before

---

34 Hørlyck, *op. cit.*,p. 376.
35 *AB 92* § 30, s. 2.
36 *AB 04* Chapter 5, § 5.
37 *AB 92* § 36, s. 3.
38 *AB 92* § 36, s. 2.
39 *AB 04* Chap. 4, §. 7
40 *AB 04* Chap. 5, § 6.
41 *YSE 1998* § 29 and 30.
42 *NS 8405* Art. 36.7

other remedies are considered. There are, however, exceptions to this general principle. First of all, if the cost of remedial works would be disproportionately high in relation to the expected benefit,[43] if the remedy seems unreasonable due to other circumstances,[44] or, in the Finnish standard, if the defect does not hinder the use of the works,[45] the contractor is not obliged to carry out remedial work, but the employer is instead entitled to a price reduction.[46] Secondly, if remedial work must be carried out in emergency[47] (for example, in case of risk of water leakage) and the contractor is not in a position to come back to the site on time, the employer is entitled to let a new contractor carry out the works at the first contractor's expense. Finally, if the contractor has attempted to remedy the defects, but the works are still not in compliance with the contract, the employer is entitled to let a new contractor carry out the works at the first contractor's expense as well.

27–031 Finally, the contractor can, in certain situations, be liable to pay damages in case of defects. If a defect causes consequential damage (either to the works themselves, or to the employer's, or a third party's person, or property), the solution varies according to the country in question. In Sweden, the contractor is bound to cover consequential damages caused by a defect for which the contractor is liable.[48] In Norway, the contractor is liable to cover the costs of remedy of damages that are caused to parts of the works not comprised in the contract[49] by a defect caused by the contractor's negligence. Furthermore, if the defect causes to the employer a loss that is not covered by the provision previously mentioned, the employer can claim that the contractor cover his loss only if the defect is due to the contractor's wilful misconduct, or gross negligence.[50] The level of fault by the contractor thus determines the extent of their liability for damages in the case of defects. In Denmark, the contractor is liable to cover consequential damages caused by defects that are the result of contractor fault, or negligence, or that relate to properties guaranteed by the contract[51] (for instance, if a roof collapses, because it does not have the guaranteed load-bearing capacity). As opposed to what the wording of the clause suggests, this provision not only concerns consequential damages caused by defects in the works, but also by the contractor's activity in relation to the contract in general; jurisprudence quotes the example from case law of a contractor obstructing a sewage pipe while pouring foundations piles.[52] However, the contractor is not liable for operating losses, losses of profit and other indirect losses.[53]

---

43 *AB 92* § 33, s. 1. Norway: *NS 8405*, § 36.2, s. 1.

44 Sweden: *AB 04*, Chap. 5, § 18, states that the contractor is not obligated to remedy defects which do not essentially influence the state, the appearance or the possibility to use the works for the intended purpose to the extent that such remedial work would be unreasonable having regard to their costs or other circumstances.

45 *YSE 1998* § 29, s. 3.

46 Denmark: *AB 92* § 34. Sweden: *AB 04*, Chap. 5, § 18, 2nd section. Norway: *NS 8405* Art. 36.4.

47 Denmark: *AB 92* § 32. S. 5. Norway: *NS 8405* Art. 36.3, s. 7.

48 *AB 04* Chapter 5 § 8.

49 The risk of damage to the works themselves remains with the contractor until taking-over and is covered by insurance during the construction period.

50 *NS 8405*, art. 36.5

51 *AB 92* § 35, s. 1.

52 Hørlyck, *op. cit.*, p. 432.

53 *AB 92* § 35, s. 2.

Conclusion

27–032 The brief discussion of key issues considered above reveals that, although the Nordic countries are generally considered by outsiders as a united family, significant differences exist between the different countries as far as construction law is concerned. Denmark and Norway can be considered as the two extremes: Danish construction law is rudimentary, pragmatic and the current Danish standards are (from an international point of view) hopelessly backwards, whereas the latest version of the Norwegian standards shows a level of formalism and sophisticated change management procedures that to some extent resemble FIDIC.

27–033 Nonetheless, the reply to the question raised at a recent conference (namely, "Is Standardisation Possible?") is (at this stage) predominantly negative, as far as the Nordic countries are concerned. In fact (and although this is difficult to establish with certainty due to the confidentiality generally surrounding international construction projects and the related dispute resolution procedures), it is the general view among construction scholars and practitioners that Nordic practice revolves around the national forms of contract and that international forms (such as FIDIC) are very rarely used, if at all.

27–034 The explanation for this situation is that FIDIC is considered foreign to Nordic contract culture for several reasons. First, FIDIC standards forms aim at regulating the entire contractual relationship as between employer and contractor and to detach this from the background law to the largest extent possible. On the contrary, Nordic standard contracts rely, often quite heavily, upon the national law under which they were created to operate.

27–035 Secondly, the FIDIC institution of the engineer (which carries the double function of being (on the one hand) the employer's representative and (on the other hand) (in theory, at least) an independent and impartial primary adjudicator when making determinations upon the parties' claims), is wholly unknown to Nordic construction law. All Nordic standards operate with parties' representatives, but none of them is granted the competence to make first instance decisions upon disagreements; if a dispute arises, it has to be settled (or mediated) by a neutral third party.

27–036 Thirdly, the drafting language of FIDIC forms is technical and complex, with long and detailed provisions and many definitions and cross-references; this is in direct contrast with the Nordic forms, whose language is generally much more plain and simple, with the exception of the Norwegian standards, which have evolved to become generally far closer to Anglo-American standards.

27–037 Finally (and although this argument is applicable in priority to Danish law), FIDIC forms show a high level of formalism and presuppose heavy contractual administration, which is contrary to Scandinavian legal pragmatism, in which judges and arbitrators are focused upon material reasonableness, rather than formal requirements and, as a consequence, refuse to enforce the latter as a condition precedent. It has been repeatedly pointed out in scholarly works that the Danish reluctance to accept formal requirements is one example of the under-development of Danish construction law[54] and that the pragmatic application of the law operated by Danish construction arbitrators is

---

54 Ole Hansen, *Formkrav og frister i entreprisekontrakter – en analyse af præklusion som retligt redskab til styring af ændringer i byggeaftaler* i Ole Hansen (red.) *Ændringsregler i længerevarende kontrakter* (Copenhagen, 2014), p. 70.

a considerable obstacle to the internationalisation of the Danish construction industry.[55] At the time of writing, it is impossible to predict whether this (internationally speaking) somewhat unusual Danish position will be maintained, or modified, in the new standard contracts currently expected for 2018. In addition, it may be that (if it eventually materialises and in what guise[56]), the UK's decision to "Brexit" may have some considerable impact.

---

55 Sylvie Cavaleri, "International Construction Disputes in Denmark" [2016] ICLR 39 at 55.
56 *"If thou art privy to thy country's fate, Which, happily, foreknowing may avoid, OI! Speak!"* Act I, Scene 1, lines 133-135, of *Hamlet, per Horatio.*

APPENDICES 1–4

Appendix 3 **Add to footnote 10:**

Following the ten-year anniversary conference, the Society of Construction Law (SCL) initially published amendments to its *Delay and Disruption Protocol* (following a consultation which concluded in April 2015), those amendments being contained in *Rider 1* thereto. The preamble to *Rider 1* explained that:

- Changes to the original *Protocol* were necessary because of developments in technology, construction law and industry practice since the *Protocol* was originally published in 2002; in addition, the *Protocol* is used increasingly overseas.
- Eight issues were specifically considered as part of the consultation, including record-keeping, global claims and concurrent delay.
- A second edition of the *Protocol* was to be published in due course, but, meanwhile, *Rider 1* provided guidance upon "common issues that arise out of construction contracts" and provided a means by which parties can resolve such issues and avoid unnecessary disputes. If they cannot, the *Protocol*'s "practical and principal guidance" can be used, in order to help to limit the costs of those disputes. Shortly before this *First Supplement* went to press, the second edition of the SCL *Delay and Disruption Protocol* was published and will be reviewed in the *Second Supplement* hereto, or the *Sixth Edition*.

Appendix 3 **Add to footnote 6:**

See also S Briggs, "*Alstom Limited v Yokogawa Australia Proprietary Limited*: a case note and commentary" (2012) 28 Const LJ 553.

Appendix 4 **Add at the end of footnote 7:**

See also D Barry, "The SCL Delay and Disruption Protocol – 10 years on" (2013) 29 Const LJ 367.

APPENDIX 5

The quantification of loss caused by disruption: how applicable is the measured mile method?

Robert J Gemmell[1]

Section

---

1 FRICS, FCIArb, Chartered Arbitrator, Manager, Dispute Services, Aquenta Consulting, Brisbane, Australia. This appendix is adapted from an LLM dissertation undertaken at the University of Salford Law School, Manchester, England. See also chapter 6 of *Quantification of Delay and Disruption in Construction and Engineering Projects* by Robert Gemmell (Thomson Reuters (Professional) Australia Limited/Lawbook Co 2017).

1. Introduction

"How should I grasp/What seemed to me immeasurable?"[2]

This appendix examines the measured mile method, which is used to estimate loss of productivity due to an impact upon the progress of a construction project. Although the measured mile concept is relatively simple, it is arguably misunderstood. Analysis of case law, texts and journal articles shows that, although the measured mile is not always used appropriately, a major issue may also be one of application, for example, a disruption analyst's use of the measured mile is sometimes flawed, and/or the methodology is not being used as effectively as it could be.

2. What is the measured mile method?

The Society of Construction Law's *Delay and Disruption Protocol* (the *SCL Protocol*) states[3] as follows:

"1.19.7...The most appropriate way to establish disruption is to apply a technique known as the "measured mile". This compares the productivity on an unimpacted part of the contract with that achieved on the impacted part. Such a comparison factors out issues concerning unrealistic schedules and inefficient working. The comparison can be made on the man-hours expended, or the units of work performed . . ."

In *Clark Concrete Contractors Inc v General Services Administration*,[4] the court said that:

"[A] measured mile analysis compares work performed in one period not impacted by events causing loss of productivity with the same, or comparable work performed in another period that was impacted by productivity-affected events."

The difference is taken "to be the loss associated with the disruption and is used to calculate loss of productivity".[5] The loss of productivity is calculated in labour hours, which in turn are multiplied by the labour rate to obtain the cost of the loss of productivity.[6]

3. Delay and disruption: the distinction

Delay and disruption are often treated as being the same thing.[7] However, they are entirely different concepts[8] and should therefore be carefully distinguished.

In *Bell BCI Company v United States*,[9] the court defined the terms thus:

"There is a distinction between (1) a 'delay' claim and (2) 'disruption', or cumulative impact claim. Although the two claim types often arise together in the same project, a 'delay' claim captures the time and cost of not being able to work, while a 'disruption' claim captures the cost of working less efficiently than planned."

---

2 Richard Wagner, *Die Meistersinger von Nürnberg*, Act 2, Scene 3.
3 Society of Construction Law, *Delay and Disruption Protocol* (2002), p. 32 [Society of Construction Law].
4 *Clark Concrete Contractors Inc v General Services Administration* 99–1 BCA P 30280 (1999).
5 Ibbs W, "Measured-Mile Principles" (2012) 4 *Journal of Legal Affairs and Dispute Resolution in Engineering and Construction* 31.
6 Ibbs, n 3.
7 Society of Construction Law, n 1; *Bell BCI Company v US* 91 Fed CL 664 (2010).
8 Society of Construction Law, n 1.
9 91 Fed CL 664 (2010).

The SCL *Protocol* further distinguishes between delay and disruption, as follows:[10]

"1.19.1 Disruption (as distinct from delay) is disturbance, hindrance or interruption to a contractor's normal working methods, resulting in lower efficiency. If caused by the Employer, it may give rise to a right to compensation either under the contract or as a breach of contract.
    1.19.2 Disruption is often treated by the construction industry as if it were the same thing as delay. It is commonly spoken of together with delay, as in "delay and disruption". Delay and disruption are two separate things. They have their normal everyday meanings. Delay is lateness (eg delayed completion equals late completion). Disruption is loss of productivity, disturbance, hindrance or interruption of progress. In the construction context, disrupted work is often work that is carried out less efficiently than it would have been had it not been for the cause of disruption.
    1.19.3 Disruption to construction work may lead to late completion of the work, but not necessarily so. It is possible for work to be disrupted and for the contract still to finish by the contract completion date. In this situation, [C] will not have a claim for an EOT, but it may have a claim for the cost of the reduced efficiency of its workforce."

In summary, therefore, delay is time-related and disruption is productivity-related. However, delay may cause disruption, disruption may cause delay and both may occur at the same time.[11]

4. Causes of disruption

The SCL *Protocol* states that:

"[T]he most common causes of disruption are loss of job rhythm (caused by, for example, premature moves between activities, out of sequence working and repeated learning cycles), work area congestion caused by stacking of trades, increase in size of gangs and increase in length or number of shifts. But these are also symptoms of poor site management."[12]

However, the AACE[13] goes further and attempts to identify factors that cause and/or contribute to loss of productivity, as follows:

"Absenteeism; Acceleration (directed, or constructive); Adverse, or unusually severe, weather; Availability of skilled labour; Variations, ripple impact, cumulative impact of multiple changes and rework; Competition for labour; Labour turnover; Crowding of labour, or trade stacking; Defective engineering, engineering recycle, or rework; Dilution of supervision; Excessive overtime; Failure to coordinate trade contractors, sub-contractors, or vendors; Fatigue; Labour relations and labour management factors; Learning curve; Material, tools and equipment shortages; Over-manning; Poor morale of labour; Project management factors; Out-of-sequence work; Rework and errors; Schedule compression; Site, or work area access restrictions; Site conditions; and Untimely approvals or responses."

5. Entitlement to payment for "loss caused by disruption"

A contractor that has suffered loss caused by disruption may have an entitlement to claim payment for that loss either under the contract and/or as common law damages, sometimes referred to as general damages. A contractor must prove liability, causation and loss or expense suffered.
    This appendix does not deal with issues of entitlement, but instead focuses on the quantification of financial loss due to loss of productivity, and whether and to what extent the measured

---

10 Society of Construction Law, n 1, pp. 31, 32.
11 Society of Construction Law, n 1.
12 Society of Construction Law, n 1, p. 32.
13 AACE International, *AACE International Recommended Practice No 25R-03: Estimating Lost Labor Productivity in Construction Claims: TCM Framework: 6.4 – Forensic Performance Assessment* (2004) [AACE International]. In this regard, see chapter 16 of *Construction Schedule Delays: 2016 Edition*, by W Stephen and Robert M D'Onofrio (Thomson Reuters).

mile method is appropriate to calculate such loss. In addition, as a result of the literature and case law reviewed, this article also covers the correct usage of the measured mile methodology.

6. Methods of calculating loss of productivity

There are several methods of calculating loss of productivity that include "actual costs, total and modified total cost, project comparison studies, speciality industry studies, general industry studies and the measured mile".[14] Ibbs says that system dynamic modelling and earned value analysis may also be used to calculate such loss.[15]

However, the measured mile is considered to be the most robust and reliable method because, compared to the other methods, as well as being based upon contemporaneous project documentation and knowledge from the project,[16] it calculates loss of productivity due to the "actual effect of alleged impact and thereby eliminates disputes over the validity of cost estimates, or factors that may have impacted productivity due to no fault of the owner".[17]

7. Literature and case law review

This section is divided into the following:

- literature review;
- case law review; and
- how the measured mile analysis should be conducted.

7.1 Literature review

This literature review is concerned with ascertaining the extent to which the measured mile is appropriate and/or is being used correctly/most effectively in calculating loss caused by disruption – disruption being a reduction in productivity that results in an increase of cost in carrying out the work.[18]

A type of damage often alleged on construction projects is loss of labour productivity. A method to assess that loss is by using the measured mile methodology.[19] Ibbs says that "problems exist with the measured mile approach, however, because the guidelines for developing and applying it are unclear".[20] The guidelines provided by Ibbs have been followed and expanded on in the section below entitled "The manner in which the measured mile analysis ought properly to be conducted".

7.2 Productivity

If productivity is impacted, labour costs in all probability will increase.[21] Even though labour effort and project programme are related, the courts consider that loss of productivity damages

---

14 AACE International, n 11.

15 Ibbs W, Nguyen LD and Lee S, "Quantified Impacts of Project Change" (2007) 133 *Journal of Professional Issues in Engineering Education and Practice* 45.

16 AACE International, n 11.

17 Society of Construction Law, n 1; Schwartzkopf W and McNamara J, *Calculating Lost Labor Productivity in Construction Claims* 2nd edn (Aspen Publishers, 2004); AACE International, n 11.

18 Pickavance K, *Delay and Disruption in Construction* 3rd edn (Sweet and Maxwell, 2005) at [1.25], [10].

19 Ibbs, n 3.

20 Ibbs, n 3.

21 Ibbs, n 3.

is not the same as programme delay damages[22] and therefore form a separate category of recoverable damages.[23]

7.3 The problem

Even though legal precedent,[24] writers[25] and groups[26] suggest that the measured mile is "the preferred method of calculating loss of productivity", it is not always appropriate.[27] Further, the success rate for loss of productivity claims is low as "there is no rigorous methodology" to calculate damages or for applying the measured mile.[28]

7.4 Measured mile analysis

In his paper in 1986, Zinc introduced the concept of a measured mile which compares productivity during an unimpacted period of work to productivity during an impacted period.[29] Schwartzkopf and McNamara[30] slate that:

"The most widely accepted method of calculating lost labor productivity is known throughout the industry as the "measured mile" calculation. This calculation compares identical activities on impacted and nonimpacted sections of the project in order to ascertain the loss of productivity resulting from the impact."

The SCL *Protocol* states: "The most appropriate way to establish disruption is to apply a technique known as the measured mile. . . ."[31] However, Schwartzkopf and McNamara[32] also point out a weakness in the measured mile:

"On highly troubled projects, however, it may be impossible to segregate one period of performance that was not impacted. Even if a nonimpacted period is available for comparison with the impacted period, it may be that wholly different types of work were performed during the two periods making the measured mile calculation impractical or inaccurate. . .."

The dilemma, then, is to know when the measured mile is appropriate. By way of some guidance, in *Re Lamb Engineering and Construction*[33] (*Lamb Engineering*) the Board emphasised that the measured mile approach is most effective when the impacted and non-impacted periods being compared are similar, are part of the same contract/project and close in time so that like is compared with like. However, disruption very often does not occur like this.[34]

It therefore appears inappropriate to use a measured mile analysis if there is no unimpacted period, if the unimpacted period is too short, or for complex projects.[35]

---

22 *S Leo Harmonay Inc v Binks Manufacturing* 597 F Supp 1014 (1984).
23 Ibbs, n 3.
24 *Re Lamb Engineering & Construction* 97-2 BCA P 29207 (1997).
25 Schwartzkopf and McNamara, n 15.
26 Society of Construction Law n 1.
27 Schwartzkopf and McNamara, n 15.
28 Thomas HR, "Quantification of Losses of Labor Efficiencies: Innovations in and Improvements to the Measured Mile" (2010) 2 *Journal of Legal Affairs and Dispute Resolution in Engineering and Construction* 106.
29 Zink DA, "The Measured Mile: Proving Construction Inefficiency Costs" (1986) 28 *Cost Engineering* 19.
30 Schwartzkopf and McNamara, n 15.
31 Society of Construction Law, n 1.
32 Schwartzkopf and McNamara, n 15.
33 *Re Lamb Engineering & Construction* 97-2 BCA P 29207 (1997).
34 Schwartzkopf and McNamara, n 15.
35 Loulakis MC and Santiago SJ, "Getting the Most Out of Your 'Measured Mile' Approach" (1999) 69 *Civil Engineering (NY)* 69.

Gulezian and Samelian[36] also say that the measured mile may not show the actual productivity of a contractor because successive cumulative data has a "smoothing effect". Professor Thomas argues, however, that cumulative data should not be used and that a "unit rate" should be used instead.[37]

Partly, or totally, as a result of the above-mentioned problems, and other problems that are covered later in this section, some quantum experts are not using the measured mile methodology correctly. For example, in *Daewoo Engineering and Construction Limited v US*,[38] the court rejected the expert's measured mile analysis and considered that the presumed efficiency regarding the impacted period was neither substantiated, nor justified, and that Daewoo's expert witness was "less than truthful".

In *Appeal of JA Jones Construction*,[39] the tribunal also rejected the quantum expert's evidence because the expert made "no attempt to isolate specific impacts allegedly caused by changes" and "the methodology used by the expert does not consider the nature of any specific changes or what locations/areas and work they directly affected on the project".

The measured mile was also found to be inappropriate in *Southern Comfort Builders Inc v US*,[40] in which a baseline, ie the measured mile, was calculated using the production rates of another contractor on the same project. The court stated, as follows:

"Based on the information presented, this court cannot adopt [the plaintiff's]. . .analysis to support [its] calculation of damages. [The plaintiff's]. . .calculation is deficient in that it does not adequately represent a comparison between the plaintiff's unimpacted work with an impacted period."

The measured mile method is more appropriate in such cases if the projects being analysed are similar.[41]

However, if used correctly, the measured mile method can be appropriate where similar work is carried out at different times, maybe even on a different project.[42] The calculation remains the same but the impacted activity and the measured mile may not be on the same activity, close in time, or even not on the same project.[43]

In summary, disruption analysts are using the measured mile method to quantify loss caused by disruption in a variety of ways with varying degrees of success in the courts. From the above literature review, the main reasons appear to be that the measured mile is not always appropriate for the circumstances in which it is being used, together with analysts not using the method in the most effective manner.

7.5 Case law review

In the following cases, the use of the measured mile method has been considered in some detail. Each case is worthy of separate review because of the issues dealt with, and the comments made in the judgment. Most of the case law considered below is from the United States, simply because the United States has by far the greatest amount of case law and also the majority of publications dealing with both productivity and, more specifically, the measured mile.

---

36 Gulezian R and Samelian F, "Baseline Determination in Construction Labor Productivity-loss Claims" (2003) 19 *Journal of Management and Engineering* 160.

37 Thomas HR and Barnard PD, *Conducting a Measured Mile Analysis – Concepts, Principles, and Procedures* (Thomas & Associates Publishing, 2013).

38 73 Fed Cl 547 (2006).

39 00–2 BCA P 31000 (2000).

40 67 Fed CL124 (2005).

41 Schwartzkopf and McNamara, n 15.

42 AACE International, n 11.

43 *Maryland Sanitary Manufacturing v US* 119 Ct Cl 100 (1951); *Appeal of Clark Construction Group Inc* 00–1 BCA P 30870 (2000).

The case illustrations are included in ascending chronological order:

Illustrations

(1) *Facts*: Maryland (C) manufactured shells with a production cost ranging from US$7.5534 each for a 12-hour per day/seven days a week period, to US$5.918 each for a ten-hour per day/six days a week. However, the cost of materials during the periods being compared was uncertain and the fact the work was being "closed out" during the lower cost period led to lower production costs. *Held*, notwithstanding these complications, that: efficiency would be impaired by working a 12-hour day, seven days per week. The court also considered a government study that was introduced in evidence. This showed that efficiency was reduced by about 20% as a result of extending the workday to ten hours and the working week from five to six days. In spite of the lack of certainty in Maryland's evidence, the court was convinced that Maryland incurred increased costs of at least half the amount claimed by reason of labour inefficiency because of the increased work day and work week. However, owing to the uncertainty in Maryland's calculations, the court awarded only half the amount (of US$30,152.95) claimed. Whilst the words "measured mile method" were not specifically referred to in the judgment, the methodology used by the plaintiff was based upon the measured mile principles. Maryland claimed for loss of productivity during a period in which its labour worked 12 hours per day, seven days per week. This unimpacted period was compared with a period immediately following the 12 hours per day, seven days per week period, ie the impacted period.

Comment: Notwithstanding that the evidence presented by Maryland was uncertain, it therefore appears that the court was persuaded, partly by a comparison of productivity during the impacted and unimpacted periods and partly by a government study, that Maryland suffered loss of productivity caused by the client. On the basis of Maryland's uncertain calculations and the government study, the court was persuaded that Maryland had suffered at least half the loss that it claimed. The court therefore awarded half the amount claimed by Maryland. Maryland was able to demonstrate that it was entitled to payment for loss of productivity. However, its calculations were uncertain, which, in turn, may have led the court to err on the side of caution and, even though Maryland was awarded some payment for its loss, if its calculations had been more "certain", Maryland might have been able to demonstrate an entitlement to an amount in excess of that awarded by the court: *Maryland Sanitary Manufacturing v US*.[44]

(2) *Facts*: Lipsett, Inc contracted with Bureau of Yards and Docks of the Department of the Navy (D) for the construction of aircraft maintenance facilities at the naval air station in Willow Grove, Pennsylvania and was later substituted by Luria Brothers Company, Inc (C). The contract was completed on 3 May 1955, 518 days beyond the scheduled completion date. On 30 January 1956 C submitted before the contracting officer, claims for $248,665.76 as compensation for certain additional items of work. D replied that the contracting officer had determined that, with the exception of a certain item, C's claims were considered "in the nature of claims for damages and therefore could not be the subject of compensation under the contract". C appealed to the Secretary of the Navy, which ruled that the settlement certificate precluded further consideration of those claims submitted to the General Accounting Office. C later withdrew this claim. On 9 November 1959, C filed a petition to the court for breach of contract claiming that: (1) the original plans were defective and faulty; (2) D was delayed in making necessary contract changes and taking other action; (3) a trial and error method was imposed by D to accomplish certain aspects of the construction and this was contrary

---

44 119 Ct Cl 100 (1951).

to the contract terms and was unreasonable and costly to C; (4) the magnitude and nature of some of the changes were beyond the scope of the original contract; and (5) the frequency and extensiveness of the revisions to other phases of the construction work were also unreasonable and beyond the scope of the contract. As a consequence, C argued that its costs had increased and performance of the contract was protracted unduly and into periods of more adverse conditions than would otherwise have occurred. *Held*: that C suffered delay damages and additional expenditures, resulting from D's breaches, amounting to $85,544.92 and was entitled to recover $62,948.33 for excess home office overhead, totalling $165,082.67.

Comment: Although the expert's lack of reasons, or substantiation, did not prove fatal to the claim, their absence probably proved to be detrimental to the amount recoverable. It is therefore necessary for an analyst making adjustments to productivity rates to reason and substantiate the adjustments made: *Luria Brothers v US*.[45]

(3)   *Facts*: In 1974, E C Ernst Inc (C) was hired by Koppers Co (D) as the electrical sub-contractor for the Aliquippa Project, Pennsylvania with Jones & Laughlin Steel Corp (J&L), which involved novel technology for loading and preheating coal prior to its conversion to coke. The completion date was set for June 1975. Difficulties arose with D requesting modifications to the original project, which required C to do extra work and costs not contemplated in the contract. The project was completely six months later in 1976. C sued claiming damages for D's delay; recovery of extra costs due to additional work and additional work done pursuant to field authorisations and directives issued by D. D in turn counterclaimed to recover for services supplied to D during the construction of the coke battery. *Held*, by the district court that: D was liable for the delays, without awarding damages; D should pay C damages of $1,421,920 for extra costs for the additional work done by C with a deduction of $500 from each separate drawing revision; that D should pay C $9,581.64 in damages for the additional work done pursuant to D's authorisations and directives. C appealed on the $500 deduction and D appealed on the other findings. *Held*, reversing and remanding judgment of the district court concerning damages payable by D to delays, and on the deduction of $500 from each claim; affirming the judgment in all other respects.

Comment: An expert's analysis may therefore be invalid if the methodology used to calculate loss of productivity is "artificial and hypothetical", for example as in *EC Ernst*, using the number of drawing revisions each year and then conducting a *pro rata* exercise based purely on the number of drawing revisions to determine loss of productivity: *EC Ernst Inc v Koppers Inc*.[46]

(4)   *Facts*: Documents were used to substantiate corrections to scraper cycle times to reflect different site conditions encountered during the impacted and unimpacted periods. The measured mile used by the expert was based upon actual records of the productivity of one scraper for six days. The scraper operator kept records of the number of hours of operation and the number of cycles (cut and fill) completed by the scraper each day. The scraper carried out between 8.35 and 12.91 cycles per day at an average of 5.44 minutes per cycle. The site conditions varied between the impacted and unimpacted periods being compared, the site conditions during the impacted period being more difficult. The expert adjusted the cycle times during the unimpacted period down by one minute per cycle. This had the effect of increasing productivity by 20%, which made the difference between the impacted and unimpacted periods greater. The expert witness then used the topographic and grading drawings to calculate the amount of material "stripped" and "cut and filled" to arrive at a number of hours for each phase as anticipated, ie the number of hours the work should have taken. The expert then

---

45 177 Ct Cl 676 (1966).
46 626 F2d 324 (1980).

prepared a separate composite hourly rate for each of the operations as planned, drawing from actual cost records, and multiplied the calculated number of hours for each phase by the relevant composite rate to arrive at a "but for" cost for each. He testified that the "but for" cost for the cut and fill operations was $94,795. *Held*, by the Board of Appeals: that, the measured mile method "is most effective when" the unimpacted and impacted periods being compared "are close in time, involve similar types of work, and occur in the same contract". So that like could be compared with like, the Board allowed the measured mile, ie the unimpacted period, to be corrected. The Board in this case said that the expert appeared to have been thorough in gathering and allocating data necessary for his calculations and concluded that the measured mile process followed was "essentially sound".

Comment: On the basis of the decision in *Lamb Engineering* (which follows *Luria Brothers*[47]), it is appropriate for the analyst to adjust the data, in order to ensure that like is being compared with like – in *Lamb Engineering*, this being adjustments made to reflect differing ground conditions impacting on scraper cycle times. Unlike the expert in *Luria Brothers*, the expert witness in *Lamb Engineering* reasoned and substantiated the adjustments made: *Lamb Engineering v Construction*.[48]

(5)   *Facts*: Centex Bateson Construction Co. (A) was awarded contract No. V101C-1567 by the Veterans Administration (R) for the construction of a medical center in Houston, Texas for the fixed price of $172,690,000. The contract price was later modified by $9,767,730, as a result of the request for information (RFI) implemented by A. Each RFI was evaluated by R, who would issue a request for proposal (RFP) for the work, or indicate the next work. A and R entered into supplemental agreements, called either the "Field Supplemental Agreement" (FSA), or the "Central Office Supplemental Agreement" (COSA). After completion of the works, A submitted to R a claim for equitable adjustment on behalf of Dynalectric, one of its sub-contractors. The claim was denied and A appealed to the Board. The Board held that all the claims were resolved by the "supplemental agreements" made between A and R and that A had not established that it was entitled to recover those impact costs that were unknowable at the time of the supplemental agreements. A appealed to the Court. *Held*: that the Board had not erred in asserting that the supplemental agreements covered all impact costs that were not knowable at the time of the agreements and that A had not proved its claim for unknowable costs, and as a consequence, the decision was affirmed.

Comment: Following *Centex Bateson*, the analyst carrying out the measured mile analysis must take out the causes of loss of productivity to which the contractor is **not** entitled. If not, that analysis will be flawed: *Centex Bateson Construction v West*.[49]

(6)   *Facts*: A sub-contractor's progress of work was disrupted because of additional concrete work, failure to respond to requests for information on time and an inexperienced engineer. *Held*, by the Board, that: (1) the government was correct in that the work carried out by Clark during the impacted and unimpacted periods was not identical; however, the court stated that it would be "surprised to learn that work performed in periods being compared is ever identical on a construction project"; (2) the works being compared did not need to be identical because the calculation of damages for labour inefficiency was "not susceptible to absolute correctness". The Board stated that it would accept a comparison if it were "between kinds of work which are reasonably alike, such that the approximations it involves will be meaningful"; therefore the Board accepted the disruption analyst's use of the impacted periods. One was "severely" impacted and the other was "moderately" impacted. However, the court

---

47   177 Ct Cl 676 (1966).
48   97–2 BCA P 29207 (1997).
49   250 F 3d 761 (Fed Cir 2000). *Appeal of Centex Bateson Construction* 99–1 BCA P 30153 (1998); affirmed in *Centex Bateson Construction v West* 250 F3d (2000).

did not accept the expert's calculation of the adjusted unimpacted productivity rate as they did not sufficiently corroborate the adjustment made.

Comment: Following *Luria Brothers* and *Lamb Engineering*, the analyst should explain and corroborate any adjustments made, but does not need to ensure that the periods being compared are identical: *Clark Concrete Contractors Inc v General Services Administration.*[50]

(7)   *Facts*: Clark Construction, also acting on behalf of its sub-contractor PKC, claimed loss of labour productivity on a complex plumbing and mechanical installation in a hospital. As a result of an instruction, the work had to be re-sequenced from a horizontal to a vertical construction methodology. PKC used three methods so as to calculate loss of labour productivity: the measured mile analysis, the MCAA method and modified total cost. The disruption analysis applies only to the PKC portion of the claim. The analyses compared productivity rates for installation of four piping systems (domestic water, interstitial heating hot water, medical gas cast iron drain, waste and vent) on the first floor with the installation productivity rates for the sixth, or seventh, floors of the main hospital structure. PKC also compared the underground piping work for the hospital with the underground work for the adjacent nursing home on which PKC was the mechanical sub-contractor for the project. The underslab utility work for the nursing home was similar to, although less complicated, or extensive than, the work on the project on which disruption loss was claimed. The underground piping analysis compared productivity rates for installation of such work with rates for installation of underground piping in the nursing home, immediately adjacent to the main hospital building. This comparison was made because of the proximity of the buildings and also because the nursing home underground piping installation was not impacted. Overall, however, there was no unimpacted area or time on the disrupted project to establish a baseline for the measured mile analysis; therefore, PKC used a lesser-impacted area (sixth and seventh floors) as the baseline. For the heating hot water piping system, PKC's expert compared the first and sixth floors because he found that PKC had improperly coded its seventh floor work, thus preventing him from determining the number of man hours actually expended to install the heating hot water system on that floor. PKC's expert also "adjusted" the first floor actual man-day per lineal foot rates. The adjustment was made because the installations on the first floor involved more and larger pipes and fittings and the adjustment was necessary, in his view, for accurate comparison of productivity rates between the floors. PKC's expert determined a percentage inefficiency factor for the first floor installations by dividing the difference of the lineal feet/man-day productivity rate between the first and sixth or seventh floor by the sixth or seventh floor productivity rate. The underslab utility inefficiency factor was determined by applying the same methodology as that used for arriving at the inefficiency factor in the main hospital and comparing this to the rates for the nursing home. Adjustments to the nursing home productivity rate were made in reaching the underground piping inefficiency factor. The overall estimated productivity loss was 44,500 man hours. Clark Construction's expert considered that the systems and the floors included in PKC's measured mile analysis presented a "representative slice" of the disputed project and that it was valid to apply the analysis to ascertain an overall project loss of productivity. The government's expert considered, however, among other things, that Clark Construction's use of average estimated productivity rates for a particular piping system where there were wide differences indicated for various parts of each floor would not provide an accurate result because of the variance in planned productivity rates for the same work. He also found that acknowledged coding errors brought into question the validity of the analysis since accurate reporting by PKC of the actual expended labour hours was

---

50 99–1 BCA P 30280 (1999).

essential for a valid report. *Held*: that PKC had approached the three analyses using total incurred labour hours, or costs, as the starting point and that to some degree, each of the three methodologies was a variant on a total cost claim. The court decided against PKC's use of the measured mile and preferred to use the productivity factors from the MCAA Manual instead, ie a speciality industry study.

Comment: There was sufficient evidence to persuade the court that there had been loss of labour productivity. However, owing to PKC's total cost approach to using the measured mile analysis, the court preferred PKC's use of productivity rates from the MCAA Manual. The total cost approach to the use of the measured mile method made the analysis unreliable and it was therefore rejected: *Clark Concrete Contractors Inc v General Services Administration*.[51]

(8) *Facts*: JA Jones claimed that due to the changes on the contract work, costs had increased by about 28–29% and, to prove this, JA Jones' expert prepared a computerised measured mile analysis. *Held*: that the expert (1) had not carried out a cause and effect analysis and consequently had not identified and singled out the specific disruptive effects that were caused by the changes; (2) had not considered specific changes and the locations, or work they affected, without considering a comprehensive knowledge of the project; (3) had not considered when the changes were ordered, or if the contractor had had enough notice to perform the changes required in an effective manner; (4) failed to link the alleged labour shortcomings with the causes of the impacts; (5) had not successfully ruled out that there were not other non-compensable causes that could have contributed to productivity losses and that the expert had "produced patently illogical results" and, as a consequence, J A Jones had "failed to prove that it was entitled to additional compensation in excess of the 'direct' costs it has already been paid for compensable changes."

Comment: Following the judgment in *JA Jones*, it is necessary for the analyst to ensure that the analysis is not subjective and is clearly explained. The analyst should account for factors that contribute to loss of productivity for which the contractor does not have an entitlement to payment for loss. Further, it is necessary to carry out a cause-and-effect analysis and correct the contractor's cost accounts if they overstate the costs incurred. The analyst should not rely on a one-day, and possibly non-representative, impact to conclude that the entire month was or was not impacted, especially if other documents demonstrate that cost overrun was caused by the contractor, high turnover of staff and optimistic productivity estimates: *Appeals of JA Jones Construction*.[52]

(9) *Facts*: At trial, it was proved that butt-welding on polyethylene pipes took between 15 seconds and two minutes per weld, and steel welding took up to 2.69 hours per weld. The expert for PW Construction, however, had left out both sets of welding and trenching work from the period before disruption took place, leaving them in for the "post-disruption" period. *Held*: that, by removing the welding work from the "pre-disruption" period, the measured mile was inaccurate, since then the impacted and unimpacted periods were not comparable.

Comment: It is therefore necessary, when comparing the impacted and unimpacted periods, that like is compared with like, ie that the comparison periods are the same or substantially similar, and that adjustments made to one period are reflected in the other period: *PW Construction Inc v US*.[53]

(10) *Facts*: The Department of Veterans Affair (R) hired PJ Dick (A) to construct the clinical addition to R's centre in Michigan. R issued over 400 orders changing the contract, which caused various delays to the project and resulted in over 5% increase of the

51 00–1 BCA P 30870 (2000).
52 00–2 BCA P 31000 (2000).
53 Fed Appx 555 (2002).

contract price. R granted 107 days of additional contract performance time, whilst A reserved its right to seek an additional impact and suspension costs. A completed the work 260 days after the original completion date and presented the contracting officer (CO) claims for additional relief. The CO denied the claims and A appealed to the Board, claiming that it was entitled to extension for all 260 days of delayed performance and sought field and home office overhead damages. The Board granted A field overhead, but not for unabsorbed home office overhead. A and R both appealed different aspects of the Board's decision and asked the Court of Appeal to determine whether the language of the contract required the Board to analyse the effect of each change separately and whether A was entitled to recover home office overheads and, if not, whether A had shown that it was placed on standby by R. *Held*, by the Court of Appeal that: (1) the express terms of the contract prevented the Board from analysing the effect of all of the "combined directives" using the computer schedule update as of the date R issued the first of the change order; rather, it must use the computer schedule current as of the date R issued each change order; (2) though the Board was right to find that A had not proved it was on standby, A was still entitled to recovery of home office overhead damages. As a consequence, the Board's construction of the parties' stipulation was reversed, affirming the Board's determination that A was not on standby and vacating the Board's analysis of the extent of the "combined directives" delay and determining that the Board should determine the length of the "combined directives" delay by analysing the effect of each of the six change orders separately using the computer schedule update, and should also determine whether A's other delay claims become controlling as a result of any reduction in the "combined directive" delay and, if so, analyse them accordingly and finally, based upon the parties' stipulation, calculate the amount of home office overhead A is entitled to for government-caused delays compensable and award that amount to A, with no costs.

Comment: *PJ Dick* therefore followed the board decision in *Clark Concrete Contractors* in that, when comparing impacted and unimpacted periods, it is acceptable in principle for the disruption analyst to compare similar work carried out by another crew with the impacted period. It is not necessary for the work being compared to be identical: *PJ Dick Inc v Principi*.[54]

(11) *Facts*: Due to the change orders, the expert witness claimed that the measured mile method could not be used, since all the late changes and out-of-sequence working had affected the whole project, subsequently different contractor's productivity rates were used to prepare a measured mile. The expert's measured mile used a higher amount than a total cost calculation to calculate productivity loss. *Held*: that the expert's analyses was wrong, in so far as the measured mile was not the appropriate comparison between the contractor's impacted and a comparison with the sub-contractor's productivity rates.

Comment: It may therefore be inappropriate to conduct a measured mile analysis based upon the productivity rate of a different contractor. However, it did not help that the expert undermined his own analysis by admitting that his measured mile analysis should not be more than a total cost calculation. The expert's admission may not be entirely correct in this regard. It is possible for a contractor legitimately to claim more than it could in a total cost claim if the tender price, and assumed resources, are found to be in excess of that required to complete the work. However, this is not normally the case: *Southern Comfort Builders Inc v US*.[55]

(12) *Facts*: As part of the treaty between the United States (R) with the Republic of Palau, in 1998, R tendered the building of a road around the island of Babeldaob. Daewoo (A) was awarded the tender, which contract required completion within 1,080 days, commencing

54 324 F3d 1364 (2003).
55 67 Fed CL 124 (2005).

in October 2000. Delays occurred due to rainy conditions and A urged R to reduce the amount of soil compaction required by the contract, with which R finally complied. In December 2002, A filed before the Court of Federal Claims seeking an increase in the "compensable and non-compensable contract performance time", monetary relief, amounting to $50,629,855.88. R counterclaimed for damages, seeking $64m under the *Contract Disputes Act* and $10,000 under the *False Claims Act*, as well as a special plea in fraud and sought forfeiture of A's claims under 28 U.S.C. § 2514. The Court awarded R $10,000 under the *False Claims Act* and $50,629,855.88 ("$50.6m") under the *Contract Disputes Act*, forfeiting A's claims under § 2514. A appealed. *Held*, by the Court of Appeals that: (1) the Court of Federal Claims was correct in concluding that A submitted a certified claim for $64m; (2) A's $50.6m projected cost calculation was fraudulent; (3) the Court of Federal Claims was right in concluding that A had violated the *False Claims Act*, since no evidence was found that R had incurred damages from A's false claim, the court only assessed the statutory penalty; (4) that A's claims against R were forfeited and consequently upheld the $50.6m award and upheld the forfeiture.

Comment: In summary, it is necessary for the disruption analyst to substantiate and justify their opinions and not just reach unsupported arbitrary opinions. This case also reinforces the need for the analyst to be truthful whenever calculating and presenting a loss of productivity claim or, indeed, any claim: *Daewoo Engineering and Construction Limited v US*.[56]

7.5.13 Summary

The main findings and the principles revealed from the above case law analysis have been used to prepare the following section concerning the appropriate manner in which a measured mile analysis ought properly to be conducted. It is uncertain whether these examples are typical of the industry as a whole and this appendix does not attempt to address this issue. However, on the basis of the case law and literature reviewed above, they appear to be typical.

8. The manner in which the measured mile analysis ought properly to be conducted

This section identifies the appropriate use of the measured mile method to calculate loss caused by disruption. Ibbs sets out four main headings under which he considers a measured mile analysis should be conducted.[57] These are:

1. Selecting the impacted period;
2. Selecting the measured mile and/or the unimpacted period;
3. Calculation of lost productivity, and
4. Presentation of the analysis.

Because there is no presentation of the analysis in the manner which Ibbs envisages in his paper, the first three headings are applicable to this appendix and will be used in the discussion of the use of measured mile analysis.

8.1 Selecting the impacted period

The measured mile method compares actual labour performance during an impacted and unimpacted period. Both these periods therefore need to be identified.

---

56 73 Fed Cl 547 (2006).
57 Ibbs, n 3.

Productivity graph(s)

A measured mile analysis should associate loss of productivity with the cause of loss – there must be a correlation.[58] To achieve this, the analyst, having to identify the impacted periods,[59] should prepare graph(s) of productivity to identify the periods of disruption.[60] A graph of the labour productivity for each phase of the project should be plotted, which will show both the unimpacted and impacted periods.[61]

If there are no production records, it may be possible to estimate the percentage completion of a project to estimate the quantities in the unimpacted parts of the analysis. However, the percentage completed approach is unreliable because it is based upon an estimate, or a guess.[62]

However, to plot the productivity graph, if possible, the quantity of work per labour hours as a measure of productivity should be used, or, if this is not possible, work per percent project complete.[63]

Productivity calculations

Once the impacted periods have been identified from the productivity graphs, the analyst should calculate productivity for periods in which there has been high production.[64] This is because the calculation of productivity must be representative of what the contractor was able to achieve.

Cause-and-effect analysis

It is necessary to conduct a cause-and-effect analysis to establish a correlation between the loss of productivity and the alleged impact.[65] When the productivity graph indicates a loss of productivity, the cause must be determined. There must be a correlation between the loss of productivity and the alleged cause.[66] Thomas says that to conduct a cause-and-effect analysis one "will likely have to resort to many information sources, including interviews with managers, project engineers, and foremen, diaries, production records, and a review of photographs and other documents".[67]

One of the biggest deficiencies typically identified in a measured mile analysis is a lack of a cause-and-effect analysis. Without a cause-and-effect analysis, the measured mile analysis remains a largely unsubstantiated "global" analysis and will fail to demonstrate the most probable cause of the loss of productivity.

This task may be difficult where the measured mile analysis is being used. Essentially, a measured mile analysis is used where direct proof of loss is not available. In this situation the dispute decider is being asked to infer from the measured mile analysis that it is more probable than not that the contractor's loss of productivity was caused by the client, or by an event for which the client is liable under the contract. However, if an inadequate cause-and-effect analysis is conducted so that the analysis gives rise to conflicting inferences of an equal degree of probability so that the choice between the inferences becomes a matter of conjecture, then the analysis will most probably fail. The measured mile analysis must give rise to a reasonable and definite inference.[68]

---

58 Thomas and Barnard, n 35, p. 20.

59 Thomas and Barnard, n 35.

60 Zink, n 27; Fink MR, "Statistical Evaluations of Measured Mile Productivity Claims" (1998) 40 *Cost Engineering* 28; Ibbs W and Liu M, "Improved Measured Mile Analysis Technique" (2005) 131 *Journal of Construction and Engineering Management* 1249.

61 Thomas and Barnard, n 35, p. 31.

62 Thomas and Barnard, n 35.

63 *Bell BCI Company v US* 72 Fed CL 164 (2006) at 168; *PJ Dick Inc v Principi* 324 F3d 1364 (2003) at 1370; *PW Construction Inc v US* 53 Fed Appx 555 (2002); *James v North Allegheny School District* 938 A2d 474 (2003); AACE International, n 11.

64 Zink, n 27; Ibbs and Liu, n 58.

65 *Appeal of JA Jones Construction* 00–2 BCA P 31000 (2000).

66 Thomas and Barnard, n 35, p. 38.

67 Thomas and Barnard, n 35, p. 38.

68 The observations made concerning legitimate and illegitimate reasoning by inference in *Penrith City Council v East Realisations Pty Ltd* (in liq) [2013] NSWCA 64 at [62]; *Luxton v Vines* (1952) 85 CLR 352; [1952] HCA 19 at 358; *Holloway v McFeeters* (1956) 94 CLR 470; [1956] HCA 25 at 477, 480; *Derrick v Cheung* [2001] HCA 48 at [13].

Adjustments for non-compensable causes
The analyst should make appropriate adjustments for non-compensable causes of loss of productivity and for the contractor's own inefficiencies.[69]

8.2 Selecting the measured mile and/or the unimpacted period

Continuous period of time
Thomas defines the unimpacted/measured mile period as "a continuous period of time when labour productivity is unimpacted".[70] Even though there may be inefficiencies for which the contractor is responsible in the continuous unimpacted period, all client-caused impacts should not be included.[71]

Selection of similar work to impacted period
It will be necessary to identify an unimpacted period that is the same as, or similar to, the impacted disrupted period.[72] It is important when comparing labour productivity that the tasks being compared are substantially similar.[73] It is also necessary to ensure that workers in the unimpacted period have comparable skill levels to the workers in the impacted period; the work carried out should represent an attainable level of productivity; and the work should have been carried out in an environment similar to the work carried out in the impacted period.

Use of productivity graphs
To identify the unimpacted period, productivity graph(s) for the entire project period prepared to identify the impacted period(s) should be used, and the quantities of work installed during the unimpacted period (and impacted period) should be recorded.[74] However, this data is rarely reported.[75]

Adjustments and corrections
The analyst should consider and adjust productivity calculations as necessary to account for discrepancies between the impacted and unimpacted management and supervision, work hours, project programme, site logistics, weather conditions, and trades to carry out the work.[76] These factors can change over time, ie from the unimpacted to the impacted period. The analyst should therefore also note and take into account that the work environment of a project changes as the project progresses and early phases can be very different from the later phases. The environment will change with more congestion, changes, sub-contractors etc.[77] Therefore, using an unimpacted period at the start of a project to calculate loss of productivity at the end of a project is inappropriate.[78]

Identification of workers
Workers with a similar level of skill and knowledge as those in the impacted period should be identified. The same or similar labour pool is desirable.[79] Thomas gives the example that "if one

---

69 Ibbs, n 3.
70 Thomas and Barnard, n 35.
71 Thomas and Barnard, n 35.
72 Zink, n 27; AACE International, n 11; Loulakis and Santiago, n 33; Presnell TW, "Measured Mile Process" (2003) 45 *Cost Engineering* 14; Serag E, *Change Orders and Productivity Loss Quantification Using Verifiable Site Data* (PhD dissertation, University of Central Florida, 2010); Thomas HR, "Why are Loss of Labor Efficiency Damages So Difficult to Recover?" (2010) 2 *Journal of Legal Affairs and Dispute Resolution in Engineering and Construction* 190.
73 Thomas and Barnard, n 35, p. 18.
74 Thomas and Barnard, n 35.
75 Thomas and Barnard, n 35.
76 Zink, n 27; AACE International, n 11; Thomas, n 69; *Re Bay Construction* VABCA No 5594 (2002).
77 Thomas, n 69.
78 Thomas and Barnard, n 35.
79 Thomas and Barnard, n 35, p. 18.

crew is composed of five journeymen and five apprentices, it may not be comparable to a crew of two journeymen and eight apprentices even though the crew size of both is ten craftsmen".[80]

Separation of labour trades
If possible, the analyst should separate the loss of productivity by labour trade.[81] This will provide a more accurate picture of which labour resources have and have not been impacted.

Owner-collected data
The analyst should use owner-collected data if it is available[82] as it will be more difficult for the owner to rebut the contractor's evidence if it is taken from owner-collected sources. Inevitably, however, much of the data will have to come from the contractor's own records.

The unimpacted period, the measured mile period and unhindered productivity
The analyst should ensure that the unimpacted period used contains contractor-unhindered productivity. To do this, the analyst should identify and adjust as necessary for contractor-caused hindrances[83] and will need to explain the adjustments.[84]

However, the analyst may need to use conversion factors to allow for differences that may exist between impacted and unimpacted periods.[85]

Where measured mile productivity actual project data is not available: other sources
If it is not possible to calculate a measured mile using actual project data, it may be possible to use other sources of information, for example, to supplement the analysis using published industry estimating guides,[86] productivity data from different projects constructed by the same contractor or by similar contractors,[87] and/or cost as a percentage of completed work and/or earned value rates.[88]

8.3 Calculation of lost productivity

Data testing
Data for productivity, change, progress etc must be tested.[89] The accuracy of the data being used is critical to a reliable analysis.[90] The analyst must therefore ensure that the data reported is correct, and if it is not, it should be corrected.

---

80 Thomas and Barnard, n 35, p. 18.

81 *Appeal of Bay West* 07–1 BCA P 33569 (2007).

82 Dieterle RA and Gaines TA, "Practical Issues in Loss of Efficiency Claims" (2011) 53 *Cost Engineering* 29.

83 *Re Lamb Engineering & Construction* 97–2 BCA P 29207 (1997); *Luria Brothers v US* 177 Ct Cl 676 (1966); *Southern Comfort Builders Inc v US* 67 Fed CL 124 (2005).

84 *Luria Brothers v US* 177 Ct Cl 676 (1966).

85 Thomas HR and Oloufa AA, "Labor Productivity, Disruptions, and the Ripple Effect" (1995) 37 *Cost Engineering* 49.

86 AACE International, n 11.

87 *Appeal of Robert McMullan & Sons Inc* 76–2 BCA P 12072 at 57947; *Maryland Sanitary Manufacturing v US* 119 Ct Cl 100 (1951); *Southern Comfort Builders Inc v US* 67 Fed CL 124 (2005); Shea TE, "Proving Productivity Losses in Government Contracts" (1989) 18 *Public Contract Law Journal* 414; Jones RM, "Lost Productivity: Claims for the Cumulative Impact of Multiple Change Orders" (2001) 31 *Public Contract Law Journal* 1.

88 *Bell BCI Company v US* 72 Fed CL 164 (2006) at 168; AACE International, n 11.

89 Dieterle and Gaines, n 79.

90 Thomas and Barnard, n 35.

Productivity factors

Loss of productivity factors should be applied to just the disrupted labour.[91] It may be necessary to combine tasks rather than just analysing each task individually.[92] However, a primary reason for the measured mile analysis being rejected is that too many tasks are combined or that the combination is inappropriate.[93]

Adjustments to be made

It is necessary to consider and if necessary make adjustments, for example, for the learning period in the early phases of the work,[94] any labour hours included in variations,[95] and any loss not recoverable under the contract and the contractor's own inefficiencies[96] etc.

Actual costs v "unit rate"

Actual costs on their own should not be used to calculate labour productivity.[97] This is because costs can be affected by several factors; for example, labour costs may not be recorded in the correct cost code, labour rates change, crew sizes fluctuate and crew functions may also change.[98] Thomas advocates the use of the "unit rate", which he describes as "commodity items", for example, square metres of partition wall, cubic metres of concrete and linear metres of pipe.[99] The unit rate is contrasted with say square metres or cubic metres of floor, this being composed of several "commodity items", therefore leading to a less reliable analysis than using the unit rate for the applicable items only.

9. Summary

A literature review and critical case law has been presented and, on this basis, an assessment made of the manner in which a measured mile analysis ought properly to be conducted.

The measured mile method is one of various methods which can be used in order to calculate loss caused by disruption and is the method preferred by the courts. However, the measured mile basis is clearly not always appropriate. Furthermore, as the literature review and case law analysis reveal, analysts and experts using the measured mile method are not always using the method in the most appropriate manner.

10. Survey

10.1 Introduction

A questionnaire survey was conducted in order to gather information about the use of the measured mile method. Questionnaires were sent to the following professional groups:

1. Experts;
2. Judges, arbitrators and adjudicators;
3. Lawyers, both solicitors and barristers;
4. Those who work in the contract/legal department of contractor organisations, and
5. Those who work in the legal/contract department of client organisations.

---

91 AACE International, n 11.
92 Thomas and Barnard, n 35, p. 25.
93 Thomas and Barnard, n 35, p. 25.
94 *Appeal of Bay West* 07–1 BCA P 33569 (2007); AACE International, n 11.
95 AACE International, n 11.
96 AACE International, n 11.
97 Thomas and Barnard, n 35, p. 17.
98 Thomas and Barnard, n 35, p. 18.
99 Thomas and Barnard, n 35.

Responses to the questionnaire were collected from 16 June 2015 to 19 August 2015. The questions asked were:

- Question 1: What is your primary profession?
- Question 2: Have you dealt with claims that concern the quantification of loss caused by disruption to the progress of a construction project?
- Question 3: In respect of the matters in which you were involved, has the measured mile method been used to calculate loss caused by disruption?
- Question 4: In approximately what percentage of cases was the measured mile method used successfully?
- Question 5: If the measured mile has not been used successfully, why?
- Question 6: Would you like a copy of the results of this survey?

10.2 Summary of survey findings

There were 228 responses to the questionnaire. Of the 228 responses, 92% of the respondents said that they had dealt with loss caused by disruption.

Of those respondents who said they have dealt with, or have decided, issues in relation to disruption, 66% said that the measured mile has been used. However, the overall "success" rate is low, with 74% of the respondents saying that the measured mile was "successful" less than 50% of the time (43% citing success between 0–25% of the time and 31% citing success between 26–50% of the time).

The main cause of the low "success" rate is a lack of records (71% of the respondents).

However, 52% said there was no unimpacted period to use as a baseline, 40% said the unimpacted period was too short and therefore not representative and 45% said the comparison periods were not comparable. 13% gave other reasons, which in most cases were an elaboration of their previous responses to the questionnaire.

Further, a few of the additional reasons given tend to reinforce the findings in the qualitative analysis section of this article, for example, the analyst was not qualified to use the measured mile method, which is a recurring theme in the case law analysis.

Based on the 228 responses received, the measured mile method is inappropriate more often than not. This finding forms the basis for recommended further research, which is set out earlier in this article.

It is not possible to determine from the survey responses whether the analyst used the measured mile methodology correctly, and/or in the most effective way. However, the survey questionnaire was not designed to obtain that information. If the measured mile is being used incorrectly, as the case law reflects, then this would suggest that the measured mile may be appropriate more often than this research suggests. However, there is no data on this point.

11. Conclusion

In general, because the measured mile method is the most accurate method to estimate loss of productivity, it is the preferred method.[100] However, it is clear from the above analysis of court judgments and from the responses to the questionnaire survey that the measured mile is inappropriate more often than not and/or is often being used less effectively than it could be. It is greatly hoped that the above guidance will provide some assistance in this regard.

---

100 Ibbs, n 3.

INDEX